THE WORLD OF WATER

WILLIAM C. WALTON

Director, Water Resources Research Center
Professor of Geology & Geophysics
University of Minnesota

TAPLINGER PUBLISHING COMPANY
NEW YORK

First published in the United States in 1970 by
TAPLINGER PUBLISHING CO., INC.
New York, New York

Copyright © 1970 by William C. Walton

All rights reserved. No portion of this book may be reproduced in any form without the written permission of the publisher, except by a reviewer who may wish to quote brief passages in connection with a review for a newspaper or magazine. No part of this publication may be reproduced, stored in a retrieval system, or transmitted in any form or by any means, electronic, mechanical, photocopying, recording or otherwise, without the prior permission of the copyright owner.

ISBN 0-8008-8610-0

Library of Congress Catalog Card Number 75-121002

AUG 12 '71

Printed in Great Britain

10.00
B+J

THE WORLD OF WATER

Contents

Preface	xi
1 The World's Water Supply and Problems	13
WATER AND LIFE	23
PROPERTIES OF WATER	28
ECONOMIC, LEGAL AND SOCIAL ASPECTS	32
2 Precipitation and Evapotranspiration	45
GENERAL CIRCULATION OF AIR MASSES	47
CLIMATES OF THE EARTH	53
WEATHER	56
Weather instruments	59
Clouds	60
Fronts	61
Thunderstorms	62
Hurricanes	62
Tornadoes	63
PRECIPITATION	63
EVAPORATION	67
USE OF WATER BY PLANTS	68
3 Oceans	72
CONTINENTAL SHORES AND ESTUARIES	75
CONTINENTAL SHELVES AND SLOPES	78
FLOOR OF THE DEEP SEA	79
CURRENTS	83
TIDES	89
WAVES	91
TEMPERATURE AND CHEMICAL CONTENTS	93
Temperature	94

Contents

Types of ice and icebergs	97
Chemical content	98
BIOLOGICAL ASPECTS	100
OCEANOGRAPHIC INSTRUMENTATION	107

4 Ice Caps and Glaciers — 112

SNOW AND ICE	114
GLACIATION	116
ANTARCTICA	122
The land beneath the ice	124
Ice surface, shelves, and sheet	125
Organisms	128
ARCTIC BASIN	129

5 Subsurface Water — 133

GROUNDWATER	134
Geologic aspects	134
Water levels	144
Hydraulic characteristics	146
Recharge	148
Discharge	149
Chemical and biological aspects	151
Well drilling	156
Resource measurement	159
Aquifer conditions	162
Development problems	166
SOIL MOISTURE	172

6 Lakes, Swamps, and Reservoirs — 175

ORIGIN OF LAKES	177
LAKE FORMS	182
THERMAL PROPERTIES OF LAKES	184
MOVEMENT OF WATER IN LAKES	186
GASES AND INORGANIC CONTENT OF LAKES	189
SOLAR RADIATION AND OPTICAL PROPERTIES OF LAKES	191
BIOLOGICAL ASPECTS OF LAKES AND BOGS	192
EVOLUTION OF LAKES	199
BOGS AND SWAMPS	199
RESERVOIRS	200

Contents

7 Streams   203
   STREAMFLOW   204
   Streamflow measurement   207
   Streamflow graphs   209
   GEOMETRY OF DRAINAGE BASIN AND STREAM-CHANNEL SYSTEM   211
   CHEMICAL AND BIOLOGICAL COMPOSITION   213
   SEDIMENT TRANSPORT AND EROSION   215
   Sediment measurement   218
   FLOOD CONTROL   220
   Dams   222
   River forecasting   223
   HYDROELECTRIC PLANTS   224
   WATER SUPPLY AND SEWAGE   225

8 Water-based Recreation and Wildlife   231
   WATER FOR OUTDOOR RECREATION   235
   FISHES   242
   WATERFOWL   254

9 Conservation   261
   CONCERN OVER POLLUTION   263
   POLLUTION AND ITS CONTROL   267
   FISHERIES   275
   FLOODS   279
   DRAINAGE   281

10 Water Resources Planning, Development, and Management   283
   RIVER BASIN COMPREHENSIVE PLANNING   285
   United States   285
   Germany   289
   DEVELOPMENT AND MANAGEMENT ORGANIZATIONS   291
   England and Wales   291
   Tennessee Valley Authority   300
   Genossenschaften in the Ruhr industrial area   304

References   309

Index   313

Plates

(Between pages 160 and 161)

1 Evaporation station at Jefferson City, Tennessee
2 Continuous plankton recorder silk showing zooplankters
3 Continuous plankton recorder
4 A scene in Antarctica
5 Large springs discharging from a basalt aquifer into a river
6 Water well-drilling rig
7 Electric analog computer for studying groundwater problems
8 A stream in a plateau terrane
9 Current meter for measuring streamflow
10 Soil erosion
11 Erosion on a large scale
12 Flooding of urban areas
13 Flooding of rural areas
14 Depth-integrating sampler for suspended sediment
15 Navigation dam and lock
16 Model for studying a dam structure
17 Barge on inland waterway
18 Fontana Dam on Little Tennessee River in North Carolina

Plates

19 Hydroelectric dam and power plant

20 Ice fishing

21 Trout fishing

22 Water-oriented recreation

23 Wetlands and waterfowl

24 Soil conservation

25 Dead waterfowl caused by accidental oil spill and associated pollution

Diagrams

1 The hydrologic cycle   15

2 Type of rock interstices and relation of rock texture to porosity   135

3 Structure and stratigraphy of the bedrock and piezometric profiles of the Cambrian-Ordovician aquifer, Chicago region   168-9

Preface

The world of water, viewed in all its aspects, is enormous; the large body of knowledge concerning water can only be found scattered through many scientific and technical books, journals, and reports. It is possible only to touch upon the highlights of the vast amounts of available information in a single volume. The writer has attempted to present, as far as possible, in nontechnical language a digest of facts to partially inform the intelligent general reader about water and its relation to everyday life. The information presented has been large abstracted from the references listed at the end of this book.

Hopefully, this book will provide a clearer understanding and appreciation of the world of water and create an awareness of the urgent need for accelerated research, planning, development and management programs. The writer will consider his efforts well spent if only this book inspires readers to become more fully informed on the subject of water and to take a more personal interest in what is happening from day to day in the field of water.

The oceans; ice caps and glaciers; subsurface reservoirs; lakes, swamps, and surface reservoirs; streams; and atmosphere contain the earth's total water. The physical aspects of these subjects are reviewed in this book together with biological, economic, legal, and social aspects. Some of the measures taken by man to develop and manage water resources and the effects of man's activities on the water environment are discussed. The problem of water conservation is stressed.

The world of water has many problems brought about largely as a consequence of man's desire to achieve higher standards of living. As we strive for increased economic activity, reduction in unemployment, increased personal income, and a general

Preface

improvement in social welfare, we create steadily growing unsatisfied demands for water resources. The world does not have an overall water shortage. All the ingredients for great cultures and agricultural and industrial economies are present. The bright prospect for the future prosperity and security of the world's peoples, however, is being dimmed by water problems created in part by our lack of a comprehensive understanding of the World of Water. Perhaps this book will in some small way assist in raising the priority mankind assigns to the importance of water. It is dedicated to Ellen, Cynthia, and Louise.

Chapter 1

The World's Water Supply and Problems

Water is to man the most important single substance, with the exception of the air he breathes. Together, the oceans and the ice caps and glaciers comprise 99.35 percent of the earth's total water. The remaining two thirds of one percent are apportioned to the waters of the rivers and lakes, the inland seas, the streams, springs, brooks and ponds, swamps and bogs, the rain, snow and vapor in the atmosphere, the snow and ice on mountain slopes, the moisture in the soil and the ground-water that supplies wells and streams. About 97.2 percent of the world's water is in the oceans; 2.15 percent occurs in icecaps and glaciers. Groundwater, in part, accounts for about 97 percent of the water which remains when the oceans, ice caps and glaciers are subtracted from the world's water supply.

Water is evaporated from the sea and land, is discharged into the atmosphere, falls as rain and snow, some of it runs off the land to form streams and rivers, some percolates into the earth to reappear in streams and springs, and then drains back into the sea. Maintaining this hydrologic cycle requires that at any moment an average of 3,100 cubic miles of water must be distributed throughout the atmosphere in the form of vapor or water droplets. This amount of moisture is slight, relative to the size of the atmosphere. If all of it abruptly fell as rain, the 3,100 cubic miles of water would cover the earth with only an inch of water. However, once every 12 days all the moisture in the air does fall and is subsequently replaced. About 95,000 cubic miles of water is discharged into the air annually; approximately 80,000 cubic miles evaporates from the ocean; about 15,000 cubic miles is derived from the land, evaporated off lakes, streams and moist soil, and transpired from the leaf surfaces of living plants. The total process is called evapotranspiration. Of the water that reaches the atmosphere, about

13

71,000 cubic miles precipitates into the oceans. Another 9,000 cubic miles precipitates on land but runs off into rivers and streams and is returned to the oceans within days or, at most, a few weeks. The remaining 15,000 cubic miles percolates into the soil and participates in plant and animal life processes (Leopold and Davis, 1966).

While the hydrologic cycle balances what goes up with what comes down over the entire earth, no such reciprocity holds for individual areas. Wide differences occur in rates of both evaporation and precipitation. Evaporation might be expected to be greatest at the equator, since most solar energy reaches that area. But heavy clouds are more frequent over the equator than in most other regions and they reduce the radiation reaching the surface. To the north and south, strong winds evaporate moisture more than the relatively calm winds of the equator. The highest evaporation rates on earth occur in the Red Sea and Persian Gulf.

Among the nine planets, the earth is uniquely endowed with large quantities of water in its liquid state. It is massive enough so that its gravitational force will hold an atmosphere of water vapor and other heavy gases. Its location 93 million miles from the sun keeps it near the center of a narrow zone where temperatures permit water to exist as liquid, solid and vapor.

In absolute terms, an enormous amount of water is available for man's use. But, the distribution of it is uneven, and so inept has man been in making use of it, that water, or its lack, has always been one of the greatest problems confronting the human race. Water has been the focus of conflict among individuals, families, tribes and nations. Flood and drought alternately have killed millions, while many more have died from waterborne diseases. Other millions have suffered more slowly as wind and rain stripped their lands of precious topsoil. There is an urgent requirement for water that is clean and pure enough for human use, water for drinking; water for cooking; water for washing and bathing. Beyond that, water for food production; water for industry; water for commerce, transportation, and electric power generation, and water for recreation.

Three billion human beings inhabit the earth today, and every day there are 200,000 more persons on this planet. By the year

The World's Water Supply and Problems

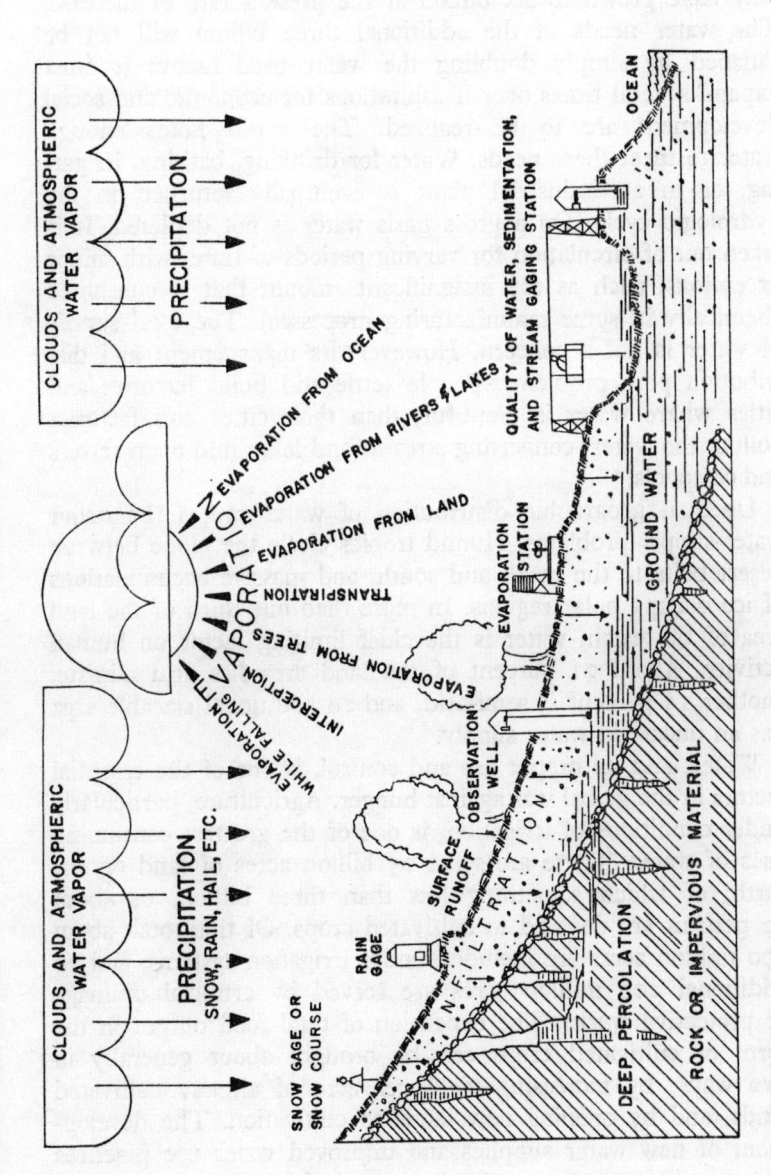

The hydrologic cycle

2000, which is about 30 years away, these three billion people may have grown to six billion at the present rate of increase. The water needs of the additional three billion will not be satisfied by simply doubling the water used today; it must expand several times over if aspirations for economic and social development are to be realized. The world holds enough water to meet these needs. Water for drinking, bathing, irrigating, or in an industrial plant is eventually returned to the hydrologic cycle. On a gross basis water is not depleted. It is taken out of circulation for varying periods of time (with minor exceptions, such as the insignificant amount that is consumed chemically in some manufacturing processes). The total supply of water is not a concern. However, its management and distribution pose problems. People settle and build factories and cities where water is plentiful; then their cities and factories pollute the water, converting streams and lakes into open sewers and cesspools.

Unequal geographic distribution of water causes the major water-supply problems. Humid tropics circle the globe between desert belts to the north and south, and massive accumulations of ice occupy polar regions. In more than one-third of the land area of the earth, water is the chief limiting factor on human activity. About 21 percent of the land area has arid climate, another 15 percent is semi-arid, and an additional sizeable area has an uncertain water supply.

Water, and its proper use and control, is one of the essential factors in the global war against hunger. Agriculture, particularly under conditions of irrigation, is one of the greatest consuming uses of water. There are some 25 billion acres of land on the earth, of which something less than three billion, or about 12 percent are devoted to cultivated crops. Of this total, about 400 million acres are included under irrigation systems, and an additional 200 million acres are served by artificial drainage or protective works. The expansion of total food output in the form of cultivated crops can be brought about generally in two ways: by increasing yield per acre of already cultivated lands, and by opening new lands to cultivation. The development of new water supplies and improved water use practices can contribute to greater food output in both situations (Water for Peace, 1967).

The oceans, rivers, and lakes comprise major sources of proteins, yielding over 56 million tons in 1964. In addition to contributing to the nutritional balance of local diets, fish are important exchange earners for the nations involved. During the last decade, the world's fishing fleets increased their landings by 70 percent. The steady increase in landings over the past decade is one of the most encouraging events in man's urgent search for food sources. There is evidence to support the belief that further large gains are possible. The productivity of fresh-water areas for fish production, when properly managed, exceeds that of the land.

The well-being of communities, both urban and rural, is highly dependent on the water available for their daily needs. Water for human consumption and sanitation are of great social and economic importance, because the effect on man's health in turn influences all his other activities. Of the 1·1 billion people living in rural areas, nearly 800 million had no water service in 1964. Less than 300 million were served by public outlets and very few enjoyed water service from house connections. Forty percent of the urban population, comprising around 140 million people, had no water service, and an additional 90 million obtained water from public outlets. More than 900 million people were without any kind of public water service, and another 365 million relied on public outlets. Only about 170 million, or one person out of nine, had water piped to his habitation. In many parts of the world women and children still spend as much as 50 percent of their time hauling water for household and stock watering purposes (Water for Peace, 1967).

Disease not only causes high death rates and short life expectancy, but saps the much-needed energy of the population. Although all nations have deficiencies in providing adequate supplies of potable water for domestic use, the problem is most critical among the developing countries. Of the $1\frac{1}{2}$ billion people in the developing portions of the free world, it is estimated that nearly a billion obtain their water from unsanitary sources. As a result, most of them are suffering or have suffered for extended periods in the past from waterborne or water-related diseases; each year an estimated 500 million people are affected by illnesses, and as many as ten million people, about half of them infants, die. Dysentery, typhoid fever, cholera, and lesser diseases are often the direct consequence of drinking polluted water, or of poor sanitation due to a lack of water. Other diseases, such as typhus and trachoma also attack those who are unable to obtain enough water to keep themselves, their clothing, and their dwellings to a minimum standard of cleanliness. In addition to those diseases whose control may be approached in the provision of water for human consumption and sanitation, there is a group of water-related diseases, those for which an insect or other carrier spends an important part of its life in, or on water. Measures to control these diseases are elements of water management directly affecting the health of people. The widely known of these diseases is malaria; eradication and control measures are now concentrated on the application of insecticides. However, there are other fly and mosquito-borne diseases, in need of control through water management.

If water quality is sufficiently degraded, it becomes unusable, and the effect is the same as a quantitative loss. The problems of water quality and water quantity are, therefore, inextricably interwoven. The control of water pollution has become the overriding consideration in providing adequate water supplies for continued global growth, health, and welfare. The limited supply of water, relative to the demands made upon it, requires that its quality be maintained for reuse by downstream communities, industries, farms, and recreation areas. Pollution has been vastly accelerated by the large increases in population, and by the measures people have taken to improve their standards of hygiene, nutrition, and public health. Organic wastes, laden with infectious agents, conveniently removed from one city arc disposed of often with insufficient treatment to areas downstream. The chemical residue that remains in the water used to treat certain materials in industrial processes does great damage to the natural chemical balance of streams, and ambient temperature of rivers may be raised several degrees by the heat laden discharge of plants which use water for cooling. Farmers who use large volumes of pesticide and chemical fertilizers contribute to the problem of pollution and irrigation return flows often degrade the quality of the water in the

The World's Water Supply and Problems

stream. Water transportation also can result in pollution from shipboard wastes and oil discharges.

Just as water is vital to human life and happiness, so also is it essential to industrial processes that provide higher standards of living. With the possible exception of agriculture, industry is the greatest consumer of water. The industrial uses of water are varied. Water is used in the minerals industry and the refining of oil. It is used in all chemical processes, such as in the making of paper and plastics. The processing of crops and fish for distribution requires water. Water is used by industry for washing, for heating, for cooling, and for many other purposes. For example, an automobile coming off the assembly line represents the expenditure of at least 30,000 gallons of water, 20,000 needed to produce its ton of steel, and 10,000 more used during the actual assembly process. Many thousands more are involved in the manufacture of its plastics, glass, fabrics, and other parts. Every gallon of gasoline represents as much as 70 gallons of water, utilized in refining. The use of water for industrial purposes has the advantage of being largely nonconsumptive, that is, after use in the industrial cycle, much of it is discharged to a stream and is potentially capable of reuse. However, all too frequently the water is altered by chemical, thermal, or other industrial pollution.

Almost all rivers have flooded at one time or another, but few have wrought so much havoc as the Hwang Ho. As early as the eighth century B.C. the Chinese were raising dikes to confine the shifting lower river in its channel. When the dikes give way, as they have many times in the past 3,000 years, the damage is appalling. The millions of acres of land in these areas are rich in topsoil washed down from upstream watersheds through centuries of erosion and are intensively cultivated for food production. Uncontrolled flooding results in loss of life, damages to crops, dwellings, and other properties, contamination of water supplies, the spreading of waterborne diseases, and the disruption of orderly social and economic processes. The Mississippi, the mightiest river in the USA, sometimes rises to flood miles of countryside. In 1965 it overflowed its banks and submerged 90,000 acres of cropland in Illinois alone. Thousands of acres more in Missouri, Iowa, Wisconsin, and Minnesota were inundated. More than 40,000 people were driven from their homes; by the time the river subsided, the damage totaled $200 million.

The reduction of flood damage, usually through the construction of storage, channelization, and containment works, has long been recognized as a public concern. In recent years, however, increasing attention has been given to the fact that the success of a project in subduing minor floods often only leads to an escalation in the damage from more severe floods, because extensive new investment is attracted to the flood-plain zone. This has led to investigation of the regulatory mechanism of flood-plain zoning as one possible means of attaining a permanent end to the public expense. Great masses of people in the developing countries, particularly in Asia and the Far East, live in vast flood-plain and deltaic areas.

On February 1, 1953, under the onslaught of wind-whipped waves from the North Sea, dikes protecting the southwestern Netherlands burst in 100 places. Some 400,000 acres were flooded and 1,800 people drowned. The catastrophe was one of the worst in Dutch history. The Netherlands always exists in the threat of a flood disaster. A tiny country with the densest population in the world, the Netherlands has been adding to its own land since the twelfth century by constructing an artificial coastline of dikes, then pumping out the impounded seawater with windmills and electric pumps. Today fully half of the Netherlands, including the two largest cities, lies below sea level. An altimeter at the Amsterdam airport reads −13 feet; near Rotterdam it reads −30 feet. The Netherlands' defenses against the North Sea require constant maintenance by a corps of 10,000 engineers and workers. Day and night, 2,000 pumps and 400 windmills labor to keep the land dry. The Netherlands allots eight percent of its national budget for dike-building and upkeep. In many places the dikes are battered and antiquated. After the 1953 flood, the Dutch government undertook a huge $650-million, 25-year construction program to prevent any recurrence of the disaster. About 25 miles of new concrete dikes are being built across the mouths of estuaries in the south-west part of the country. These new barriers will form an outer wall to protect the vulnerable older dikes, and will shorten the coastline by 435 miles. One scheme now being considered would pump 600 billion cubic yards of earth into the interior of the country from the North Sea and end the threat of the sea for all time (Leopold and Davis, 1966).

Everywhere in the world, including the developing nations, the demand for energy is climbing steeply. This is especially true of electrical energy. Historically, the consumption of electrical energy has more than doubled for each of the past several decades and no diminution of the trend is evident. Gross world electric power consumption amounted to just over three trillion kilowatt-hours in 1964, an increase of eight percent over the previous year. For countries blessed with conditions suitable for its development, hydro-electric power, especially when developed in concert with other purposes such as flood control and irrigation, can be a means to rapid growth. Hydropower is estimated to account for roughly a third of all electricity generated in the world. Construction began in 1961 on the world's first tidal-power dam, near the mouth of the Rance estuary on the Coast of France. Twice a day, a tidal flow nearly equivalent to that of the Mississippi River will flow through the dam's 24 turbines and raise or lower the water level 28 feet. The turbines are designed to generate 240,000 kilowatts of electricity when the tide is flowing in and the same amount when it is ebbing out. Because this amount is not always adequate to meet the region's power needs, the blades of the turbines driven by electricity from nearby steam generators can slowly pump water into the reservoir during periods of slack tide. The stored water can then be released to generate power at times of peak demand.

Civilizations have grown up along rivers, lakes, and oceans, which offered the facility for easy and cheap transportation of goods. Waterways are made more useful by dredging and silt control and benefit from such measures as large storage projects which may permit year-round navigation otherwise possible only during the rainy season, systems of locks around navigational obstacles, and the improvement of port and harbor facilities. The opportunities for further navigation development are enormous, since the cheapest way to ship bulk cargo is still by water.

The booming industrial sections of Germany, France, Belgium, and the Netherlands depend on a 13,000-mile network of barge canals and rivers. The Great Lakes ports, benefiting

The World of Water

from the access to the Atlantic Ocean provided by the $1.3-billion St. Lawrence Seaway, now handle 70 percent as much cargo as all other US ports combined. The titans among canals are the lockless Suez, 35 feet deep and 165 yards wide, and the six-lock Panama Canal. Traffic on the Panama waterway has reached 1,000 ships a month and plans for a second canal across Central America are receiving serious attention. The Suez provides passageway, blocked in 1969, for 40 ships a day between the Mediterranean and the Red Sea. On the Hooghly river stands the bustling port of Calcutta, 128 miles from the sea. Keeping the Hooghly navigable from port to sea is an endless operation that keeps 18 dredges at work around the clock. In 1963, this fleet dredged 9,190,746 tons of silt from the river, working a total of 5,781 hours at a cost of $2,300,000. The silt is ultimately dumped at the mouth of the river. The fleet includes the biggest dredger in the world, a $4.5-million ship that can suck up 100,000 cubic feet of silt (about 5,000 tons) every 50 minutes.

Fresh water may be processed from saline water by several means. One group of processes separates water from its dissolved salts either by distillation or by freezing. Large amounts of energy are required to change water from a liquid to a vapor, or a solid, to accomplish the separation process. Of the two processes, distillation has long been used, and accounts for most of the installed capacity today. The heat energy required may be supplied by nuclear reactors or by burning oil, gas, or coal. In sun-rich areas, solar energy may be used for small plants where other heat sources are uneconomical or unavailable. The freezing process theoretically requires less energy than does distillation but in 1969 the technology was not as far advanced. A second group of processes separates the dissolved salts from the water by utilizing membranes. Of these, electrodialysis already has practical application in more than 100 small plants throughout the world. Reverse osmosis is theoretically the most efficient known process, and is showing great promise for brackish and perhaps sea water as it moves into the pilot plant phase of development. Other processes, such as ion exchange, are currently under investigation and with further development may have useful application in certain circumstances. Cost is inherently the most important consideration in determining the extent to which desalination should be adopted as a method for providing water at a specific location.

Effective water development cannot proceed unless basic information is at hand with respect to a wide range of physical, social, and economic factors. In addition to data on water resources, realistic planning for water development programs cannot be accomplished unless adequate information is available with respect to such socio-economic matters as the incidence of disease, population density and projected growth, per capita income, agricultural production and potential, tax revenues, gross national product, and so forth. The compilation and analysis of data of this kind is a necessary part of every water program. Basic physical data are obtained only by systematic observation, analysis, and interpretation of hydrological phenomena. Hydrologic observations generally consist of river stage or flow records, records of well yields, flood and drought data, sediment loads, water-quality data, soil-moisture measurements, rainfall data, snow depths and accumulations, and measurements of evaporation. Even with the best possible arrangements for all aspects of collection, dissemination, and application of present knowledge on water resources development and management, there is still a great need to learn more. Research is required in many fields of water knowledge: water chemistry and biota; the interplay of soil moisture, fertilizers, pest and weed control, seed varieties, and cultivation practices on crop yields in different areas; sewage disposal and treatment, dissipation of heat and industrial wastes, and other aspects of pollution control; reduction in water losses by evaporation and seepage; soil conservation and erosion control; desalting; and weather modification, among others.

WATER AND LIFE

Before birth, much of man's life is spent in water, in the sheltering membranous sac of his mother's womb, and water flows through his body till death. Man can live several weeks without food; one Indian fakir survived 81 days with no nourishment whatever. But without water, the longest any human being can live is ten days. Some bacteria flourish without oxygen, but neither they nor any other form of life can grow without water.

The World of Water

The amount of water in the human body, averaging 65 percent, varies considerably from person to person and even from one part of the body to another. A lean man may have as much as 70 percent of his weight in the form of body water, while a woman, because of her larger proportion of water-poor fatty tissues, may be only 52 percent water. The average man has approximately 50 quarts (about 100 pounds) of water in his body and every day he must replace about two and a half quarts of it. Drinking supplies about one and half quarts and the water content of food brings in another quart; an extra half-pint is produced by the metabolizing of food. The driest food man can eat, baked sunflower seeds, is five percent water; the wettest is the watermelon, which is 97 percent water. A tomato is 94 percent water; meats are 50 to 70 percent water, and bread contains about 35 percent. Water permeates all human tissue, fills cellular gaps and bony hollows, and flows through 60,000 miles of arteries and veins. Water in the cells make up 41 percent of the body's weight, the blood plasma provides four percent, and the fluid occupying empty cavities, such as the intestines or eyeballs, comprises five percent. This distribution is not static; water knows no anatomical boundaries and passes constantly through membranes from one compartment of the body to another (Leopold and Davis, 1966).

Water is involved in the most fundamental process of the human body. Acting on food, with the help of chemical accelerators called enzymes, it breaks up the great molecules of carbohydrates into simple molecular groups, chiefly the sugar glucose, that are small enough to be absorbed through cell membranes. These molecules combine with oxygen, also transported into the cell in water solution, and become metabolized; the food is oxidized, or 'burned,' to produce energy for the body. The products of this combustion are organic compounds such as starch, which can be stored, heat, which must be distributed at once, and carbon dioxide, which is carried to the lungs. Another product of this metabolic 'burning' is additional water, which remains in the body. The heat of the body's metabolic fires is great; water helps control this heat. It absorbs large quantities of metabolic heat with little increase in temperature; its rapid circulation throughout the body via the bloodstream enables it to carry heat to the surface of the body for quick release to the surrounding air. A related property, water's high latent heat of vaporization, further helps to protect the body from high temperatures. Water in the form of perspiration disposes of almost three times as much heat in the process of evaporation as the same weight of alcohol. In addition, water protects the internal chemical processes of the body from violent fluctuations in pressure, acidity and chemical composition.

Water leaves the body by several routes. About 15 percent is exhaled in the breath, and perspiration evaporates another 20 percent; this last figure may be 33 percent in hot weather. The rest is released by direct excretion. While these proportions may vary, the combined rate of disposal is always held within narrow limits. Excretion rarely falls below the minimum of about four pints per day. Most of the body's water loss is through kidney waste fluid, or urine, which is roughly 95 percent water.

The balance of water within the body must be precise; a variation of one or two percent from the normal immediately makes itself felt as thirst or pain. The master control center is the hypothalamus, a small section in the center of the brain just above the spinal cord. The hypothalamus governs processes that must respond automatically without any delay for conscious decisions: heart action, sleeping and waking, appetite, sex, digestion, and thirst. It maintains water balance by secreting a hormone that regulates the kidneys and also stimulates nerves at the back of the throat. True thirst is sensed mainly there, even a man dying of lack of water might feel no thirst if his throat could be kept moist. Either too much or too little water can be disastrous. When a man loses only five percent of his normal body water, his skin will shrink, his mouth and tongue will go dry, and he may experience hallucinations; a loss of 15 percent is usually fatal. Too much water causes nausea and weakness, and enforced drinking, the water 'cure' inflicted by some savages on their enemies, leads successively to mental confusion, disorientation, tremors, convulsions, coma, and death (Leopold and Davis, 1966).

The body must carefully meter the materials dissolved in it. Too great a loss of salt through heavy perspiration brings on heat cramps. The muscles react to the loss of salt by contracting into hard and painful knots. Organisms keep the amount of salt in their bodies in balance, using water to remove excessive amounts of the substance. No animal can tolerate a body-salt concentration of more than 0·9 percent. Water in human kidneys serves as the medium which purges wastes from the bloodstream. Fifteen times an hour, all the blood in the body passes through the two kidneys. A total of about 2,000 quarts of blood is washed every day; from this amount, two quarts of waste are removed as urine. The rest is absorbed back into the bloodstream. The kidneys are so efficient that even if one is incapacitated the other can continue cleaning the entire blood supply by itself. If both kidneys fail, however, a condition known as uremia results; salts and other wastes pollute the blood. A man cannot live more than three weeks with uncleansed blood.

Animals must maintain fairly rigid percentages of water in their bodies. Most however, have adapted their physiology to match the moisture or their environment. The donkey can survive in a desert for four days; in the process it may lose 30 percent of its body weight in water, doubling the amount that would fatally dehydrate a human. Desert animals conserve water by foraging at night, when lower temperatures make water losses far less than they would be during the day. They keep out of the sun and often live underground. Many of them, like the armadillo and the desert-dwelling lizards, have developed hides that are virtually impervious to water loss by perspiration. The pocket mouse and the kangaroo rat, small rodents inhabiting the deserts of the southwestern USA, may drink no free fluid as adults. These animals manufacture the water they need by combining the oxygen in the air with hydrogen from dry seeds. A diet of succulent plants supplies the water requirements of the desert tortoise. In a pair of bladder-like sacs located along the inner surface of its upper shell, it can store as much as a pint of liquid for use in time of drought (Leopold and Davis, 1966).

The amount of salt an animal can concentrate in its urine is directly related to its need for water. Creatures such as the camel and kangaroo rat, which live where water is scarce, cannot afford to use much of it for flushing; as a consequence, the amount of their urine is slight, but the concentration of salt in it is high. The kidneys of the horse, an animal which consumes large quantities of water and excretes freely, produce a very low percentage of salt.

Plants, like cities, often find their need for water far greater than the available supply. They tend to develop elaborate supply systems as water becomes harder to find. For some plants, like the aquatic algae, the system is simple. They absorb water, which makes up 95 percent of their substance, by direct contact, and would quickly perish, if removed from their water-filled environment. The semi-aquatic marsh plant merely extends its body an inch or two into the damp ground for its water needs. By contrast, the land plant has evolved a root system that can absorb moisture from as far as 30 feet underground. A single rye plant may have 14 billion root hairs, with a root network totaling 380 miles. In a single growing season, a plant may soak up 20 times its dry weight in water.

With a few exceptions, plants make their own food from water and air. The water, absorbed through the fine root hairs underground, travels upward through long, microscopic tubes penetrating the stem and branches, and passes back to the atmosphere as transpiration through tiny leaf pores called stomata, which also serve as entrance and exit ports for the carbon dioxide and oxygen essential to photosynthesis and growth. One square inch of leaf may contain as many as 300,000 stomata, most of which are on the underside. Although transpiration varies with conditions of temperature, humidity, light, wind, and soil moisture, it usually totals several hundred times the dry weight of the plant itself during a single growing season. During its lifetime, a crop of corn, for example, may release water sufficient to cover its entire field to a depth of 11 inches. In one warm day a single birch tree can dispose of 60 to 80 gallons of water (Leopold and Davis, 1966).

Plants which must cope with occasional droughts can shut off or drastically reduce transpiration. The guard cells of the leaf stomata hold the pores open only when the cells are turgid with water; when the plants wilt, as they do when water becomes deficient, the pores close. Plants of the driest deserts carry this process further; their stomata normally opens only at night. Plants like ocotillo accomplish the same end by dropping their leaves during droughts and growing new foliage following a rain. Cacti, whose leaves have been reduced to spines, have a thick, waxy cuticle which prevents the escape of water. The barrel cactus is well known for its ability to absorb and conserve large amounts of water. After a rain, its thousands of roots take in moisture from the soil. This moisture is then carried up into the plant, whose cylindrical body swells to barrel-like proportions as it makes room for its water supply and shrinks again as the supply is depleted.

The movement of water in certain plants, very tall trees, for example, poses one of the most intriguing puzzles of biology. There are Douglas firs which tower 400 feet; since their roots may sink 50 feet into the ground, some of the water that reaches the treetop must be lifted a total of 450 feet. The pressure required for this task is more than 30 times greater than the pressure of the atmosphere at sea level.

PROPERTIES OF WATER

Water exists in three states: the solid, the liquid, and the gaseous. Water may partially cover a lake as ice, form the bulk of the lake as a liquid, and in a gaseous state float in the sky above the lake within a visible cloud. As a solid, water exhibits rigidity and is a body having length, breadth, and thickness. Water in the liquid state lacks rigidity and, though it has a definite volume, the liquid assumes the shape of the vessel containing it. Liquid water flows under an imbalance of force. As a gas, water has indefinite expansion and assumes the shape and volume of the vessel containing it. Water vapor has neither rigidity nor definite volume.

The stage of water depends upon its temperature; as the temperature goes up, frozen water melts to become a liquid and the liquid boils to become a gas. Heat, being a form of energy, increases the motion of the atoms and molecules of water. In ice, molecules are fixed in relationship to one another. As the temperature increases thermal agitation of molecules occurs and the arrangement of molecules becomes more and more random. Changes in state are not instantaneous; there are transitional periods of time during which two states coexist: a mixture of ice and liquid water at the melting-freezing point and a mixture of liquid and gas at the boiling-condensation point. The temperature of water remains unchanged by the continued application of heat during the transition periods. The temperature at which the transitions from one state to another occur depends upon the atmospheric pressure. The heat required for a change in state increases with higher pressures; the effect of pressure is greater upon the liquid to gas change than it is upon the solid to liquid change.

During transition periods, heat is absorbed without producing a change in the temperature of the water. This heat is called latent; water's latent heats are higher than any other widely prevalent substance. Water has a great capacity to store heat which is released when the temperature declines. Water in freezing releases the same amount of heat that it absorbs in melting; the condensation of vapor into liquid releases heat in the same amount that the vaporization of liquid absorbs it. At the melting point one gram of water absorbs 79.7 calories without a rise in temperature; at the vaporization point one gram of water absorbs 539.4 calories before its temperature rises again.

Water has about five times the heat capacity of a sandy soil. Water vapor in the air absorbs mid-day heat for release during the night, thus, moderating surface temperatures. Over deserts, dry air is unable to moderate temperatures and during the night sands are rapidly drained of heat, resulting in wide fluctuations in surface temperatures. Water in the process of freezing releases heat. Thus, a greenhouse is often kept warmer than outside air by use of a container of water which may partially freeze and release heat. Our human bodies are cooled during the summer by perspiration because heat is absorbed by the evaporation of liquid water.

Oceans receive the major portion of the energy radiated by the sun on the earth. The amount of energy absorbed varies with the amount of water vapor present and with the scattering effect of dust particles. Of the total solar energy absorbed by the ocean, approximately 50 percent is used for evaporating sea water. The energy is made available to the atmosphere in the form of latent heat of vaporization of water. This constitutes a most important component of the atmospheric heat budget.

Water, over a wide range of temperatures, contracts or shrinks in volume as it is cooled. As a liquid down to a temperature of

The World of Water

39°F, water shrinks in volume; between 39°F and the freezing point, water gradually expands and becomes less dense. Almost any substance can be dissolved in water; about half the known chemical elements are dissolved in natural waters. Streams, lakes, oceans, and other bodies of water are aqueous solutions. Metals, non-metal substances in ionic form, and organic and inorganic compounds are contained in aqueous solutions.

Water, with the exception of mercury, has the highest surface tension of all common liquids and in its natural state has a tensile strength close to that of most steels. Water coheres or clings to itself and adheres or clings to other substances. Water adheres strongly to almost every particle of organic and inorganic matter forming soil. In soil openings of small size, the combination of surface tension and adhesion causes water to rise to appreciable heights. Partly because of this 'capillary action' water circulates in the soil and vital solutions reach roots and stems of plants. Water's abnormally high surface tension increases its erosive ability.

Pure water is a very poor conductor of electricity because it provides very few charged particles to constitute a current between two electrodes. The water molecule resists dissociation into ions and has a strong tendency to orient itself in an electrical field with its positive end toward the negative plate and its negative end toward the positive plate. The strength of this tendency, called 'dipole movement,' depends upon the magnitude of the charge separation within the molecule. The charge separation within the water molecule is great and water is said to have a large dipole movement. Water molecules tend to neutralize an electrical field and as a result of its large dipole moment, water has a large dielectric constant. In part, water's large dielectric constant is responsible for its ability to dissolve substances, especially substances whose molecules are held together mainly by ionic bonding. Broken ionic bonds are not likely to be reestablished in water, because the attraction between the dissociated, oppositely charged ions is reduced by water's high dielectric constant to a fraction of what it would be in air (Davis and Day, 1961).

The hydrogen bond, a bond between molecules of water, is partly responsible for water's remarkable abilities as a solvent. Water molecules are joined together in rare tightness and continuity of structure by means of a hydrogen bond. Water molecules are attracted to one another by the extra force of the hydrogen bond which is electrostatic in nature.

In the water molecule, two hydrogen atoms share their electrons with the oxygen atom, thereby exposing their nuclei (single protons). The exposed positive charges exert attractive forces upon unpaired electrons. An oxygen atom has two unpaired electrons, therefore, each water molecule is able to form four hydrogen bonds. The two molecules bonded together in a complex have a great ability to neutralize an electrical field. Hence, water's ability to form hydrogen bonds accounts for its large dielectric constant and its great capacity as a solvent.

Hydrogen bonding accounts in large part for water's remarkable heat capacity, high latent heats of fusion and evaporation, and its ability to adhere strongly to substances. Ice can float because of hydrogen bonding. Water's density increases as its temperature reduces until a point is reached at which the hydrogen bonding influence exceeds the tendency to contract or shrink. At this point, 39°F, molecules start to arrange themselves along the directional lines of the hydrogen bonds and openings are left between these lines. The water expands until, at 32°F, it solidifies into a very open structure.

Water called pure H_2O is actually a complicated compound, a mixture of eighteen isotopes and fifteen ions, 33 different substances in all. In 1934 it was discovered that pure water contained minute portions of a substance containing water molecules made up of atoms of hydrogen having twice the atomic weight of ordinary hydrogen, each of their nuclei having a neutron in addition to the single proton which is the nucleus of ordinary hydrogen. The substance is called 'deuterium,' its oxide, 'heavy water' has the formula D_2O. The boiling point of D_2O is a little higher than that of H_2O, its freezing point is much higher than that of H_2O. Although D_2O has the same chemical formula as H_2O, its molecular weight is greater than that of H_2O. D_2O is physiologically inert.

Progress in the development of nuclear energy has increased the practical importance of heavy water. To induce a chain reaction in ordinary uranium an abundant supply of very slow neutrons is needed. Fast neutrons must be slowed down. A moderator is required, a substance which will absorb the excess energy of the fast neutrons without capturing the neutrons themselves. D_2O is a highly effective moderator; nuclei of heavy hydrogen, each consisting of a neutron and a proton, are poor neutron absorbers, but light enough to absorb large portions of the neutrons' energy upon impact (Davis and Day, 1961).

Heavy isotopes of hydrogen are particularly fusible. Nuclear fusion could some day prove superior to nuclear fission as a source of industrial power. Deuterium will have increased practical importance in supplying the energy needs of mankind in the future. There is no practical limit to the amount of fusion fuel present in the oceans. The deuterium in a single gallon of sea water has an energy content equivalent to that of 350 gallons of gasoline.

ECONOMIC, LEGAL AND SOCIAL ASPECTS

The task of developing and managing water resources for man's benefit would be hopeless but for the great advances in scientific and technical knowledge that have been made over the past few generations. Although we still have much to learn, we are no longer ignorant of the basic cause-and-effect relationships between man, air, soil, water, and the biota of a given environment. Technologically speaking, we generally know what must be done if the water resources of a country are to be developed. Development, however, is not a matter of technology alone. The technology of one people cannot simply be grafted onto the social structure of another with the expectation that it will thrive and produce the same benefits. Technology, in the absence of relevant data, organization, planning, institutions, human skills, available capital, and above all, the understanding and motivation of the people who are to employ it, is like an automobile without a driver. Technology can specify what must be done to develop the water resources of a nation. It requires the purposeful articulation of human effort, skills, and institutions to apply the technology to obtain effective results.

A number of economic and financial considerations are involved in selecting and planning water development programs. These may be grouped under the headings of economic policy, reimbursement policy, and project evaluation. Informed judgements as to individual water programs cannot be made in isolation from overall economic policy. Water development must be placed in its total economic perspective.

Who owns the water in a river? Who owns the water in the ground? These questions seem of little interest to a village housewife who washes her clothes in the river and dips out enough to carry back for household use; or to an enterprising farmer who sinks a well to supply the needs of livestock, crops, and home. But, to the modern water planner the answers to these questions are of vital concern. The success of a new project may depend as much upon questions of water rights and water law, as upon the considerations of engineering and finance. It is not unknown for reservoirs to empty, not because of drought, but because upstream users have diverted the flow of the river to their own uses; or for a well to dry up because excessive pumping of a common underground source has lowered the water table beyond economically feasible reach. In areas where water is plentiful questions of property rights in the use of water are not so critical. The places in the world where these conditions exist are not many, and their number declines each year as population, urban and industrial growth place increasing demands on the available supply.

In many areas of the world, conditions of water surplus have never existed. The inhabitants of these areas have long struggled to develop workable doctrines to accommodate the conflicting interests and to provide a sound legal base for economic progress. The lessons they have learned, and the legal institutions they have created can provide a valuable guide to other peoples faced with similar problems. One such area is the American West. There the early settlers found that the common law doctrine of riparian rights, that permitted each owner of property bordering a watercourse to take what he needed for his reasonable use, while allowing the flow to continue otherwise undisturbed, would not serve the development needs of a more arid land. Instead, a new doctrine was evolved to govern water rights of individuals within a state based on the concept of 'first in time, first in right.' Called the law of prior appropriation, these rules protect the right of the first person to use a known quantity of water to continue to use this amount as against any subsequent upstream or downstream user. The importance of legal institutions in water development has too often been overlooked. The development of water law must parallel and in many cases precede that of water works (Water for Peace, 1967).

Cultural institutions, like legal ones, usually evolve slowly. They are shaped by religion, by history, by language and by the natural environment. Shared convictions about the relationships among individuals and between the individual and the group; assumptions regarding initiative and responsibility; concepts of justice; attitudes of fatalism or optimism toward the environment; policies regarding payment for water; and many other cultural precepts will determine whether any given institutional arrangement will succeed or fail. The study of institutional transfer from one culture to another is an important requirement for facilitating the strengthening of institutional support for water development. Parallel with the development of legal institutions relating to the distribution and use of water are a host of legal arrangements dealing with construction, operation and maintenance of water projects and the important matter of providing revenues to defray the costs of these services.

In addition to the legal institutions relating to water rights and to project implementation, another area of concern deals with the public authorities regulating the management and use of water resources. The long range objective in the control of river and streams is to maximize the next benefits, to the extent practicable, from development of the land and water resources for all purposes necessary to meet man's future needs. Such an objective can be advanced through systems analyses of the effectiveness of the various control and development measures, both in the upstream watershed and on the mainstem and principal tributaries of the river system. These measures include multiple-purpose reservoirs to store floodwaters and use them for power, irrigation, improvement of navigation depths and of water quality. They also include local flood protection works, levees, floodwalls, channel stabilization measures, and bank protection. Additionally, there are nonstructural measures, such as flood-plain zoning and flood-warning systems, which should be considered in the analyses.

The World's Water Supply and Problems

Up until this century nearly all waterworks were built for a single purpose: to provide power for a mill, to impound water for a town's use, to provide a means of transportation, to divert it for irrigation, to prevent floods, or dispose of waste. As a result, these separate and unrelated ventures contributed nothing to one another's effectiveness. Thus, a dam might be built for municipal use that was too low for power generation or too small for the additional demands of industry. Gradually the realization evolved that many of these disparate purposes were indeed compatible, and that often it was possible to build a dam that would not only provide water for irrigation, for industry, and for electric power, but could also serve beneficially the purposes of navigation, and flood control as well. Thus, the notion of multiple-purpose development of water resources grew. At the same time, there also developed an increasing awareness of the interdependence that exists among the inhabitants of a common drainage basin and the tenuous balance between the forces that continuously operate upon the basin's land, water, vegetation, and animal life.

In the industrial Ruhr area of Germany, a highly effective system has been evolved that permits multiple-purpose management for waste-carriage, water supply, and recreation of a vital water resource. The system is administered principally by seven large water resources cooperative associations called *Genossenschaften*, with origins dating back to 1904. Membership, consisting principally of municipal and rural administrative districts, coal mines and industrial enterprises, is compulsory and the associations have the power to assess costs against their members based, among other factors, on the quantity and quality of waste water discharged.

The integral nature of river valleys and the interdependence of those who live in them have led to rivalries, irritations, and armed warfare that have taxed the efforts of peacemakers for thousands of years. Water, fully as much as land, has been fought over, disputed, and otherwise contested by rival claimants at every level from the individual to the nation. However, where a supervening authority exists over the disputed region, the differences can be settled by mutual consent, if possible, or by law if necessary. But since integrated authority ends at the level of the nation-state, rivers which are shared by two

35

or more nations present a problem of great magnitude to the peaceful relationships of the nations who seek the benefits of the waters they carry.

International rivers do not merely bring problems. They provide matchless opportunities for cooperation between people and nations for the peaceful development of their potentials. The enormous advances in science and engineering over the past half century have accentuated these opportunities by making possible many essential features of cooperative development that formerly could not have been accomplished at all. To an ever-increasing degree, the management of international rivers is becoming not merely a matter of distributing existing benefits, but of increasing them greatly through cooperative action. The possibility of developing the water resources of the international river for the benefit of all parties can be highly instrumental in settling age-old disputes over water rights. Of vastly more importance, however, is the stimulus that a successful venture of this nature can give to the solution of other issues which trouble the relations of neighboring countries (Water for Peace, 1967).

So much attention has been focused for so long on the active hostilities in Vietnam that a peaceful enterprise of international scope in that region seems scarcely to belong in such a setting. It is remarkable that an effort to develop the region's principal river for peaceful purposes could even exist, let along progress. The Mekong flows 2,600 miles from the snows of Tibet to the China Sea; 1,500 miles is in the Lower Mekong, below China. The Lower Mekong drains an area with a population of some 30 million. The lower river has 34 principal tributaries. It is one of the largest rivers in the world, with an annual discharge of 400-million acre feet. The area through which it flows is so little developed that in all its 1,500 miles there is not a single bridge across the river.

The UN Economic Commission for Asia and the Far East (ECAFE) recommended in 1957 the establishment of a Committee of the riparian nations to look into the possibilities of developing the river. The Governments of Cambodia, Laos, the Republic of Vietnam, and Thailand thereupon jointly established the Committee for the Coordination of Investigations of the Lower Mekong Basin with one member from each nation and with 'plentipotentiary authority to promote, coordinate, supervise and control the planning and investigation of water resources development projects in the Lower Mekong Basin.' The Committee may also solicit and administer funds. The UN has confirmed its interest and support of the Mekong project through the Special Fund, ECAFE, and ten other UN cooperating agencies. In addition 21 nations, the Ford Foundation, the Adia Foundation, and four major private industries are contributing money and technicians (Water for Peace, 1967).

The Mekong Project seeks the development of the water resources of the Lower Mekong Basin, including main streams and tributaries, with respect to hydroelectric power development, irrigation, flood control, drainage, navigation improvement, watershed management, water supply and related developments for the benefit of all the people of the basin, without distinction as to nationality or politics. Work is broadly divided into categories of: pre-investment planning, (including basic data collection, overall basin planning, planning individual mainstream and tributary projects, planning navigation improvements, and ancillary projects); construction; finance; and management. Thus far the Committee's attention has been directed primarily to pre-investment activities: basic data collection and the preparation of an overall basic plan. The Committee realizes explicitly that no single project should be undertaken without knowing how it will fit into the overall plan and that it will not prejudice a project needed to be undertaken later in the general scheme. The basic overall plan was stated in a 1957 ECAFE report. The Committee decided in 1962 to prepare an amended and amplified plan in the light of accumulating data to be completed in 1967. To help in this work it is establishing an electronic computer facility in Bangkok to make a system analysis to help determine the optimum system, sizes and functions of dams, and reservoirs. Three projects were given priority by the Committee as early as 1957: the Pa Mong, Sambor, and Tonle Sap. The Pa Mong mainstream project, high up on the river on the Laos-Thailand border above Vientiane, would help control the flow of the entire river down to the sea. It would irrigate approximately a million hectares of land in northeast Thailand and Laos and could operate generators of up to a million kilowatts.

The World of Water

The Committee has recognized that physical development without concurrent social and economic planning will be wasteful and even dangerous. It has therefore undertaken an organized program to examine the social and economic effects of the development program and the steps needed to keep them in proper phase. The Committee has also extended its activities beyond water development to comprehensive regional agricultural planning, mineral development, experimental and demonstration farms, surveys of potential uses of power, a pulp and paper industry, health studies, and the legal aspects of international construction and operation of its mainstream projects. The Committee seeks to finance its preinvestment work by grants and its construction projects by grants and loans. Thus far its total resources have amounted to more than $100 million. Of this, nearly one-third has come from the four member governments and two-thirds from the UN, co-operating countries and other organizations. The comparatively heavy contribution of the local countries, considering their shortage of funds, indicates the sincerity of their determination to make the cooperative work succeed (Water for Peace, 1967).

There are many principal entities engaged in water resources development assistance and scientific and technical cooperation throughout the world (Water for Peace, 1967). Working under the authority of the United Nations General Assembly, the Economic and Social Council examines and makes recommendations on international economic, social, educational, health and related issues, and calls international conferences when needed. Composed of 27 member states, nine of which are elected each year by the General Assembly for a three-year term, the Economic and Social Council usually meets for two sessions a year. There are four regional economic commissions which report to the Economic and Social Council: The Economic Commission for Europe, the Economic Commission for Asia and the Far East, the Economic Commission for Latin America, and the Economic Commission for Africa. The UN Secretariat is represented in the field of water resources through the Department of Economic and Social Affairs. The work is done through the Resources and Transport Division and the secretariats of the regional economic commissions. The Department is represented by the Bureau of Technical Assistance Operations, which administers UN technical assistance. The Resources and Transport Division (UNRTD) is responsible for overall surveys designed to meet multiple objectives, reconnaissance of river basins, ground-water inventories, hydropower development, river navigation, water for industry, desalination and conveyance of water and research and support of UN technical assistance. The Water Resources Development Center under UNRTD serves as a clearing-house for the assembly, dissemination of information on water matters, and for the study of administrative, legislative, and related aspects of water problems. The UN Development Program (UNDP) is a recent amalgamation of the UN Special Fund (SF) and the UN Expanded Program of Technical Assistance (EPTA). The UNDP provides funds for preinvestment surveys, such as resources surveys and feasibility studies, and for technical education institutes. Projects approved under this program are executed by the UN Secretariat or by one of the other organizations of the UN system. In recent years the predecessor groups (SF and EPTA) have financed water resources activities (excluding hydropower) at a rate of about $12 million per year.

The International Bank for Reconstruction and Development (IBRD), and its affiliates, the International Development Association (IDA) and the International Finance Corporation (IFC), provide funds in the form of loans to finance projects of high priority in member countries. The IBRD, organized in late 1945, concentrates on so-called 'hard loans' with generally higher interest rates and shorter repayment periods; IDA, formed in 1960, makes relatively 'soft loans' with lower rates and longer terms; and IFC, a separate but affiliated corporation established in 1956, specializes in investment in manufacturing enterprises, often on a mixed loan and equity basis, and in standby and underwriting arrangements. Funds are derived from both public and private sources, and the Bank group regularly makes a profit on its lending operations. Particular emphasis has been given to projects in the fields of transportation and electric power, which together account for two-thirds of all lending. Other specific economic sectors include industry, agriculture, water supply, communications, and education. In the 19 years since the Bank started, total loans for single-purpose and multiple-purpose power projects amount to approximately $3,256 million, and for other water projects, to $340 million.

The Inter-American Development Bank (IDB) is a regional hemispheric agency created in 1959 to accelerate economic development of member countries through promoting investment of public and private capital for development purposes and providing technical assistance for the preparation, financing, and implementation of development plans and projects. The Bank also administers the Social Progress Trust Fund. As of March 1966, loans for water projects, comprising approximately one-fourth of its loans authorized to date, amounted to $425 million, and the total costs of these water projects exceeded $1 billion. In addition, the IDB has made a number of reimbursable and nonreimbursable technical assistance grants for preinvestment studies and resource investigations, and expanding its support for countrywide surveys and preinvestment feasibility studies.

The Pan American Health Organization (PAHO) traces its lineage back to the International Sanitary Bureau established in 1902, which in turn became the Pan American Sanitary Bureau in 1923. The purpose of the Organization is to promote and coordinate efforts of the countries of the Western Hemisphere to promote the physical and mental health of the people, and it serves as the regional office of the World Health Organization. PAHO's programs encompass technical collaboration with governments in the field of public health, including sanitary engineering and environmental sanitation, community water supply, maternal and child health, and eradication and control of communicable diseases.

The Organization of American States (OAS), consisting of the 21 republics in the Western Hemisphere, was organized in 1948 as an outgrowth of a series of hemispheric cooperative arrangements which began in 1890. The Pan American Union serves as its secretariat. In 1961 OAS endorsed the Alliance for Progress, a far-reaching 10-year program of economic and social development.

An African Development Bank has been established by the developing countries of Africa to provide among themselves lending facilities similar to those of the Inter-American and Asian Development Banks. Lending functions have not started.

Unlike these other Banks, the African Bank has no developed countries as members either from within or from outside the region. Through international agreements the Asian Development Bank is being established to finance economic development projects in Asia.

A most important association of bilateral donors is the Organization for Economic Cooperation and Development (OECD), which was formed in 1961 under the sponsorship of the Organization for European Economic Cooperation (OEEC). This body in turn was formed in 1948 to allocate Marshall Plan aid and to work together to restore the economies of the European countries after World War II. Twenty-one countries are members, including, outside of Europe, the United States, Canada, and Japan. OECD serves as a forum for discussion and coordination of economic, scientific and trade problems of mutual interest, including the coordination of programs of aid given to the developing countries. Coordination of the bilateral assistance extended by most of the OECD countries is provided through the Development Assistance Committee (DAC), which was created in 1960 to provide a central point where suppliers of assistance to less developed countries might consider together common problems such as the volume, form, organization, and effectiveness of assistance efforts. DAC has no funds of its own, but is rather a center where new policies, problems and practices are discussed and old ones reviewed. DAC is made up of 15 countries, Australia, Austria, Belgium, Canada, Denmark, France, Germany, Italy, Japan, Netherlands, Norway, Portugal, Sweden, the United Kingdom, and the United States.

The purview of the Food and Agriculture Organization of the United Nations (FAO) in the field of water resources is the investigation and development of surface and groundwater resources in relation to agriculture, which also includes forestry and watershed management, and fisheries. The World Food Program (WFP), undertaken jointly by the United Nations and the FAO, assists economic and social development, including water projects, mainly through contributions in kind. The World Health Organization (WHO), provides special competence on all aspects of community water supplies and waste disposal. It is also concerned with the reduction and prevention of water-borne and water-related diseases on all projects involving water resources development, and with the control of pollution.

The UN Educational, Scientific, and Cultural Organization (UNESCO) concentrates, as regards water resources, on the scientific and educational aspects involved, including the provision of the secretariat for the International Hydrological Decade (IHD). Growing recognition of hydrology as a unified science and profession has emerged in recent years with the awareness that fragmented and single-focus efforts to understand, to manage, and develop water resources cannot succeed in the face of the massive demands placed upon them. Efforts to stimulate international cooperation in hydrology were initiated by the United States in 1961 through discussions in several international forums. In the spring of 1964, UNESCO convened an intergovernmental meeting of experts in Paris to discuss formulation of an international cooperative program. This led to the formal adoption by UNESCO, at its thirteenth session in November 1964, of a resolution calling on interested countries to establish national programs within the framework of an International Hydrological Decade to begin 1965. Pursuant to this resolution a coordinating council for the Decade consisting of 21 rotating members had been established and held its first session May-June 1965. Approximately 100 member states are participating in the program, and most of these now have formed national committees to coordinate their activities in the program.

The IHD is promoting worldwide assembly and analysis of information about water, its quantity, its distribution, and its behavior. It is also serving to promote worldwide realization that a science of hydrology exists, that teaching, training, and research must be expanded greatly, and that many varied career opportunities are open for hydrologists. Specific activities in the program will include the assembly of basic data about water, the preparation of inventories of water and the study of water balances, including its chemical quality and its sediment load. Requirements for water will be studied. Many countries plan to establish representative and experimental basins. Also included will be education and training programs; fellowships and faculty exchanges; and numerous supporting activities, such as standardization of instruments, methods, units of measure and terminology, advice on data network design and operation, and dissemination of information including publication of handbooks, manuals, and textbooks. Strong support for the IHD is uniquely appropriate for inclusion as part of the Water for Peace Program. Both share the common objective of promoting attention to water as a separate subject for study and development. IHD will have a major responsibility for the scientific aspects of the Water for Peace Program dealing with hydrology, as well as for sponsoring of education, training, and scientific exchanges in hydrology.

The World Meteorological Organization (WMO) work in the field of water resources is principally in the field of hydrometeorology, which includes surface hydrology. The International Atomic Energy Agency (IAEA) plays a role in the field of water resources through its activities relating to research, development, and application of isotope techniques in the investigation and development of water resources, the application of nuclear energy to desalination, and also through its competence as regards the disposal of radioactive wastes. The International Biological Program (IBP) is a cooperative scientific effort initiated by the International Council of Scientific Unions. About 48 countries, including the United States, are participating in the planning. The objectives of the IBP are to stimulate and coordinate comparative studies in contrasting environments: on organic production, nutrient cycles and system regulation on the land, in fresh waters and in the seas; and on the adaptability of man as a component and manager of these ecosystems. The World Weather Watch is a program sponsored by the World Meteorological Organization as an international undertaking aimed at the improvement of weather services for all the nations of the world. It is a system for the observation, collection processing, and dissemination of global weather data using the most recent developments in space, communication, data processing, meteorological, and instrumentation technology. It is an essential step toward developing the capability for improving forecasts of precipitation and resultant streamflow, as well as a basic requirement for large-scale weather modification.

There are many special or general intergovernmental groups which become involved in water matters through the sponsorship of studies, conferences or institutes, exchange of information, coordination of policies, or provision of technical assistance. This category includes such diverse entities at the Afro-Asian Rural Reconstruction Organization (AARRO), the Caribbean Organization, the Central Treaty Organization (CENTO), the Colombo Plan Council for Technical Cooperation in South and Southeast Asia, the Commission for Technical Cooperation in Africa (CCTA), the League of Arab States, the Organization of African Unity (OAU), the Organization of Central American States (OCAS), the South Pacific Commission (SPC), the Southeast Asia Treaty Organization (SEATO), the Inter-American Association of Sanitary Engineering, the International Association for Hydraulic Research, International Association of Hydrogeologists (IAH), International Association of Meteorology and Atmospheric Physics, International Association of Scientific Hydrology (IASH), International Association of Sedimentologists, International Association of Soil Science, International Association of Theoretical and Applied Limnology, International Association on Water Pollution Research, International Commission on Irrigation and Drainage, International Commission on Large Dams of the World Power Conference, International Geographical Union, International Union of Geology and Geophysics, International Water Supply Association, Permanent International Association of Navigation Congresses, and the World Power Conference. Some of the more important international journals of hydrology are: Journal of Hydrology (Netherlands), Bulletin of IASH (Belgium), Water Resources Research (USA), and Journal of IAH (France).

Chapter 2

Precipitation and Evapotranspiration

The atmosphere is the zone from which rain falls and to which water returns by evaporation and transpiration. The atmosphere is fluid and mobile; anything that happens in one part of it affects it all. The troposphere reaches from the earth's surface to a height that ranges from five miles at the Poles to eleven miles at the equator. It is the layer of clouds and changing weather, and it is marked by a steady drop in temperature with increasing altitude. The air of the earth's lower atmosphere is a uniform mixture of many gases, but most of the mixture is nitrogen and oxygen.

Although water vapor comprises only a very small part of the total atmosphere, averaging less than two percent and ranging from nought to five percent of the total mass, it is the single most important component of the air from the standpoint of climate. If the space above a given area to the top of the atmosphere were saturated, it would not as a vial contain enough water to make more than an inch of rain. However, complete saturation never occurs, and only a small part of the moisture in the air is removed by the processes of condensation. Hence, one necessary condition for a heavy rain is a continuous supply of moist, rising, inflowing air.

Water vapor enters the air from any place on the earth's surface where water exists either as a liquid or as ice. Most of the water vapor in the atmosphere comes from the oceans, lakes, marshes and glaciers that comprise about three-fourths of the earth's surface, but additional amounts are supplied by moist ground, by transpiration from the leaves of plants, and by gases of erupting volcanoes. The ocean is the atmosphere's principal source of water vapor.

Dust is an important part of the air; certain kinds of dust particles act as 'condensation nuclei' around which water vapor condenses to form cloud and rain droplets. Most moisture in the air moves horizontally. It travels as vapor and clouds, often for thousands of miles, before it drops to the earth as precipitation. The average yearly precipitation for the whole earth is estimated to be about 39 inches. Over the lands where the humidity of the continental air is less, the yearly precipitation is estimated to be only about 26 inches while over the oceans the comparable figure is 44 inches.

The variability of weather leads to continuing efforts to modify it, particularly to increase or direct rainfall by making clouds precipitate. Drop-forming particles (condensation nuclei) of exactly the right size are introduced into clouds that are at the right temperature and ready to make rain. Two decades ago, scientists successfully 'seeded' clouds by plane, using particles of dry ice and later particles of silver iodide. Ground generators burning coke impregnated with silver iodide have also been employed. There is no doubt that properly handled seeding can cause precipitation, but argument persists as to whether it increases total rainfall or merely causes rain to fall in one place instead of another. There remain some knotty legal problems; suits have been brought for damage from unwanted rain, and for depriving areas of rain they might otherwise have had. While orbiting satellites add to our knowledge of meteorological conditions, promising ever more accurate forecasting, useful manipulation of the weather seems likely to remain out of reach unless we can learn to harness the vast natural forces that determine it. For the near future, we must count on living with the precipitation nature makes available.

The close relationship between the climate, the totality of weather conditions over a period of years, of a region and the kind of plant life it supports is obvious. Nature decides what use can be made of the land, and man adapts himself to her limitations and variations. Precipitation is essential to supply the moisture by which food is taken from the soil in solution and carried throughout the plant by the sap. It is also necessary to prevent the drying and wetting of leaves, from which large quantities of water are transpired to the air in the growth processes. Climate largely determines what shall be the staple crops of a region; the weather of the individual seasons largely determines the yields of those crops.

Precipitation and Evapotranspiration

The characteristics of weather and climate, and the way in which they vary in time and place, have many important relationships to the life and labors of man; they are fundamental factors conditioning our life on this planet. The present center of world progress is in the middle latitudes, where there is considerable daily variation in weather and still greater annual variation. Many persons are depressed and discouraged on dark days, or nervous and irritable on windy days, and others feel the changes in atmospheric conditions in twinges of rheumatism, neuralgia, or old wounds. Temperature, relative humidity, wind, and sunshine are the four weather elements that most directly affect man's physical condition. A number of investigations have indicated that the most favorable temperature for persons engaged in active work either indoors or outdoors is about 64°F. Vital statistics indicate that the death rate is lowest when the mean temperature is between 60°F and 75°F. The same conditions are not ideal for all persons in all states of health. In general, ideal weather may be defined as follows; a daily mean temperature of about 65°F, with moderate changes from day to night and with variation from day to day sufficient to avoid monotony; a relative humidity continuously moderate, say from 50 to 60 percent; moderate to brisk air movement; and abundant sunshine, but not monotonously cloudless and arid weather. When a person moves from the climate to which he is accustomed to a climate having a different cooling power, there is normally a gradual adjustment of the body to the new climatic conditions. The process of adaptation to a new climate is called acclimatization. The change occurs primarily in the capillary blood vessels of the skin.

GENERAL CIRCULATION OF AIR MASSES

Pressure, temperature, and winds are related phenomena of the distribution of the air over the earth, the changes in air distribution, and the processes by which the transportation of great masses of air is achieved. The average annual pressure and prevailing winds are closely related and their distribution may be generalized into a simple system dividing the earth into a few large zones or belts. The average distribution of wind movement is known as the general circulation of air masses.

The World of Water

Pressure maps of the world show a number of lows and highs that cover large areas of the earth's surface for the entire year or a large part of it. These lows and highs are known as primary lows and highs. They result from movements of air caused by unequal heating of the earth's surface. Temperature decreases from equatorial regions towards polar regions. The decrease is due to the different amounts of insolation received; the amount of solar radiation received is dominant in determining the general course of isotherms (lines drawn through points of equal temperature). Isotherms do not follow the parallels of latitude closely, but bend irregularly northward and southward. Two major influences produce the irregularities of the annual isotherms: the differing responses of land and water to the influence of insolation, and the transportation of warm and cold water by ocean currents. The January isotherm of 90°F includes only a small area in South Africa and in Australia. In January, the lowest mean temperatures are in Siberia (−50°F) and in Greenland (−40°F). In July, the average temperature is 90°F or over in parts of southwestern United States and in large areas in North Africa and southwestern Asia. A portion of the Sahara Desert has a mean temperature of 100°F. The lowest mean recorded is −126.9°F at Vostak, Antarctica on August 25, 1960. The highest temperature recorded is 136°F at Axixia, Tripoli on September 13, 1922. The highest average annual temperature in the world is 88°F, at Lugh, Somalia (Flair and Fite, 1965; Trewartha, 1954).

An air mass is a huge section of the troposphere in which temperature and humidity are fairly uniform at any given level. Air masses originating in the tropics have temperatures that are higher than normal and are called tropical. Those that originate in high latitudes have relatively low temperatures; they are called polar. Air masses with source regions over continents are called continental; air masses with source regions over oceans are called maritime. Together these make four main kinds of air masses with the following general characteristics: continental polar—dry, cold; maritime polar—moist, cold; continental tropical—dry, warm; and maritime tropical—moist, warm. Air masses are carried in the general circulation from their source regions to other parts of the world. Warm, moist, tropical air is transported northward, and cold, dry, polar air southward. When an air mass moves from the area in which it acquired its characteristic properties to a region of different surface conditions, it immediately begins to be modified by the new influences to which it is subjected; and the longer it remains under the new conditions, the more the original characteristics are modified.

At the surface, air moves from regions of higher pressure toward regions of lower pressure. Movement of air more or less parallel to the surface is called winds, while up or down movements, such as those that exist at the center of a conventional system are usually called currents. The coriolis force causes winds in the Northern Hemisphere to be deflected to the right of the pressure gradient direction. In the Southern Hemisphere the deflection is to the left of the pressure gradient direction.

There is an orderly sequence of high and low pressure belts girdling the earth (Flair and Fite, 1965; Trewartha, 1954). In equatorial regions a belt occurs where the pressure is less than 29.9 inches (1,013 millibars, mb) throughout, and less than 29.8 inches in parts of the Eastern Hemisphere. The belt varies in width, but completely encircles the earth and its center is somewhat north of the equator. Within the equatorial belt, the winds are generally light and variable, with frequent calms, but with an average slow drift from east to west. The entire belt is called the doldrums. In January, the continuous equatorial belt of low pressure has its centers of lowest pressure over the land areas in the Southern Hemisphere, where it is midsummer. In July, the belt is almost entirely north of the equator, and low pressure extends far northward over North America and Asia, with minima in northwestern India and southwestern United States.

Centered at about 35° north and 30° south latitude, there are irregular belts where the average pressure is above 30 inches (1,016 mb) and within which are certain areas averaging more than 30.1 inches. These are the subtropical high-pressure belts or the horse latitudes. These belts are regions of variable winds, averaging light and changing with the seasons. In January, the subtropical high-pressure belt is practically continuous in the Northern Hemisphere near latitude 30°, with somewhat higher pressure in the eastern parts of the Atlantic

The World of Water

and Pacific than in the western parts of these oceans. In the Southern Hemisphere, where the land is warm in January, there are three maxima over the relatively cool oceans, in each case where the ocean water is abnormally cold for the latitude because of cold ocean currents moving northward. In July, in the Northern Hemisphere, the high-pressure belt is broken by the development of low pressure over the hot interior regions of southwestern United States and southwestern Asia, but there are well-developed and extensive cells of high pressure over the cool ocean areas. South of the equator, although pressure has risen over the land areas, the centers of highest pressure remain over the oceans as in January. These two cells, Pacific High and Azores High, influence the weather in all temperate regions of the Northern Hemisphere.

Between the doldrums and the belts of higher pressure, there are steady, moderate winds, known as trade winds, blowing out of the high-pressure areas toward the equator. As they move equatorward, they are deflected to the west and become northeast trades in the Northern Hemisphere and southeast trades in the Southern Hemisphere. They are confined to the belt between 30° north and 30° south latitude.

There is a continuous belt of low pressure in the Southern Hemisphere between latitudes 60° and 70°. This belt overlies a water surface. In corresponding latitudes in the Northern Hemisphere there are large, cold land masses, and their effect is to increase the pressure; but over the northern oceans there are areas of low pressure. These are centered in the vicinity of the Aleutian Islands in the Pacific and between Greenland and Iceland in the Atlantic. Winds from the west or southwest blow into these regions of low pressure from the equatorward side. In the summer, the temperature gradient reverses and the center of low pressure moves to the continents, and the Aleutian low practically disappears. These lows exercise an important influence on the weather of North America and Europe and are separated in winter by areas of high pressure over the continental interiors. The regions of highest pressure are Mongolia in the center of Asia, and the Mackenzie Valley in northwestern Canada.

In the Arctic and Antarctic regions there exist more or less permanent caps of high pressure with prevailing easterly winds.

Precipitation and Evapotranspiration

In the Northern Hemisphere, the cap is not centered at the pole, but extends from northern Greenland westward across the northern islands of Canada.

Winds blowing out of the poleward sides of the subtropical belts of high pressure are deflected as they move into higher latitudes and become southwest winds in middle northern latitudes, and northwest or west winds in middle latitudes. These are known as the prevailing westerlies. They begin about 35° north and south latitudes and extend to the subpolar lows. Winds persist throughout the year but are stronger in winter, especially in the north Atlantic and north Pacific. Winds blowing out of the Antarctic cap of high pressure and deflected to the left are known as polar easterlies. The relatively warm prevailing westerlies meet the cold polar easterlies or the cold air from continental interiors along an irregular shifting boundary which is known as the polar front. From day to day, this boundary changes its position, swerving far northward or southward, especially in the Northern Hemisphere in winter. It is along this moving polar front that the storms, or barometric depressions, characteristic of the weather outside the tropics, develop.

In conformity with this general distribution of the pressure in alternating belts of high and low pressure, the general circulation of air masses is divided into three zones in each hemisphere. One of these is the zone between the subtropical high-pressure belt and the equator, in which winds move equatorward with a large component from the east. The second zone lies between the subtropical high-pressure and the polar-circle low-pressure belts, that is, between latitudes 30° and 60°, approximately, in each hemisphere. In this zone, the air moves poleward but by deflection becomes largely westerly. Finally, in the third zone, the air moves out of the polar cap of high pressure toward the lower pressures at about latitude 60°, becoming easterly by deflection. Thus, instead of a continuous circulation between equator and poles, each hemisphere is divided into three more or less independent circulation zones. A closer examination of the pressure belts shows that they are not of uniform pressure throughout, but that they are divided into a number of centers or cells. The latitudinal (east-

The World of Water

and -west) circulation is much greater than the meridional (north- and -south) movement of air.

Much transposition and interchange of air occurs from one pressure belt to another. Some of the processes by which this mixing is accomplished are: by the shifting of the center of the doldrums north and south of the equator, by the circulation of the air around the semi-permanent centers of high and low pressure as they gradually change their position with the changing seasons; by the movement of great quantities of cold air equatorward and of warm air poleward along the polar front as it rapidly alters its position; and by the rising and settling of air in various parts of the world, displacing surface air with air from aloft and involving new circulations. To move the masses of air involved in the general circulation requires an immense amount of work. The factors contributing toward the accomplishment of this work are: insolation, gravitation, condensation, and the earth's rotation.

With practically no friction aloft, the winds in the upper levels of the atmosphere respond to the existing forces to create gradient winds or geostropic winds, according to the pressure pattern (Flair and Fite, 1965). Although there is considerable zonal transport of air at high levels as the winds meander over pressure troughs and ridges, the principal air movement is west to east. At heights between 3,000 and 13,000 feet above the trade winds direct reversal of the wind direction has sometimes been observed. These winds, from the southwest over the northeast trades and from the northwest over the southeast trades, are known as the antitrades.

The jet stream is a narrow meandering band of swift westerly winds that circles the globe in the prevailing westerlies of middle latitudes. It may range from 25 to 400 miles in width and up to a mile or two in depth. Wind speeds up to 300 miles per hour have been recorded. Sometimes the jet stream forms a continuous band around the entire earth. More frequently it is found to be made up to two, three, or even more disconnected segments. Its height ranges from about 20,000 to 45,000 feet. The snakelike course of the jet streams, particularly during their southward migration in winter, is believed to create great waves in the polar front at high elevations. As a result of these waves, massive outbreaks of polar air may penetrate far to the south, and tropical air may reach the far north. Such outbreaks appear to bring cold waves, warm spells, stormy weather, and heavy precipitation.

CLIMATES OF THE EARTH

The climate of a region is made up of its temperature, moisture, winds, storms, cloudiness, and other weather elements. The principal climatic controls include latitude, altitude, prevailing winds, topography, distance from the sea or large lakes, and ocean currents. A broad general description of the climates of the earth has been made, following a more or less latitudinal division into four zones: tropical zones, subtropical zones, intermediate zones, and polar zones (Trewartha, 1954, Namowitz and Stone, 1965).

The central portion of the tropical zone is the equatorial low-pressure belt that has a large annual rainfall and frequent and heavy thunderstorms in all months of the year. It is the doldrum region of variable winds and calms, a region of dense tropical forests of rapid growth. Bordering this wet belt on the north and on the south, there are regions which receive rain during the summer of that hemisphere, as the doldrums migrate toward the regions, but little or no rain during a short period of the opposite season, when the doldrums are farther away. The vegetation of this climatic regime constitutes the true jungle, with many trees and a dense undergrowth of tangled vines and other tropical plants. In the western hemisphere, these jungles extend intermittently northward into southern Mexico and southward into central Brazil.

Toward the poleward sides of these belts, where the rainfall becomes light, there are open grasslands, or savannas, bordering the forests. The savannas include the Sudan of Africa, the Llanos of Venezuela, the Campos of Brazil, and the Downs of Australia. In the equatorial and savanna zones, seasonal temperature changes are light. There are practically no seasons, except where there is a wet and dry season. Temperatures average high throughout the year, and the climate is oppressive, especially when the humidity is high, but maximum temperatures are usually not so high as in continental interiors in so-called temperate zones. In large areas of the tropical zones temperatures never reach 100°F. High humidity, dense vegetative cover, and days that are shorter than summer days in higher latitudes are factors in keeping the maximum temperature moderate.

In the central portions of the trade-wind belts, on the poleward sides of the savannas, the winds blow with great regularity at a moderate speed, storms are very rare, and the temperatures are uniformly mild. There are no frosts; the climate is tropical. Although the trade winds move for long distances over the oceans, they move from colder to warmer regions and are dry except when there is orographic uplift. On the windward sides of highlands the rainfall is heavy and frequent at all seasons. In other areas the skies are bright, sunshine is abundant, and rainfall is light. Though not stimulating, this trade wind climate is comfortable and healthful in contrast with the mugginess of equatorial climates.

In the poleward portions of the trade winds and the equatorward portions of the subtropical high-pressure belts, there are transition zones in each hemisphere with subtropical types of climate, not entirely free of frost. On the west coasts of the continents in these latitudes is the Mediterranean climate. These areas have moderate temperatures throughout the year, with moderate rainfall in winter under the influence of the westerlies, and with dry, sunny summers under the influence of the subtropical belts of high pressure. The Mediterranean climate is of greatest extent in the countries bordering on the sea from which it is named, but there are small areas of this type of climate in California, South Africa, southern Australia, and central Chile. The east coasts of continents in these transition areas have a humid subtropical climate, more nearly continental in character than is the Mediterranean type, with greater annual temperature ranges, and with no dry season. In parts of southeastern Asia and the Netherlands Indies, a humid, monsoon climate prevails, having a short moderate dry season but a heavy annual rainfall from onshore winds. In the main, the subtropical zones are deficient in rainfall, with large arid and semi arid areas. The subtropical zones include most of the great desert areas in each of the five continents. Deserts may go without rain for years. Iquique, Chile, has a record of 14 years without measurable rainfall.

The intermediate zones of each hemisphere are regions of

the prevailing westerlies, much interrupted and confused by local conditions and by traveling disturbances resulting from the meeting of polar and tropical air masses. There is much variability of rainfall, which is generally heavier on the coasts and lighter in the interiors of the continents. In Russia and Siberia, in the intermediate zones, there are large, unwooded, grassy, semi-arid plains called steppes. These and similar regions in Hungary and the Great Plains of the United States have what is called a steppe climate. Such a climate occurs only in large continental interiors. There are large inland areas and coastal regions within the intermediate zones that have adequate rainfall.

About eight percent of the earth's surface is included in the polar zones, in which only a minimum of plant and animal life exists. There is almost continuous sunlight for a short time in summer, with some warm days, but the season is so short that the ground remains frozen except in a thin surface layer. Precipitation is light.

In the interiors of continents the climate is usually rather dry and clear, that is, rainfall is light to moderate, relative humidity is low, and sunshine is abundant. Within the tropics, temperature contrasts are small over large land areas as well as over the oceans. In middle latitudes, continental climates are marked by severe winters and hot summers; in polar regions, the winters are long and severe and the summers short and cool. Steppe climates are dry continental, while a desert is an extreme type of dry continental climate.

The climate of the oceans and of lands that are largely influenced by ocean conditions, islands, for example, is characterized by small daily and yearly ranges of temperature, with nights and winters relatively warm and days and summers cool. Because water warms slowly, the springs are late and cool; because water cools slowly, the autumns are late and warm. Except in the trade-wind belts, marine climates usually have greater humidity and cloudiness than continental climates.

The climate along the coasts of continents is intermediate between the marine and the continental types. The prevailing winds and mountain barriers largely determine the distance inland to which oceanic influences penetrate. In the zones of the prevailing westerly winds, west coasts of continents have belts of distinctly coastal climate; but, on the east coasts, continental climates extend practically to the shore. In trade-wind belts, east coasts are under marine influence and west coasts, under continental influence.

Robert Raikes (1967) presents a most interesting account of the role of water in environment and the effect of post-glacial climate and water resources on early human societies. He concludes that there have been no major world-wide past-glacial climate changes and that any changes that there may have been have not been of a magnitude sufficient to cause observed ecological change. Ecological changes have been due mainly to: the built-in year-to-year variability of climate and particularly of rainfall; the intervention of biotic factors such as fire or plant diseases; the intervention of man and animals; and changes in drainage caused by geomorphological processes such as change of sea level, tectanic and volcanic activity, and the erosion, transportation, and deposition of sediments, often themselves originating indirectly from changes in ecology wrought by one or more of the other factors.

Raikes further concludes that botanical evidence of climatic changes must be interpreted not in terms of weather extremes but as short-term examples of the built-in variability of rainfall and temperature or drainage changes. If the identification of postglacial climate phases is relevant to archeology, the relevance of an understanding of the basic elements of hydrology cannot be doubted.

WEATHER

Similar weather tends to persist for several days. Reasons for this persistence may be found in the influence of the semipermanent areas of high and low pressure of the general circulation, and in the slow movement or stagnation of lows (cyclones) and highs (anticyclones), resulting in the continued inflow of warm air or outflow of cold air. There is a tendency for similar types of weather to continue for several months. Changes in the general circulation affect the whole atmosphere and consequently result in weather changes throughout the world, but not necessarily changes of the same kind. For example, a rise of pressure in one part of the world may show itself several months later in changed weather conditions in a distant part of the globe, not necessarily in the same hemisphere.

A few dry years often occur in succession, followed by a series of wet years, and again by another group of dry years. Such short-period fluctuations are constantly occurring with other weather elements and are called weather cycles. There are so many of these cycles and they are so irregular that it is impossible to find periodicities that would be useful as indicators of future conditions (Flair and Fite, 1965). Weather cycles are characteristic of climate throughout the world and often have important social and economic consequences. In addition to the short-period variations called weather cycles, there are tendencies that persist over longer periods and are known as secular trends. In the study of annual growth rings of sequoia trees, glaciers and lake levels, evidence of oscillations in climate in periods of a few centuries have been found. For example, there is evidence that Persia and Turkestan, Arizona, and New Mexico, are drier than they were at the beginning of the Christian era, and that Yucatan and southern Mexico are wetter. However, in most parts of the world, there is no evidence of important trends persisting through centuries. Considering geological eras, climate has changed greatly, but also cyclically.

The practical value of accurate weather prediction is evident (Flair and Fite, 1965). The first step in making a weather forecast is the collection of available weather information. Many of the countries of the world maintain a grid of observation stations and a teletype network for the collection and distribution of regular weather reports. These reports are transmitted in numerical weather codes which can be decoded into the various languages of the world. Plotters and analysts must do their work quickly if a reliable forecast is to be made in time to be of value to the public. Facsimile machines and circuits for the transmission of weather maps and charts are commonly used. The following types of data are available for charting at forecast centers: the simultaneous surface observations, giving pressure, temperature and humidity of the air at various levels above the stations; and pilot-balloon observations and rawins, giving wind direction and force at known upper air elevations. These upper-air data are the basis for the construction of constant-pressure charts, winds-aloft charts, verti-

The World of Water

cal cross sections, and mean pressure charts of the atmosphere.

Areas of precipitation and other special weather conditions are carefully analyzed and related to their causes. Having charted the data, the next step in the preparation of the forecast is to estimate the movement, future position, and development of patterns of isobars, fronts, and areas of high and low pressure. A synoptic weather chart is designed to present a view of the whole weather situation at one time. Weather observations are made at selected stations over the area to be represented. This information is collected by teletype and plotted on the chart at each station location. Analysis lines and symbols are drawn showing the distribution of pressure, temperature, air masses, fronts, precipitation areas, etc. On a complete surface chart, data are also entered in station-model form showing amounts and types of clouds, wind direction and velocity, visibility, pressure changes, etc. Charts may also be drawn for levels other than the surface when upper-air data are available. Such charts are usually prepared for the 850-, 700-, 500-, and 300-mb surfaces. They do not show all the details of the surface chart, but they give a good picture of the distribution of pressure, temperature, humidity, and wind at those levels. From the picture of the existing weather before him, the meteorologist is able to estimate with fair accuracy the changes that will occur in a given area during the next 24 to 48 hours.

A short series of weather maps have isobars that do not have the same regularity of spacing and direction that is shown on the charts of the general circulation. Instead, the isobars are disturbed by irregularities of pressure. Two patterns of great importance in understanding the weather are those which enclose areas of low and high barometric pressure. A low-pressure center which is enclosed by one or more isobars is often called a cyclone. The cyclone is a barometric depression marked by a series of roughly circular or oval isobars enclosing an area of low pressure, that is, where pressure decreases from its outer rim to its center. Individual lows differ greatly in size ranging in diameter from 100 to 2,000 miles. The typical round or elliptical low has, near the surface of the earth, moderate winds directed inward and around the center of low pressure, making an angle of from 20° to 40° with the isobars. The direction movement is counter clockwise in the Northern Hemisphere and

Precipitation and Evapotranspiration

clockwise in the Southern Hemisphere, responding to the influence of the earth's rotation and the pressure gradient.

Weather instruments

Thermometers are instruments used to measure temperature and operate on the principle that a rise in temperature will cause expansion. Liquid thermometers use mercury or alcohol as the expanding material. Metal thermometers use a compound metal bar which will bend up or down as temperatures rise or fall, or a coil which tends to wind or unwind itself. A thermograph is a self-recording metal thermometer. Maximum-minimum thermometers record highest and lowest temperatures that occur during a given period.

A barometer is an instrument used to measure atmospheric pressure. The mercury barometer is a very accurate instrument and is generally used as a standard barometer. The barograph is a recording aneroid barometer. An aneroid barometer contains a flexible metal can sealed airtight after most of the air has been pumped from it. The can is prevented from collapsing by a strong spring. Changes in air pressure result in movements of the top of the can which are recorded.

The direction of the wind is usually determined by use of a wind vane. Wind speed near the surface is measured by the cup anemometer. Cups catch the wind causing them to turn in proportion to the velocity of the wind. The speed and direction of upper-air winds may be determined by tracking the flight of special weather balloons either by telescope or by radar. In the rawin method, a special weather balloon carries a radio transmitter aloft.

Instruments used to measure relative humidity are called hygrometers. In the hair hygrometer, changes in the length of a bundle of human hairs very sensitive to moisture changes are recorded. The psychrometer consists of two identical thermometers, one of which has a water-soaked wick wrapped around its bulb. Air is forced past the two bulbs by fanning or whirling the thermometers. Relative humidity is measured based on the principle that evaporation causes cooling, and dry air causes more rapid evaporation than moist air.

In the standard rain gage, a brass funnel directs the rain into a narrow cylindrical tube. A marked stick is dipped into the tube to measure the depth of water. The tipping bucket rain gage and the weighting rain gage automatically record the amount of rainfall.

The radio sonde is a tiny combination thermometer, barometer, hygrometer, and radio transmitter. The transmitter automatically emits signals that indicate the temperature, pressure, and relative humidity of the air through which the radio sonde is passing. The radio sonde is carried to heights up to 125,000 feet by a large helium filled balloon. An automatic radio receiver at the weather station records the transmitted signals.

Weather detection radar equipment can determine the location of rain areas in storms within the range of the radar set. Television and infra red observation satellites discover storms by transmitting television pictures of the atmosphere to stations at the earth's surface. The use of radar in weather observation depends on the fact that radar waves are reflected as radar echoes from the water droplets and ice crystals in clouds, rain, and other forms of precipitation. Like television signals, the radar echoes form images on the radarscope that represent the surfaces from which they are reflected. Thus, pictures may be seen of thunderstorms, hurricanes, and other areas of heavy precipitation. Ground-based radar can detect and track such storms within a radius of 200 miles. Radar echoes are sometimes useful in measuring the rate of rainfall and in distinguishing between snow and rain or between ice clouds and water clouds.

Clouds
Clouds are chiefly the result of the dynamic cooling produced by expansion under reduced pressure (Flair and Fite, 1965). The most important cause of clouds is the adiabatic cooling resulting from upward movement of the air. The exact process or processes by which the minute cloud droplets grow to sufficient size to fall to the earth as precipitation, are not fully known. One theory is that the saturation vapor pressure over super cooled water drops is greater than that over ice. When the two exist together in a cloud, there will be evaporation from the droplet and condensation on the crystal and the crystals grow to sufficient size to fall. As they fall through the cloud they grow in size by further condensation and by coalescence with other drops after they melt. Other processes that may be effective

in the growth of small raindrops are: the presence of unusual hygroscopic nuclei, a vapor-pressure gradient due to the presence of drops of differing temperature, and the coalescence of drops of differing size as they collide in the turbulent air.

Cirrus clouds are thin, feathery, or tufted, and so high (20,000 to 40,000 feet) that they are always composed of tiny ice crystals. Cirrostratus clouds are high, thin, feathery sheets or veils of ice crystals in clouds. They may indicate the approach of rain or snow. Cirrocumulus clouds are patches of small globular ice-crystal clouds heaped up from cirrus or cirrostratus clouds. Altostratus clouds at lower heights (6,500 to 20,000 feet) look like thick cirrostratus at lower altitudes and are grey or bluish in color. Altocumulus clouds look like higher, thinner stratocumulus clouds in smaller masses. Stratocumulus clouds at heights of 1,600 to 6,500 feet are layers composed of globular masses of rolls, often covering the whole sky, especially in winter. Stratus clouds are low, uniformly dense and threatening, from which steady rain or snow may develop. Cumulus clouds are formed at heights of 1,600 to 40,000 feet by vertically rising air currents and are piled high in thick, fleecy masses. Cumulonimbus clouds are characterized by heavy showers of rain, snow, or hail, often accompanied by thunder and lightning. Air may be forced upward by the movement of winds across a mountain range (orographic uplift). Continuous sheets of cloud of the stratus type with flat bases, as well as continuous rain often result. As the air moves downward on the other side of a mountain range, it is dynamically warmed and becomes dry and clear.

Fronts

A front is a boundary between two air masses (Flair and Fite, 1965). Frontal surfaces generally have a gentle slope that averages about 1 mile in 100 miles, but may be as steep as 1 mile in 40 or as gentle as 1 mile in 200. When a front passes a particular place it invariably means a change of weather. Fronts are almost always accompanied by precipitation.

The weather undergoes certain definite changes across a front; temperatures are usually lower on one side of the front than on the other, wind velocities are usually higher on one

The World of Water

side of the front than on the other and air pressure usually changes abruptly as the front is crossed.

If the cold air is pushing warmer air ahead of it, the front is a cold front; if warm air is pushing colder air ahead of it, the front is a warm front. If neither air mass is being displaced, the front is said to be stationary. The occluded front is a front that results when a cold front overtakes a warm front. All fronts, warm, cold, stationary, or occluded, usually bring rain with them. Warm-front rains are steady and extensive and are usually associated with stratiform clouds. Cold-front rains are showery, are of short duration, and are usually associated with cumuliform clouds. Cold fronts move more rapidly than warm fronts and cause sharper changes of weather.

Thunderstorms

Thunderstorms are local, relatively small-area storms generated by the strong upward movement of warm, moist air. It is estimated that 44,000 thunderstorms occur everyday across the surface of the earth (Flair and Fite, 1965). Air-mass thunderstorms occur within an air mass when warm moist air is heated strongly at the earth's surface and powerful convection currents are developed. Frontal thunderstorms occur when warm moist air is forced to rise over upward sloping frontal surfaces. Thunderstorms are most frequent in the rainy regions of the tropics where heat and moisture are abundant and where light winds favor convection. At some places within the tropics, as in Panama, Java, and equatorial Africa, the average number of days with thunderstorms is as great as 200 per year. Thunderstorms are rare in polar regions and in cold areas.

Hurricanes

A hurricane is a tropical low pressure area having an average diameter of about 200 to 480 miles. Its pressure gradients are very steep, and its central air pressure may be as low as 26.35 inches. A hurricane has no fronts, it has a central area of descending air currents (eye) usually from 10 to 30 miles in diameter (Flair and Fite, 1965). Here the sky is clear, there is no rain, and there are almost no winds. Around the eye the wind speeds may exceed 150 miles per hour. A hurricane may travel over a path of more than 1,000 miles. The rains of a hurricane are very heavy. The world's record for a 24-hour rainfall is 46 inches. All hurricanes originate on the western sides of the oceans in the doldrums.

Tornadoes

Tornadoes are barometric depressions resembling hurricanes but much smaller, of much shorter life, and with much steeper pressure gradients. Tornadoes are primarily an atmospheric phenomenon of North America and Australia. When tornadoes occur at sea they are known as waterspouts. Such waterspouts are known to occur in the United States off the East Coast and in the Gulf of Mexico, and off the coasts of China and Japan in regions where cold, continental air extends over warm water. Tornadoes are narrow, funnel-shaped, spiral whirls in which wind velocities may exceed 500 miles per hour and up drafts may have a speed of over 100 miles per hour (Flair and Fite, 1965). The air pressure at tornado centers is very low. Air rushing into the center cools below its dew point by expansion to form a dense, black, funnel-shaped cloud from which thunder and lightning, heavy rains, and hail are discharged. Tornadoes touching ground cause extensive destruction through the action of their violent winds and updrafts and their suction-producing vacuum centers. They travel at rates from 25 to 40 miles per hour and have life spans measured in hours.

PRECIPITATION

Precipitation occurs in a variety of forms. Drizzle consists of fine drops close together falling slowly. Raindrops are larger and farther apart than drizzle, ranging in diameter up to 0·1 inch. Snow consists of branched hexagonal crystals or stars, except at very low temperatures, when fine ice needles are formed. Frozen rain is called sleet. Hail is formed exclusively in thunderstorms and has an icy center surrounded by alternating layers of snow and ice.

The ratio of the amount of water vapor in the air to the amount that the air would contain if saturated at the same temperature is called the relative humidity. The temperature

The World of Water

at which saturation occurs is the dew point. Condensation of water vapor take place when air is cooled below its dew point. In general, condensation that is vigorous enough to lead to precipitation takes place in rising currents only, where air in large quantities is being cooled below its dew point by expansion. Wherever air rises high enough and in large quantities, precipitation will occur. Within limits, the higher the air rises, the more moisture it can drop.

When air ascends, the pressure decreases, and gases expand according to the gas laws. Expansion constitutes work in the physical sense and uses emergy. The energy expended is heat energy, and the effect is to cool the air. Ascending air cools as it expands under decreasing pressure and descending air is warmed by compression as it comes into regions of greater pressure. The air becomes cooler or warmer without any conduction or radiation. The change in temperature is an internal change as a result of the change of pressure upon it. Such changes in temperature are called adiabatic changes. The dynamic cooling due to expansion is at the uniform rate of $5.5°F$ per 1,000 feet. When considerable moisture is present in rising air, the cooling caused by expansion may result in saturation and then in condensation of some of the water vapor. Descending air is dynamically warmed by compression. The capacity of the air to hold water vapor is thereby increased.

Average annual precipitation is greatest in equatorial regions (often 40 to more than 477 inches) and decreases irregularly towards the poles. Average annual rainfall decreases toward the interior of large continental masses, because the chief source of supply of the moisture of the air is the oceans. Much of the moisture is often precipitated on near-by land areas, and little is left for the distant interiors. Average annual rainfall shows a relation to the general wind systems of the world and to the direction of the wind, especially when onshore or offshore.

Ocean currents influence the distribution of rainfall. Warm currents increase precipitation on the neighboring coasts, where there is much water vapor over warm water, and this vapor is cooled when it moves inland. Cold ocean currents diminish precipitation; the air moving over them is cool and stable and of moderate humidity. Mountain systems influence precipitation

Precipitation and Evapotranspiration

by giving rise to ascending and descending air currents. Most mountain systems have a wet and dry side, the wet side being toward the ocean or toward the prevailing winds. Outside the tropics, the wettest parts of the world are mountain slopes facing prevailing winds from the oceans.

The average annual precipitation is above 100 inches in small areas in Central America, Panama, western Columbia, and southern Chile, as well as in the East Indies, the Himalayas, and along the north coast of the Gulf of Guinea. Annual precipitation averages between 80 and 100 inches at places on the west coast of North America, in tropical South America, many tropical islands, and large areas of the tropical oceans. Mt Waialeale, Kauai, Hawaii (altitude 5,075 feet) is the wettest place on earth, and has an average annual rainfall of 450 inches. Mt Waialeale receives copious rains during all months, whereas Cherrapunji receives nearly all of its rainfall during the summer monsoon. Precipitation extremes during a single month include Manoyuram, India with 264 inches and Helen Mine, California with 71 inches. In Romania, there is a record of a rainfall of 8·07 inches in 20 minutes (Flair and Fite, 1965).

At the other extreme, there are areas of less than ten inches of average annual precipitation in southwestern United States, the Sahara and Arabian deserts, much of the interior of Asia from the Caspian Sea to China, the tradewind belts of the eastern Atlantic, and in north polar regions north of latitude 70°. In the Southern Hemisphere there are regions of less than ten inches in South America, southwest Africa, and in much of the interior of Australia. The average annual rainfall is 1·33 inches at Helivan, Egypt; 1·66 at Greenland Ranch, California, 1·84 inches at Aden, Arabia; 4·16 inches at Arequipa, Peru; and 0·02 inch at Arica, Chile (Flair and Fite, 1965).

Amounts of average annual rainfall between 20 and 100 inches are favorable for agricultural use of the land. Areas receiving between 10 and 20 inches of rainfall a year are semi-arid. They are suitable for grazing and dry farming, but not for intensive agriculture except under irrigation. Where rainfall is below 10 inches, desert conditions prevail, and water for irrigation must be brought from wetter regions. Percentages of land areas of the earth with rainfall between various values are: less than 10 inches—25 percent, 10 to 20 inches—30 percent, 20 to

40 inches—20 percent, 40 to 60 inches—11 percent, 60 to 80 inches—9 percent, and more than 80 inches—5 percent.

Regions of heavy precipitation include: the entire doldrums belts of warm, humid, convectionally rising air that reaches up to the stratosphere to form gigantic cumulonimbus clouds and almost daily thunderstorms; the windward sides of mountain ranges, where prevailing winds are forced to climb to great heights; and storm areas of all kinds, such as hurricanes, typhoons, cyclones, fronts, thunderstorms, and tornadoes, for in all of these there are great masses of moist rising air. Places over which the doldrums pass have almost daily rains while the doldrums are over them. Places windward of mountains have heavy rains whenever the winds blow from a moist source. Other locations have rain only when they have storms of one kind or another.

In regions of descending air, the air is warmed by compression, and no precipitation can occur. Descending air may become so warm and dry that it causes excessive evaporation and creates desert conditions. Regions of descending air include: the two horse-latitude belts, on the leeward sides of the mountains, in middle-latitude highs, and in the great polar highs. Rising air in the moist, hot doldrums or equatorial low-pressure belt brings almost daily thundershowers and heavy annual precipitation to the entire equatorial belt around the world. The reverse is true in the horse-latitude high-pressure belts, where dry descending air brings desert conditions to the latitudes of 30° to 35° around the world in both hemispheres. Lands lying between the rainy doldrums and the arid horse-latitudes have alternative rainy and dry seasons caused by the shifting of the wind belts with the seasons.

For most regions in the tropics, rains come almost entirely with the arrival of the doldrum belt. In addition, however, heavy rains fall on the windward slopes of coastal mountains when the normally dry trade winds blow from the oceans onto the east coasts of Africa and South and Central America. The heavy monsoon rains of India and southeast Asia are similarly due to warm ocean winds rising over the Great Himalayan mountain range of India and Burma. Storms play little part in bringing precipitation to the tropics, except for the occasional hurricane or typhoon that may strike island or coastal areas.

The middle latitudes in both hemispheres are covered for most of the year by the prevailing westerly winds. There are no world-circling belts such as the wet doldrums or the dry sub-tropical high pressure belts. Instead, the chief causes of raininess or dryness are mountain range, distance from the oceans, and storms. The rainiest regions are the windward slopes of high coastal mountains.

There are large areas in equatorial regions where the rainfall is heavy throughout the year, and other areas within the tropics with alternate wet and dry seasons. In the middle latitudes, the west coasts of continents have a winter maximum of rainfall and dry summers. The precipitation is cyclonic in origin and is often increased by orographic factors. In the interiors there is a marked summer maximum, largely of thunderstorm type. On eastern coasts there is a fairly even distribution through the year, partly cyclonic and partly convectional, but usually with a summer maximum.

EVAPORATION

Moisture continually evaporates from exposed water and land surfaces into the air where it exists in vapor form. Vapor is transported in accordance with the atmospheric circulation and is finally condensed into fog or clouds, from which a part is precipitated as rain or snow. The amount of water evaporated from a given surface of water in a given time depends upon the following factors: temperature of the water surface, vapor pressure of the air, wind movement, and salinity. Evaporation into the air is balanced by condensation from the air. Over the earth as a whole, precipitation plus deposits of dew, frost, and fog must equal evaporation. There is little quantitative information about the rate of evaporation. Evaporation must be determined indirectly.

Our present knowledge of evaporation from the oceans is derived partly from pan observation and partly from computations based on consideration of the energy budget and the mass transfer by turbulent processes of water vapor from the ocean to the atmosphere. The water-budget method, whereby evaporation is determined by measuring inflow, outflow, and changes in storage, cannot be applied to the oceans. Total evaporation from the oceans is about 275,000,000,000 acre-feet. Annual evaporation from land surfaces and from inland seas is about 51,000,000,000 acre-feet (Flair and Fite, 1965). In the United States average annual lake evaporation ranges from 80 inches in the southwest to less than 25 inches in the northwest and northeast. In arid regions, evaporation may consume a large portion of the water stored in reservoirs.

USE OF WATER BY PLANTS

The successful growth of plants requires light, suitable temperatures, an adequate supply of the essential nutrient elements, and an abundance of water. Light is seldom limiting to plant growth. During the growing season, temperature becomes limiting only at high altitudes and in the far north. Most soils contain sufficient of the essential nutrient elements for the growth of a variety of plants and any deficiencies for the maximum growth of crop plants are easily supplied by the application of fertilizer. Over large areas of the earth's surface, however, plant growth is severely limited by the lack of water. This is reflected in the development of natural vegetation which consists chiefly of forests in the best-watered areas, grasslands where rainfall is deficient or uncertain during the growing season, and areas of very limited rainfall which bear so little vegetation that we call them deserts (Water, 1955).

Water is used in plants as a constituent of the living protoplasm, in the maintenance of turgidity of the cells, as a reagent in chemical reactions, and as a solvent in which food and minerals are translocated. Water is the chief constituent of growing plants. A growing tree consists of at least 50 percent water, while leaves of such plants as cabbage or lettuce contain over 80 percent, and the growing tips of roots and stems contain over 90 percent. Only those cells of plants which are completely filled with water or which are in a turgid condition supported by a high water content, will function normally. When the water content of plant tissues decreases only a few percent, the cells lose their turgidity and wilting occurs, accompanied by cessation of growth and interference with various physiological processes. Water is also an essential reagent in such processes as photosynthesis and the digestion of

Precipitation and Evapotranspiration

stored foods into simple, soluble compounds. It serves as the solvent in which food and minerals move from place to place in the plant. All substances enter and leave cells in water solution.

Continued growth involves the formation of new cells by cell division, the enlargement of these cells to many times their original volume, and their differentiation into various tissues of the plant. Lack of water interferes with all of these processes, but cell enlargement is particularly dependent on maintenance of a high moisture content. Increase in size of growing cells seems to be caused largely by turgor pressure produced by the diffusion of water into them. Whenever a water deficit develops in plant tissue, either because of excessive transpiration or slow absorption, the cells lose their turgidity and cease to enlarge.

The chemical composition of plants is materially affected by water deficit. Starch often disappears from wilting leaves. This is sometimes accompanied by an increase in sugar content, but not always. The nitrogen metabolism is often disturbed, but the exact effects vary among different species. In some plants drought conditions result in the production of abnormal amounts of pentosan, hemicelluloses, and other compounds. In many instances moisture stress causes unusually large proportion of the food to be converted into cell wall materials, resulting in woody plant tissue which is low in nutritive value.

Since growing plant tissue is essentially saturated with water and the air surrounding plants is usually relatively dry, large quantities of water evaporate from them, a process called transpiration. Various methods have been used to determine the amount of water consumed by agricultural crops and native vegetation. Unit values of consumptive use may be determined from different kinds of native vegetation and agricultural crops by soil moisture studies, lysimeter or tank measurements, analysis or irrigation data, analysis of climatological data, and other methods. For irrigated crops, data on the depths of the irrigation water, number of irrigations in a year, irrigation efficiency, water-holding capacity (field capacity) of soil, and length of growing season may be used in estimating unit values of consumptive use. Unit values observed in one area may be used in estimating consumptive use for other areas with somewhat similar climatic conditions, if temperature and precipitation records are available for both areas.

Plants have been observed to lose twice their own weight of water per day during periods of hot, dry weather which favors high rates of transpiration. Studies made at Manhattan, Kansas, USA showed that the average corn plant required only 2.2 quarts of water to provide for all the internal uses of water during the entire growing season, but actually absorbed a total of 54 gallons. Thus, only about 1 percent of all the water absorbed by the Kansas corn plant is used in it and the other 99 percent evaporates from its leaves in the process of transpiration. While the relative proportions used in the plant and lost by transpiration vary considerably with different crops and climatic conditions, by far the larger portion is used in replacing water lost in transpiration.

More than half of the precipitation which reaches the land surfaces of the earth is returned to the atmosphere by the combined processes of evaporation and transpiration, called evapotranspiration. From the various methods of determining evapotranspiration scientists know how much water is transpired and evaporated under different conditions. Scientists find that the rate of evapotranspiration depends on climate, supply of soil moisture, plant cover, soil type and structure, and land management.

Evapotranspiration, if the supply of water to the plant is not limited, is called potential evapotranspiration. When the adjustments are made for variations in day length, a close relation exists between mean temperature and potential evapotranspiration. Study of the available data has resulted in a formula that permits the computation of potential evapotranspiration for any place whose latitude is known where temperature records are available. The average annual potential evapotranspiration ranges from less than 18 inches in the high mountains of the West to more than 60 inches in three isolated areas in the deserts of Arizona and southern California in the United States. It is less than 21 inches along the Canadian border of the eastern United States and more than 48 inches in Florida and southern Texas. The march of potential evapotranspiration follows a uniform pattern through the year in most of the United States. It is negligible in the winter months as far south as the

Gulf Coastal Plain, and is only two inches a month in southern Florida. It rises in July to a maximum that ranges from five inches along the Canadian border to seven inches on the gulf coast. In some mountain areas and along the Pacific coast, it does not reach five inches in any month (Water, 1955).

Water is essential to all plant life, but trees, the giants of the plant world, require exceptional amounts. Nearly three-fourths of the weight of a living tree is either water or is made from water, and one old-growth redwood tree may weigh as much as 300 tons. The amount of water that is retained by trees, however, is insignificant compared to the amount that is transpired from the leaves. As much as 1,000 pounds of water may be transpired for every pound of dry wood produced. The large water requirements of trees limit them to the wetter parts of the world. The distribution of forests and of tree species is controlled primarily by climate in terms of heat and water. The broad-leaved deciduous trees such as oaks and maples, require the most moisture. They occupy the super-humid and humid provinces that have a moist atmosphere and precipitation evenly distributed throughout the year. The conifers tolerate more hardship. They dominate superhumid and humid provinces in which the precipitation is concentrated in winter, parts of the humid and even subhumid provinces that are too dry for the deciduous broad-leaved kinds, and the taiga province. The broad-leaved evergreen trees of the North Temperate Zone are small trees with thick, small and often sparse leaves. Uniquely adapted to dry environments, they live in subhumid environments. Forests generally are the dominant vegetation wherever annual precipitation exceeds about 25 inches. Lands too dry for forests commonly support grasses or drought-resisting shrubs.

Chapter 3

Oceans

The world ocean extends over about three-fourths of the surface of the globe. If the shallow areas of the continental shelves and the scattered banks and shoals are subtracted, there still remains about half the earth that is covered by deep water. In the Northern Hemisphere, a total of 60·7 percent of the surface is covered by water, and in the Southern Hemisphere, 80·9 percent is water covered. Only 1 percent of the 70·8 percent of the earth's surface that is covered by water is occupied by areas with depths of more than 19,600 feet. More than half of the earth's surface (53·6 percent) covered by water shows depths between 9,800 and 19,600 feet, and the remainder, between 0 and 9,800 feet. While the greatest heights of land are roughly comparable with the greatest depths of the sea, the average depth of the sea is much greater than the average elevation of the land. If the earth had a smooth surface, the waters of the ocean would cover it to a uniform depth of about a mile and a half. As it is, the average depth of the oceans is about 12,500 feet, while the average elevation of the continents is about 2,500 feet. The oceans represent only 1/790 of the volume of the earth (Dietrich, 1963; von Arx, 1962).

The race for space is undoubtedly glamorous and important, but a full understanding and use of the oceans presents an even greater challenge for the future. One of the foremost uses man makes of the world ocean is as a highway with straight great circle roads to travel. Another use that men have made of the sea is to gather food from it. But food from the sea is not properly exploited. Some desirable species of fish are overfished to the extent of threatening extermination; some are not used at all. Countries with ample food within their land, such as the USA, use less fish than heavily populated countries surrounded by the sea, such as Japan. People in Asia use seaweed as an important part of their diet.

Methods of producing fresh water artificially from brackish or sea water are being pursued vigorously, and without question this endeavor will be a big industry of the future. The ocean is the earth's greatest storehouse of minerals. In a single cubic mile of sea water there are, on the average, 166 million tons of dissolved salts, and in all the ocean waters of the earth there are about 50 quadrillion tons. This quantity gradually increases, for although the earth is constantly shifting her component materials from place to place, the heaviest movements are seaward. Wherever climate has permitted it, men have evaporated salt from sea water. Many valuable elements are so diluted that it is not economical to extract them from sea water, yet nature concentrates them in high-grade deposits on the floor of the sea. Nodules on the sea bottom are already being mined for phosphorus; nodules of manganese, not valuable enough in themselves, may contain enough valuable nickel, cobalt, molybdenum, and zirconium to warrant scraping them off the bottom in a deep-sea mining enterprise (Long, 1964).

Oil is extracted from areas under the sea on the continental shelves, which are merely extensions of the land, the shoreline being an accident of the present sea level. As our ability to drill in deeper water increases, oil rigs will push farther and farther offshore.

All types of modern warfare are critically dependent on oceanographic knowledge. But even these warfare or operational systems do not take into consideration other items of naval interest such as navigation, seamanship, corrosion from sea water, fouling organisms which attach themselves to ship bottoms, shark repellents, underwater construction, sedimentation of harbors, and construction of artificial harbors. All facets of a Navy man's life are affected by the oceans, as are all phases of modern naval development and technology.

The continents and their islands divide the world ocean into three branches. The Atlantic branch is the longest, stretching from the Antarctic Ocean to the Arctic Sea. The Pacific branch reaches northward to the Bering Strait and is effectively cut off from the Arctic basin. In spite of this abbreviation, the

Pacific Ocean is so wide it covers nearly one-third of the globe. The Indian Ocean branch is the shortest, covering roughly one-seventh of the earth's surface. The Atlantic Ocean system covers one-fifth of the earth. The Atlantic Ocean has a mean depth of 12,700 feet, the Indian Ocean 12,900 feet, and the Pacific Ocean 14,100 feet.

Continents and island chains more or less separate certain oceanic areas from the open ocean, forming adjacent seas. Such seas are called marginal when they form an indentation on the continental coast, and mediterranean when they are enclosed to a great extent by land. The latter can be subdivided into larger intercontinental and smaller intracontinental mediterraneans. The group of the large mediterraneans consists of the European, the American, and the Arctic mediterraneans, which are extensions of the Atlantic ocean; and the Austral-Asiatic mediterranean, which is an extension of the Pacific Ocean. Considered intracontinental mediterraneans are the Baltic Sea, Hudson Bay, the Persian Gulf, and the Red Sea; the North Sea, the Gulf of St Lawrence, the Bering Sea, the Sea of Okhotsk, the Sea of Japan, and the Sea of East China must be considered marginal seas (Dietrich, 1963; von Arx, 1962).

The areas of ocean surfaces are: oceans, not including adjacent seas—122·3 million square miles; mediterraneans, intercontinental—11·27 million square miles; mediterraneans, intracontinental—0·89 million square miles; marginal seas—0·09 million square miles; and oceans, including marginal sea—137·5 million square miles.

Oceanography is the unlimited science of the sea. Basic studies on oceanography include investigations of marine life; the analyses of ocean water; examination of the ocean floor; investigation and measurement of currents, waves, and tides; and analyses of the interaction of atmosphere and sea. Oceanographic studies can be grouped by their primary scientific interest into studies of the physical, biological, geological, geophysical, or chemical aspects of the sea. All of these endeavors are interrelated and dependent on one another. Thus, it is necessary to study all phases in order to comprehend the field of oceanography.

CONTINENTAL SHORES AND ESTUARIES

A composite profile of a shoreline from a point above high tide seaward to some point below low tide reveals features that change constantly as they are influenced by the nature of waves and currents along the shore. All features are not present in all shorelines, but several are present in most shore profiles. The offshore section extends seaward from low tide. The shore or beach section reaches from low tide to the foot of the sea cliff and is divided into two segments. In front of the sea cliff is the backshore, characterized by one or more berms, resembling small terraces with low ridges on their seaward edges built up by storm waves. Seaward from the berms to low tide is the foreshore. Inland from the shore lies the coast. Deposits of the shore may veneer a surface cut by the waves on bedrock and are known as the wave-cut-terrace. In the foreshore section, there may be an accumulation of unconsolidated deposits comprising a wave-built terrace (Leet and Judson, 1954).

The shoreline profile is ever changing. During great storms the surf pounds directly against the sea cliff, eroding it back and scouring through the beach deposits to abrade the wave-cut terrace. As the storm subsides, new beach deposits build up in front of the sea cliff. The energy that works upon and modifies a shoreline comes from the movement of water produced by tides and wind-formed waves, movement of currents, stream deposition, and glaciation.

Wave-cut cliffs are common erosional features along a shore, particularly where it slopes steeply down beneath the sea. Here waves can break directly on the shoreline, and expend the greatest part of their energy in eroding the land. Wave erosion pushes the wave-cut cliff steadily back, producing a wave-cut terrace or platform at its foot. Since the surging water of the breaking waves must cross the terrace before reaching the cliff, it loses a certain amount of energy there through turbulence and friction. The farther the cliff retreats and the wider the terrace becomes, the less effective are the waves in eroding the cliff. If sea level remains constant, the retreat of the cliffs becomes slower and slower. Waves pounding against a wave-cut cliff produce various features; wave action may hollow out cavities or sea caves or sea arches.

Features of deposition along a shore are built of material eroded by the waves from the headlands, and of material brought down by rivers. Part of the material eroded from a headland may be drifted by currents into the protection of a neighboring bay, where it is deposited to form sandy beaches called spits and bay barriers. Often marshy lagoons are separated from the open sea by narrow sandy beaches. Another depositional feature, a tombolo, is a beach of sand or gravel that connects two islands, or connects an island with the mainland.

In tropical and semitropical waters, many shorelines are characterized by coral reefs of varying sizes and types. These reefs are built up by individual corals with calcareous skeletons as well as by other lime-secreting animals and plants. The coral-reef shorelines are of three types: the fringing reef, the barrier reef, and the atoll. A fringing reef grows out directly from a landmass, whereas a barrier reef is separated from the main body of land by a lagoon of varying width and depth opening to the sea through passes in the reef. An atoll is a ring of low, coral islands arranged around a central lagoon.

Over the long span of geologic time, the ocean waters have come in over continents many times and have retreated into their basins. Probably the greatest submergence in the history of the earth took place in the Cretaceous period, about 100 million years ago. Then the ocean water advanced upon North America from the north, south, and east, finally forming an inland sea about 1,000 miles wide that extended from the Arctic to the Gulf of Mexico, and then spread eastward to cover the coastal plain from the gulf to New Jersey. At the height of the Cretaceous flood about half of North America was submerged. All over the world the seas rose. They covered most of the British Isles, except for scattered outcroppings of ancient rocks. In southern Europe only the old, rocky highlands stood above the sea, which intruded in long bays and gulfs into the central highlands of the continent. The ocean moved into Africa and sandstones were deposited on the ocean floor; later weathering of these rocks provided the desert sands of the Sahara. From a drowned Sweden, an inland sea flowed across

Russia, covered the Caspian Sea, and extended to the Himalayas. Parts of India, Siberia, Australia, and Japan were submerged. On the South American continent, the area where later the Andes were to rise was covered by the ocean (Leet and Judson, 1954).

Movement of the earth's crust are partly responsible for the invading seas together with the displacement of ocean water by land sediments. For the past million years, all other causes of marine transgressions have been dwarfed by the dominating role of the glaciers. Along the coasts of the USA a continuing rise of sea level has been perceptible on tide gages since 1930; the rise amounted to about a third of a foot along the Atlantic shores between 1930 and 1948.

An estuary is a body of water in which river water mixes with and dilutes sea water and is the wide mouth of a river or arm of the sea where the tide meets the river currents, or flows and ebbs. The basic physiography of coastlines and shores is due primarily to submergence or emergence. Either or both of these may form estuaries. Once the shoreline is submerged, stream and sea processes of erosion, transport, and deposition begin to modify the topography of the immediate region and eventually of the entire coast. The dropping of sediments by the stream as it meets the encroached sea intiiates the building of a delta in the upper reaches of the drowned mouth. Continued building by sedimentation gives rise to broad, level mud and silt deposits eventually becoming tidal flats. Meanwhile, currents and tidal action of the sea erode the peninsulas, or headlands, depositing the materials on the bottom of the seaward region of the estuary. These deposits may develop as bars and spits in various positions relative to the mouth of the estuary. In time, the estuary may become filled by stream and tidal deposits. The rate and extent of sedimentation and filling of an estuary are primarily dependent upon the original size of the estuary, its age, the present rate of erosion upstream and deposition by the stream at its mouth, and marine forces such as tides and longshore currents (Leet and Judson, 1954).

The shores of coastal-plain estuaries are composed of mixtures of silt, mud, and sand in varying proportions. Near the mouth of the estuary where predominating forces of the sea build spits or other depositional features, the shores and substrate of the estuary are sandy. Just inside the entrance, the sand contains considerable quantities of mud. From the estuary mouth with its generally coarse bottom sediments, there usually exists a gradation toward finer materials in the head of the estuary. In the head region, fine muds are deposited, while in the main channel and in the mouth where stream and tidal flow carry greater loads, coarser sediments make up the bottom. Tidal, or mud, flats are commonly built up in estuarine basins. Depending upon the composition of the substrate and tidal action, vegetation may eventually occupy the flats. The high-tide shoreline of estuaries is frequently the lower margin of tidal marshes. Marshes support an abundant flora as grasses, sedges, and other aquatic plants. Along the estuary-stream shore from the saltwater zone inland, the salt marsh grades into a freshwater marsh or swamp (Reid, 1961).

CONTINENTAL SHELVES AND SLOPES

Once the tide lines have been passed, the three geographic provinces of the ocean are the continental shelves, the continental slopes, and the floor of the deep sea. The shelves begin at tidelines and extend seaward as gently sloping plains. The boundary between the continental shelf and the slope occurs wherever the gentle decline of the shelf changes abruptly to a steeper descent. The average depth at which this change occurs is about 72 fathoms; the greatest depth of any shelf is probably 200 to 300 fathoms. The widest shelves in the world are those bordering the Arctic. The Barents Sea shelf is 750 miles across, it is also relatively deep, lying for the most part between 100 to 200 fathoms below the surface. It is scored by deep troughs between which banks and islands rise. The deepest shelves surround the Antarctic continent, where soundings in many areas show depths of several hundred fathoms near the coast. The Pacific coast of the USA has a continental shelf only 20 miles wide, a narrowness characteristic of coasts bordered by young mountains. All shallow shelf areas with depths of 0 to 656 feet combined represent 7·8 percent of the area of the world and only 0·2 percent of its volume (Dietrich, 1963; von Arx, 1962).

On glaciated continental shelves, sand mixed with gravel and cobbles comprises a large part of the total amount of deposited material. Also common on the continental shelves are deposits of mud, especially off the mouths of large rivers and along the course of ocean currents that sweep across the river-laid deposits. Mud also tends to collect in shallow depressions across the surface of the shelves, in lagoons, sheltered bays, and gulfs.

The continental shelves are most important to man as a source of resources. The great fisheries of the world, with only a few exceptions, are confined to the relatively shallow waters over the shelves. Seaweeds are gathered from their submerged plains to make scores of substances used in foods, drugs, and articles of commerce. As the petroleum reserves left on continental areas by ancient seas become depleted, petroleum geologists look more and more to the oil that may lie, as yet unmapped and unexploited, under these bordering lands of the sea.

The continental slope, which has a relatively strong incline, occurs at the margin of the continental blocks. Echo soundings show that the continental slope does not consist simply of an inclined surface. Great irregularities and deep furrows (so-called submarine canyons) cut into the continental block. They are most pronounced at depths less than 6,560 feet. Sometimes the canyons are continuations of submarine depressions which cross the continental shelf; these, in turn, are considered to be continuations of continental valleys. Recently submarine canyons have been discovered in all three oceans and in the large mediterraneans, proving that this conspicuous topographic form has a worldwide distribution. The slopes are the longest and highest escarpments found anywhere on the earth; their average height is 12,000 feet, but in some places they reach the height of 30,000 feet. Evidence indicates that on the continental slopes, gravel, sand, mud, and bedrock are found on the bottom (Dietrich, 1963; von Arx, 1962).

FLOOR OF THE DEEP SEA

Deep-sea trenches are longitudinal depressions with depths generally in excess of 19,600 feet. In the oceans, there are at least 15 such trenches. Almost all these deep-sea trenches are located at the margins of the oceans; most of them are found in the Pacific Ocean. Without exception, the deep-sea trenches contain the greatest depths of the world ocean. The depth of 35,800 feet is considered the deepest, is located in the west Pacific Ocean, and was discovered during a systematic investigation of the Tonga-Kermadec Trench. The greatest depth in the Indian Ocean, 24,500 feet, was found in the Sunda Trench, and in the Atlantic Ocean, 30,300 feet in the Puerto Rico Trench. One of the deepest trenches of all, the Mindanao, lies east of the Philippines and is six and a half miles deep. The Tuscarora Trench east of Japan, nearly as deep, is one of a series of long, narrow trenches that border the outer rim of a chain of islands including the Bonins, the Marianas, and the Palaus. On the seaward side of the Aleutian Islands is another group of trenches. The greatest depths of the Atlantic lie adjacent to the islands of the West Indies, and also below Cape Horn. In the Indian Ocean the curving island arcs of the East Indies have their accompanying deeps (Dietrich, 1963; von Arx, 1962). The areas in which the deep-sea trenches are located have been and are still subjected to deep-reaching and large-scale tectonic activities, concentrated on the margins of the Pacific Oceans.

The Mid-Atlantic Ridge, which extends from the Bear Islands in the north to Bouvet Island in the south, over a distance of approximately 9,300 miles, together with several developed cross ridges, impress a lattice-like pattern on the topography of the Atlantic Ocean. With the exception of the Bermuda Islands, all the oceanic islands of the Atlantic belong to this system of ridges. The ridge rises in mid-Atlantic near Iceland. It runs south midway between continents, crosses the equator into the South Atlantic, and continues to about 50° south latitude, where it turns sharply eastward under the tip of Africa and runs toward the Indian Ocean. Its general course closely parallels the coastlines of the bordering continents, even to the flexure to the equator between the hump of Brazil and the eastward-curving coast of Africa. From its western foothills across to where its slopes roll down into the eastern Atlantic basin, the range is about twice as wide as the Andes and several times the width of the Appalachians. Near the equator a deep gash cuts across it from east to west, the Romanche Trench. This is the only point of communication between the deep basins of the eastern and western Atlantic. The greater part of the ridge is submerged, its central backbone rises some 5,000 to 10,000 feet above the sea floor, but another mile of water lies above most of its summits. Here and there a peak thrusts itself above the surface of the ocean, these are the islands of the mid-Atlantic. The highest peak of the ridge is Pico Island of the Azores. It rises 27,000 feet above the ocean floor, with only its upper 7,000 to 8,000 feet emergent. The sharpest peaks of the ridge are the cluster of islets known as the Rocks of St Paul, near the equator. The volcanic bulk of Ascension is another peak of the Atlantic Ridge; so are Tristan da Cunha, Gough, and Bouvet (Dietrich, 1963; von Arx, 1962).

The relief of the Indian Ocean resembles that of the Atlantic Ocean. A continuous central ridge, the Arabic-Indian Ridge, together with its southern extension, the Kerguelen-Gaussberg Ridge, which connects with the Antarctic continent, separates the eastern basin from the western basin. All oceanic islands in the Indian Ocean are situated on this ridge and on the attached cross ridges, with the exception of the Cocos and Christmas islands. The Pacific Ocean exhibits a topographic structure which is different from that of the Atlantic and Indian Oceans. This ocean possesses a rise, elongated in the direction of the meridians of the East Pacific Ridge which together with its extension the South Pacific Transverse Ridge can be traced from Mexico to the Ross Sea. This rise, in contrast to the longitudinal ridges of the other oceans, manifests itself only as a flat broad sill. The shallower regions, from Japan to New Zealand, have also been considered as a ridge composed of several parts. The North, Central, and South Pacific basins, with depths of over 16,400 feet, form the main part of the Pacific Ocean. They contain several elevations which run in a west northwest direction and which are too short to be considered cross ridges (Dietrich, 1963; von Arx, 1962).

One of the few exceptions to the almost universal rule that oceanic islands have a volcanic origin seems to be the group of islets known as the Rocks of St Paul. Almost from the moment of its creation, a volcanic island is foredoomed to destruction. It has in itself the seeds of its own dissolution, for new explosions, or landslides of the soft soil, may accelerate its disintegration. Whether the destruction of an island comes quickly or only after long ages of geologic time may also depend on external forces: the rains that wear away the loftiest of land mountains, the sea, and even man himself. Navigators' charts are marked with numerous, recently discovered submarine mountains. Many of these are the submerged remnants of the islands of geologic yesterday. Increased knowledge of the topography of the floor of the world ocean led to the discovery of isolated submarine peaks, also called guyots, which have been found within the deep-sea basins. More than 500 guyots have been found, since 1941, in the North Central Pacific basins as well as in the Mariana Basins. Others have been discovered in the North American Basin between Bermuda and the Grand Banks. The Basins are characterized by steep slopes and, in general, a flat plateau of 3,280 to 6,560 feet depths.

The continental blocks of the earth's crust are generally composed of material of lesser density than that of the crust underlying the oceans. Crystal aggregates of the land are rich in aluminum silicates, whereas the denser rocks underlying the ocean tend to contain iron and magnesium in preference to aluminum. Seismic data show that the crustal rocks of continents have an average thickness of about 20·5 miles, whereas the crust under the oceans is relatively thin, averaging about 3·1 miles. Observations show that the foundation of the Atlantic and Indian Oceans consists of granite rocks, as does the foundation of the continents (Dietrich, 1963; von Arx, 1962).

The numerous bottom samples obtained have shown that, in general, the ocean bottom does not consist of a firm rocky foundation but of sediments. Measurements taken in the open Atlantic basin show sediment layers as much as 12,000 feet thick. In contrast to the 12,000-foot thickness found in parts of the Atlantic, oceanographers have never found sediments thicker than 1,000 feet in the Pacific or in the Indian Ocean. The deposits that spread across the floors of the deep sea are generally much finer than those on the slopes and shelves lying off the continents, although occasional beds of sand have been found in the deeps. Around the foundations of the continents, in the deep waters off the borders of the continental slopes, are the muds of terrestrial origin. These are muds of many colors: blue, green, red, black, and white—apparently varying with climatic changes as well as with the dominant soils and rocks of the lands of their origin. Farther at sea are the oozes of predominantly marine origin; the remains of tiny sea creatures. In addition to the silt load of every river that finds its way to the sea, there are other materials that compose the sediments. Volcanic dust, blown perhaps half way around the earth in the upper atmosphere, comes eventually to rest on the ocean floor. Sands from coastal deserts are carried seaward on offshore winds, fall to the sea, and sink. Gravel, pebbles, small boulders, and shells are carried by icebergs and drift ice, to be released to the water when the ice melts.

CURRENTS

Ocean currents are determined by various forces: primary forces, which induce and maintain currents and which may be subdivided into internal and external forces, and secondary forces, which only influence already existing motion. The internal forces are equivalent to pressure forces; processes at the sea surface are primarily responsible for maintaining these pressure forces. Here, the wind stress acts, and the field of mass is subjected to external influences such as temperature and salinity. The temperature may change as a result of that exchange between ocean and atmosphere, and the salinity because of water exchange, which is determined by evaporation, precipitation, ice formation, melting of ice, and run-off. Complications are introduced by mixing processes that result from turbulence, which are associated with ocean currents and which vary with time and space, influencing the distribution of temperature and salinity (Dietrich, 1963; von Arx, 1962).

External forces causing ocean currents are wind stress and tidal forces and changes of the atmospheric pressure. The wind stress is the main force. It induces drift currents and affects the internal pressure forces. A stationary distribution of air pressure over the globe cannot cause currents because the ocean would adjust to it, but changes in the atmospheric pressure distribution may induce currents. Those forces that do not cause motion but only modify existing motion are called secondary forces. Among them are the frictional forces which reduce velocity, and the deflecting force of the earth's rotation which influences the current direction. The Coriolis force always

The World of Water

acts perpendicular to the motion, towards the right in the Northern Hemisphere, in the Southern Hemisphere towards the left looking in the direction of the current.

A great similarity exists between the distribution of oceanic regions and areas with major wind systems. Currents of the trade wind regions are characterized by a persistent westerly current during the entire year. Two regions of trade wind currents exist in each ocean with the exception of the Indian Ocean where only one such region is found in the Southern Hemisphere. The corresponding region in the northern part of the Indian Ocean does not develop because of the seasonal changes of the Monsoon winds. Trade wind current regions are known as Canaries and Benguela Currents in the North and South Atlantic Ocean, as California and Peru (Humboldt) Currents in the North and South Pacific Ocean, and as the West Australia Current in the South Indian Ocean. Since they flow from higher to lower latitudes, they carry water that is colder than average for the corresponding latitudes. These temperature anomalies become larger because the winds in the areas where the trade winds originate contribute to the formation of a cross circulation in the currents; this causes cold water from deeper layers to ascend in the off-shore region. Zones of upwelling occupy a special position within the eastern region of the trade wind currents.

The entire area of the eastern trade winds current region is low in precipitation; in fact, it is an area of minimum precipitation on the globe. Oceanic islands in these regions such as the Cape Verde Islands in the North Atlantic Ocean and Galapagos Islands in the South Pacific Ocean, have desert-type climates. In regions of trade wind currents with currents moving westward, the North and South Equatorial currents move westward uniformly and persistently. They are areas of violent storms known as typhoons in East Asia, as Mauritius hurricanes in the South Indian Ocean, and as hurricanes in the West Indies. Regions of the trade wind currents with components directed toward the poles are distinguished by their high surface temperatures, which, together with the high evaporation, contribute greatly to the formation of instability in the lower atmospheric layers. Thus, a tendency to precipitation develops (Dietrich, 1963; von Arx, 1962).

Regions of the three oceans where equatorial counter currents occur, are known as regions of equatorial currents. In the Atlantic and Pacific Oceans north of the equator, equatorial counter currents are present during the entire year. They vary seasonally and are most strongly developed during the northern summer.

In regions of monsoon currents the changes in direction of the monsoon winds in spring and fall cause a change of direction of the surface currents. The season of the winter monsoon lasts from November to March or April. During this time, under the influences of cooling, a strong atmospheric high develops over Asia, and the air in the lowest atmospheric layers flows out. Over the North Indian Ocean, under the influence of the deflecting force of the earth's rotation, the winds blow from the northeast, whereas over the waters around Indochina they blow from the north, and, over the east Asiatic marginal seas and the adjacent open Pacific Ocean, they blow from north to northwest. The winds blow off-shore from Asia. In this season the hydrographic conditions in the north Indian Ocean resemble those of a region of trade wind currents; the surface water flows toward the west and becomes more saline because the dry continental air of the northeast monsoon does not show any tendency toward precipitation, and evaporation alone is effective in the water exchange between ocean and atmosphere. The season of the summer monsoon lasts from May to September. During this time the wind blows from the southwest over the North Indian Ocean, and from the south to southeast over east Asiatic waters; that is, the wind always has an on-shore component toward the Asiatic continent.

Between the region of the trade wind currents and the region of the west wind drift lies the region of the horse latitudes. In this region currents exist during part of the year that either assume the characteristics of trade wind currents or the characteristics of currents of the west wind drift. Such currents flow in winter in those parts of the regions that face poleward.

A strong gradient current develops in the region of the jet stream at the west sides of the oceans and creates a discharge of those water masses that are set in motion toward the west by the stress of the trade winds. The currents concentrate in narrow, lateral, sharply defined current bands. These discharge currents of the trade wind currents are known as the Gulf Stream and Kuroshio in the Northern Hemisphere and as the Brazil current, East Austral current, and Agulhas current in the Southern Hemisphere (Dietrich, 1963; von Arx, 1962).

The ocean is the great regulator; the great stabilizer of temperatures. Without the ocean, the world would be visited by harsh extremes of temperature. It is an excellent absorber and radiator of heat. Because of its enormous heat capacity, the ocean can absorb a great deal of heat from the sun without becoming hot, or it can lose much of its heat without becoming cold.

Through the agency of ocean currents, heat and cold may be distributed over thousands of miles. It is possible to follow the course of a mass of warm water that originates in the trade-wind belt of the Southern Hemisphere and remains recognizable for a year and a half, through a course of more than 7,000 miles. This redistribution function of the ocean tends to make up for the uneven heating of the globe by the sun. Ocean currents carry hot equatorial water toward the poles and return cold water equatorward by such surface drifts as the Labrador Current and Oyashio, and by deep currents. The redistribution of heat for the whole earth is accomplished about half by the ocean currents, and half by the winds.

The Atlantic currents of the Southern Hemisphere are practically a mirror image of those of the Northern. The great spiral moves counter-clockwise-west, south, east, north. Here the dominant current is in the eastern instead of the western part of the ocean. It is the Benguela Current, a band of cold water moving northward along the west coast of Africa. The South Equatorial Current, in mid-ocean a powerful stream, loses a substantial part of its waters to the North Atlantic off the coast of South America. The remainder becomes the Brazil Current, which circles south and then turns east as the South Atlantic or Antarctic Current. The whole is a system of shallow water movements, involving throughout much of its course not more than the upper fathoms.

The North Equatorial Current of the Pacific is the longest westerly running current on earth, with nothing to deflect it in its 9,000-mile course from Panama to the Philippines.

There, meeting the barrier of the islands, most of it swings northward as the Japan Current, Asia's counterpart of the Gulf Stream. A small part persists on its westward course, around Asiatic islands; part turns upon itself and streams back along the equator as the Equatorial Countercurrent. The Japan Current, called Kuroshio or Black Current, rolls northward along the continental shelf off eastwards, northward along the continental shelf off eastern Asia, until it is driven away from the continent by a mass of ice water, the Oyashio, that flows out the Sea of Okhotsk and Bering Sea. The Japan Current and Oyashio meet in a region of fog and winds, as in the North Atlantic the meeting of the Gulf Stream and the Labrador Current is marked with fog. Drifting toward America, the Japan Current forms the northern wall of the great North Pacific eddy. Its warm waters become chilled with cold polar water from Oyashio, the Aleutians, and Alaska. When it reaches the mainland of America it is a cool current, moving southward along the coast of California. There it is further cooled by up-drafts of deep water and has much to do with the temperate summer climate of the American west coast. Off Lower California it rejoins the North Equatorial Current (Dietrich, 1963; von Arx, 1962).

The South Equatorial Current has its course interrupted by islands, which deflect streams of its water into the central basin. By the time it approaches Asia it is a comparatively feeble current. Around the East Indies and Australia the West Wind Drift or Antarctic Current, the poleward arc of the spiral, is born of the strongest winds in the world, blowing across stretches of ocean almost unbroken by land. The Humboldt Current, sometimes called the Peru, flows northward along the east coast of South America, carrying waters almost as cold as the Antarctic from which it comes. The current is reinforced by almost continuous upwelling from lower oceanic layers. Leaving the coast of South America at about the latitude of Cape Blanco, the Humboldt Current turns westward into the Pacific, carrying its cool waters almost to the equator. About the Galapagos Islands it gives rise to a strange mixture of waters, the cool green of the Humboldt and the blue equatorial waters meeting in rips and foam lines (Dietrich, 1963; von Arx, 1962).

The World of Water

The Gulf Stream system includes the complex of currents, having relation to the waters passing through the Straits of Florida, that extends as various branches, eddies, and closely coupled countercurrents along the east coast of North America onward toward the eastern North Atlantic. The Florida Current portion of the Gulf Stream system includes the water moving toward the Atlantic through the Straits of Florida. The Gulf Stream portion of the system extends from the Atlantic and the Florida Straits to the vicinity of the Flemish Cap. The North Atlantic Current is that portion of the Gulf Stream system lying to the eastward of the Flemish Cap.

The Gulf Stream system forms the western and northern boundary of the waters of the Sargasso Sea. The limits of this area are characterized by the distribution of Sargasso weed, a brown algae which floats near the sea surface in small clumps or extensive pads. Sargassum is scattered throughout a large oval area delimited roughly by the Bermuda-Azores high-pressure cell. The eastern and southern margins of the Sargasso Sea are rather difficult to place, but the hydrographic limits of the western and northern boundaries of this area are situated at the seaward margin of the Gulf Stream system (Garson, 1961).

The surface water of the Gulf Stream is mainly derived from the southern part of the north Equatorial Current. Water driven by the trades moves slowly across the equatorial North Atlantic, through the Antilles into the Caribbean Sea, and onward through the Yucatan Channel into the southeastern portion of the Gulf of Mexico before entering the Straits of Florida and the Gulf Stream system. In addition to the surface water from the north Equatorial Current, the Gulf Stream is fed by a part of the south Equatorial Current, which appears to divide against the easternmost promontory of South America. The Gulf Strean system is probably composed of a couple of filamentary flows, eddies, and meanders. These are confined within diverging limits along the western perimeter of the Sargasso Sea. Near the Florida Straits and again at Cape Hatteras these limits may be as little as 60 nautical miles apart. Off Newfoundland, the total width of the system may be as much as 300 nautical miles. The velocity of the Gulf Stream is usually greatest at or very near the surface, where it may range from 100 cm/per sec to values approaching 300 cm/per sec.

Unless local winds have mixed the surface momentum downward, the velocity will decrease regularly with depth to about the 1,640-foot level. At this level there is often a slight inflection of secondary maximum below which the velocity again decreases with depth, reaching values in the order 1 to 10 cm/per sec in depths between the 4,920 to 6,560-foot levels. The Gulf Stream changes its position and therefore cannot be charted once and for all (Dietrich, 1963; von Arx, 1962).

The three most important factors operating to produce currents in estuaries are oceanic tides, stream flow, and wind. The interactions of these forces, particularly the processes of oscillating tides (their vertical ranges and lengthwise flow) and unidirectional stream flow (its velocity and volume), serve to make the estuary a restless and complex system of water movements. The morphology of the basin of the estuary and the channel of the stream modify and determine the stream and tidal dynamics. Within most estuaries there exists a relatively regular and uniform rate of water transport. The volume of estuarine water discharged to the sea through the mouth of the estuary compensates for the amount of fresh water introduced by the stream into the upper region of the estuary. In many estuaries the typical current pattern is one wherein the lighter, fresh water flows seaward over the upstream movement of denser saline waters (denser by virtue of having a greater concentration of dissolved salts).

TIDES

The tides are a response of the waters of the ocean to the pull of the moon and the more distant sun. In theory, there is a gravitational attraction between every drop of sea water and even the outermost star of the universe. In practice, however, the pull of the remote stars is so slight as to be negligible in the greater movements by which the ocean is affected by the moon and the sun. The moon, far more than the sun, controls the tides. Twice each month occur the strongest tidal movements, the highest flood tides, and the lowest ebb tides of the lunar month. These are the spring tides which occur when the sun, moon, and earth are directly in line and the pull of the two heavenly bodies is added together. Twice each month, at the quarters of the moon, when sun, moon, and earth lie at the apexes of a triangle, and the pull of the sun and moon are opposed, there are moderate tidal movements called the neap tides. Then the difference between high and lower water is less than at any other time during the month.

That the sun, with a mass 27 million times that of the moon, should have less influence over the tides than a small satellite of the earth is at first surprising. But in the mechanics of the universe, nearness counts for more than distant mass: the moon's power over the tides is more than twice that of the sun. The influence of sun and moon is constantly changing, varying with the phases of the moon, with the distance of moon and sun from the earth, and with the position of each. Every body of water, whether natural or artificial, has its own period of oscillation. The ocean contains a number of basins, each with its own period of oscillation determined by its length and depth. The disturbance that sets the water in motion is the attracting force of the moon and sun. But the kind of motion, that is, the period of the swing of the water, depends upon the physical dimensions of the basin. Local topography is all-important in determining the features that make the tide (Dietrich, 1963; von Arx, 1962).

The range of tide varies greatly in different parts of the world. The highest tides in the world occur in the Bay of Fundy, with a rise of about 50 feet in Minas Basin near the head of the Bay at the spring tides. At least half a dozen other places scattered around the world have a tidal range of more than 30 feet, Puerto Gallegos in Argentina and Cook Inlet in Alaska, Frobisher Bay in Davis Strait, the Koksoak River emptying into Hudson Strait, and the Bay of St Malo in France. At many other places high tide may mean a rise of only a foot or so, perhaps only a few inches. The theory of tidal oscillation seems to offer the best explanation of such local differences, the rocking up and down of water in each natural basin about a central, virtually tideless node. The tidal rhythms, as well as the range of tide, vary from ocean to ocean. Flood tide and ebb succeed each other around the world, but as to whether there shall be two high tides and two low in each lunar day, or only one, there is no rule.

Among unusual creations of the tide, perhaps the best known

are the bores. The world possesses half a dozen or more famous ones. A bore is created when a great part of the flood tide enters a river as a single wave, or at most two or three waves, with a steep and high front. There must be a considerable range of tide, combined with sand bars or other obstructions in the mouth of the river, so that the tide is hindered and held back, until it finally gathers itself together and rushes through. The Amazon is remarkable for the distance its bore travels upstream, some 200 miles, with the result that the bores of as many as five flood tides may be moving up the river at one time.

The following seas have negligible tides: Baltic Sea (including the Belt Sea), Kattegat and Skagerrak, European Mediterranean (with the exception of the northern Adriatic Sea and the northern Aegean Sea), the Sea of Japan, and the Arctic Ocean (including the north Siberian marginal seas). In the American mediterranean (the Caribbean), only the semi-diurnal tide is poorly developed.

WAVES

Water waves are observed not only at the sea surface but also at boundaries between water masses having different densities. Surface and long waves differ mainly in their propagation velocities. For surface waves, the propagation velocity depends on the wave length and is independent of water depth. The reverse is true for long waves, for which the wave length is determined by the water depth. The wave length for surface waves is small compared to the water depth, for long waves, the wave length is large compared to the water depth.

A wave has height, from trough to crest, and it has length, the distance from its crest to that of the following wave. The period of the wave refers to the time required for succeeding crests to pass a fixed point. None of these dimensions are static, but are related to the wind, the depth of the water, and many other factors. The water that composes a wave does not advance with it across the sea; each water particle describes a circular or elliptical orbit with the passage of the wave form, but returns nearly to its original position. Not all consecutive waves have the same height; high waves appear in groups. Usually the third or fourth waves are the highest; the waves may have very low amplitudes in between. Although wave groups progress, the individual wave does not maintain its position within the group but travels through it as the results of interference of waves with different wave lengths.

The fetch is the distance that the waves have run, under the drive of a wind blowing in a constant direction, without obstruction. The greater the fetch, the higher the waves. A fetch of perhaps 600 to 800 miles, with winds of gale velocity, is required to get up the large ocean waves. Waves higher than 25 feet from trough to crest are rare in all oceans. Storm waves may grow twice as high, and if a full gale blows long enough in one direction to have a fetch of 600 to 800 miles, the resulting waves may be even higher. The greatest possible height of storm waves at sea is probably 60 feet (Dietrich, 1963; von Arx, 1962).

Waves normally observed at sea are composed of two varieties: the swell, which is a long and relatively symmetrical wave having a period in the order of ten seconds and produced by winds and storms at some distance from the point of observation; and sea, which is the local wind-generated wave motion usually of shorter period with unsymmetrical slopes and steep or white-capped crests depending upon the wind speed and fetch. As the waves gradually pass out of a storm area, their height diminished, the distance between successive crests increases, and the sea becomes a swell, moving at an average speed of about 15 miles an hour. Near the coast a pattern of long, regular swells occurs. As the swell enters shallow water, a transformation takes place. The wave feels the drag of shoaling bottom, its speed slackens, crests of following waves crowd in toward it, abruptly its height increases, and the wave form steepens, then with water falling down into its trough, it dissolves.

Forces within the sea itself may greatly affect a wave. Out in the open sea, a train of waves encountering a hostile wind may be rapidly destroyed, for the power that created a wave may also destroy it. Rocky ledges, shoals of sand or clay or rock, and coastal islands in the mouths of bays all play their part in the fate of the waves that advance toward the shore. Ice, snow, and rain may knock down a sea or cushion the force of surf on a beach.

The term tidal waves is applied to two very different kinds of waves, neither of which has any relation to the tide. One is a seismic sea wave produced by undersea earthquakes; the other is a vast wind or storm wave, a mass of water driven by winds of hurricane force far above the normal high-water line. Most of the seismic sea waves called 'tsunamis' are born in the deepest trenches of the ocean floor. The Japanese, Aleutian, and Atacama trenches have each produced waves that claimed many human lives. The waves produced by a recent Aleutian quake were only about a foot or two high in the open ocean and would not be noticed from vessels. Their length, however, was enormous, with a distance of about 90 miles between succeeding crests. It took the waves less than five hours to reach the Hawaiian chain, 2,300 miles distant. Along eastern Pacific shores, they were recorded as far into the Southern Hemisphere as Valparaiso, Chile, the distance of 8,066 miles from the epicenter being covered by the waves in about 18 hours.

There are other great waves, usually called 'rollers,' that periodically rise on certain coasts and batter them for days with damaging surf. These are wind waves, but they are related to changes in barometric pressure over the ocean, perhaps several thousand miles distant from the beaches on which the waves eventually arrive. Storm surges can be destructive. In recent years there have been major losses of life and property associated with winter gales over the North Sea, with hurricanes in the North Atlantic, and with typhoons in the North and more rarely in the South Pacific (Dietrich, 1963; von Arx, 1962).

A considerable transport of water masses towards the beach is associated with surf waves. These water masses do not return with the wave but flow back along the bottom in the form of a current. The so-called undertow can cause a person to lose balance and may become dangerous in heavy surf. If the waves hit the beach at an angle, a current along the beach develops that intermittently feeds into rip currents, which flow into the open ocean and are another danger for swimmers. Alongshore currents are of considerable importance for the sand transport along the beach.

TEMPERATURE AND CHEMICAL CONTENT

Certain regions of the oceans possess characteristic associations of salinity and temperature. In general, the density of the sea

The World of Water

becomes less with elevation above the bottom. Oceanic areas and layers are distinguished from one another as water masses. Ocean temperatures vary from about 28°F in polar seas to 96°F in the Persian Gulf, which contains the hottest ocean water in the world. Some 93.3 percent of the ocean volume is colder than 50°F, 76.5 percent is colder than 39°F, the temperature at which fresh water reaches maximum density.

Temperature

The sea surface temperatures are, on the average, higher than the temperatures of the lowest atmospheric layers. The annual variation of the surface temperature depends geographically on different factors, particularly on the annual variation in radiation, on the ocean currents, and on the prevailing winds. In equatorial and polar regions, the annual variation remains small. However, the North Atlantic and the North Pacific Oceans are exceptions, especially the western parts. There, the prevailing westerlies bring very cold continental air masses over the oceans in winter, thus decreasing the surface temperature appreciably. In small mediterranean and marginal seas the corresponding variation in water temperature follows the variation of the air temperature. The annual variations and the annual mean of the surface temperature are subject to long-range variations. A warming can be observed for wide oceanic areas. The greatest temperature increase, 0.6-0.7°C, can be found at the extension of the Gulf Stream system near the Faroe-Shetland area. The mean daily variations in oceanic surface temperature approach 0.2-0.3°C (Dietrich, 1963; von Arx, 1962).

The vertical temperature structure of the ocean results in a layering of water masses. The summer thermocline is a typical phenomenon of all areas with large yearly variations in surface temperatures. The thermocline drops from approximately a 49-foot depth north of 35°N, to a depth of more than 164 feet near the Hawaiian Islands. In the fall, when cooling begins, the surface water becomes denser, and a vertical thermal convection becomes effective. In time, the thermocline will diminish until the temperature differences disappear, which is typical for winter conditions. If salinity differences do not contribute to the density stratification, the water column from the surface to the bottom becomes isothermal in marginal seas. In temperate latitudes, the isothermal layer extends to approximately 656 to 982 feet in the open ocean. In some areas of higher latitudes, the thermal convection can be followed to great depths. It leads to the formation of cold North Atlantic deep water south of Greenland, the formation of very cold Arctic bottom water in the Greenland Sea between Spitsbergen and Greenland, and the cold Antarctic bottom water in the Weddell Sea.

Three facts concerning the thermal behavior in the oceans are particularly interesting: the contrast between the east and west sides of the oceans in lower and middle latitudes, the differences between the Atlantic, Indian and Pacific parts of the Antarctic Ocean, and the extraordinarily high surface temperatures in the northeast Atlantic region. Each of these three facts can be explained by the heat transport of the ocean currents because the continents prevent a purely zonal circulation. As a result, water motions are induced and the current, which on the east side of the ocean transports cool water from middle latitudes toward the equator, on the west side of the ocean transports warm water from lower latitudes toward the poles. These contrasts between east and west sides are further emphasized by the upwelling of cold water at the east sides. The second fact can be explained by the eccentric position of the Antarctic Continent with respect to the geographic South Pole. The center of the continental mass lies in the East Antarctic along the 66°S latitude, whereas the coast of the West Antarctic in the Pacific Ocean runs along the 73°S latitude, with the exception of the Palmer peninsula. Since the isotherms in the Antarctic Ocean run parallel to the coast of the Antarctic, as the winds do, the water in the Pacific sector appears to be warmer than water at the same latitude in the Indo-Atlantic sector. The third fact is explained by the heat transport of the Gulf Stream extensions. The Gulf Stream not only carries warm tropical and subtropical water of the North Atlantic Ocean toward higher latitudes, but also carries tropical water of the South Atlantic Ocean. Part of the South Equatorial Current north of Cape Sao Roque is forced to enter the Northern Hemisphere owing to the position of South America. Therefore, the South Atlantic Ocean as a whole is colder as a result of the heat flux into the North Atlantic Ocean (Dietrich, 1963; von Arx, 1962).

The World of Water

Between 50°N and 45°S, the vertical temperature distribution shows a two-layer structure: an upper shallow warm-water sphere, on the average only 1,640 feet thick, and an underlying cold-water sphere, which reaches the bottom. The transition from the warm to the cold-water sphere occurs in a relatively thin boundary layer. Its center in the open ocean coincides with the depth of the isotherm for 8-10°C. This transition zone, which lies at a 982 to 1,310-foot depth in the tropics and at 1,640 to 3,280-foot in the subtropics, rises to the surface beginning at 40 latitude and intersects the surface at the well-pronounced boundary between water types, the oceanic polar front, which is nearly always associated with a convergence of surface currents. The vertical temperature distribution in marginal and mediterranean seas behaves quite differently than in the open ocean.

On a global scale, the oceans, with an average temperature of 39°F, form a cold water sphere. Even at the equator, the mean temperature of a water column amounts to only 41°F. Only a shallow surface layer in lower and middle latitudes serves as heat storage. This, however, can accumulate a great amount of heat as a result of the high specific heat of water. Higher latitudes benefit from this fact because of the heat transport by ocean and air currents which carry water vapor to higher latitudes where heat is released by condensation.

In the open ocean the temperatures determine the density distribution. The cold water of higher latitudes reaches the highest density. Even the high surface salinities in sub-tropical regions cannot increase the low density, which is caused thermally, to such an extent that a deep-reaching convection is initiated. Adjacent water masses of different densities cannot remain in equilibrium. The horizontal density differences, maintained by climatic influences of the atmosphere at the sea surface, cause large-scale water motions in the oceans, which follow the fundamental principle that the water spreads along the shortest path to that layer in the ocean with a corresponding density.

The temperature of the estuary is primarily a function of the temperatures of entering streams and the sea together with tidal stages. Where conditions of climate and sufficient depth are met, estuaries may exhibit a vertical temperature gradient.

Types of ice and icebergs
Depending on the state of the sea surface and currents in the Arctic regions, different types of ice are formed. If the sea surface is calm, predominantly clear crystalline new ice is formed, whereas during periods of rough sea surfaces ice mush develops which appears turbid as a result of enclosed air bubbles. If no further disturbances occur during the freezing process, a primary ice cover is formed from the new ice, as occasionally encountered in the one-year-old winter ice of marginal seas. Primary drift ice is formed when the ice mush grows to disks, which assume a circular form all nearly the same size with roll-shaped edges from the constant rubbing against each other caused by waves. A different kind of drift ice, called secondary drift ice, develops when a strong new ice field is forceably broken up under external influences (wind, currents, waves, ship traffic). This drift ice consists of ice floes of different sizes and irregular shapes and is prevalent in marginal seas. During longer periods of freezing, drift ice and ice floes may be connected by new ice and ice mush, and freeze together to form a solid, secondary ice field. If the freezing of drift ice occurs under pressure, thus causing ice floes to hummock and pile up, a third form of sea ice develops, namely pack ice. This is encountered along the coasts in the form of walls of pack ice reaching heights of 66 feet. Pack ice is also present in the narrow passages of the adjacent seas. The main areas of its distribution are the polar regions, especially in the Northern Hemisphere. In addition to the types of ice formed in the ocean, two other types of ice which trace their origins to the continents may occur in the ocean, namely river ice and glacial ice.

Two different types of icebergs can be distinguished depending on whether they originate from valley glaciers or from shelf ice. The distribution of icebergs of the shelf ice type is almost exclusively restricted to the south polar regions where the Antarctic ice sheet does not advance in separate glacial tongues but presents a well-defined boundary toward the ocean surrounding Antarctica. In part, this ice sheet lies directly on the bottom of the shelf; in part it floats. The depth of the submerged part of an iceberg is governed by the specific weight of the ice, which depends strongly on the air content of the ice.

The World of Water

With a density of sea water of 1·027 and an air content of 1 percent, 88·6 percent of the total volume of the iceberg is submerged; with an air content of 10 percent, only 80·8 percent is submerged (Dietrich, 1963; von Arx, 1962).

Chemical content

The constituents of ocean water are salts, atmospheric gases dissolved in ocean water, organic matter, and insoluble particles suspended in ocean water. Sea water is a very complex solution of organic and inorganic salts derived over the course of geologic time from the solution of rocks, the gaseous diffusion of volcanoes, biological activity, and probably from meteoritic material in the earth's atmosphere.

There is a limited return of salts to the land. While the process of evaporation, which raises water vapor into the air, leaves most of the salts behind, a surprising amount of salt does rise into the atmosphere and rides long distances on the wind. Areas nearest the sea receive the most salt; the Sambhar Salt Lake in northern India receives 3,000 tons of salt a year, carried to it on the hot dry monsoons of summer from the sea, 400 miles away.

When ocean water evaporates or freezes, most of the salt remains in the water, resulting in an increase of salinity near the surface. Conversely, precipitation, river discharge from the continents, and melting water decrease the surface salinity. Ocean currents and mixing processes decrease the salinity contrast not only at the surface but through all layers. The saltiest ocean water in the world is that of the Red Sea. The Sargasso Sea is the saltiest part of the Atlantic, which in turn is the saltiest of the oceans. The polar seas are the least salty, because they are constantly being diluted by rain, snow, and melting ice.

Samples of ocean water from different parts of the world ocean have been analyzed and these show that regardless of the absolute concentrations of the individual constituents, the relative proportions of the major constituents are nearly constant. Thus, it is possible to estimate the total salt content of sea water from measurements of the concentration of only one constituent, usually the chloride ion. Sea water on the average contains about 3·5 percent of dissolved salts, a salt content of 35 parts per thousand. This is, in general, the salinity of the open oceans at a depth of about a thousand feet. Surface waters vary considerably around this average, and there are also variations at different depths in the great ocean basins. At the surface, salinity is highest in the tropics, where evaporation is greatest, and lowest toward the poles, due to dilution from melting ice. The Red Sea, with no inflow of fresh water and with high evaporation, has salinities over 45 parts per thousand; in the Mediterranean, salinities vary from nearly 40 parts per thousand off the Syrian coast to 37 parts per thousand near the Straits of Gibraltar. The Baltic Sea with a large inflow of fresh water, has low salinities, below 10 parts per thousand.

Common salt, sodium chloride, predominates and accounts for over three-fourths of the dissolved salts in oceans. Of the metallic ions, magnesium, calcium and potassium rank next in abundance after sodium, and a great variety of chemical elements have been found to be present in traces. Sea water differs from an ordinary salt solution in one major respect: whereas in an ordinary salt solution the amount of cations is generally equivalent to that of anions, this relation does not hold in sea water, at least as far as the ions of strong bases and acids are concerned (Dietrich, 1963; von Arx, 1962).

In general, the proportion of dissolved salts in estuaries resembles that of sea water, while the total concentration is variable along the axis of the estuary. In some instances, however, the concentration of inflowing fresh waters may be such as to modify the normal ionic relationships in estuaries. Where this occurs, the result is usually an increase in the ratios of carbonate and sulfate to chloride, and of calcium to sodium over those of average sea water. Even though there is typically a decrease in turbidity seaward along the axis of an estuary, its waters are decidedly more turbid than the sea.

Although all the gases found in the atmosphere are also present in the ocean, the most important are oxygen and carbon dioxide. Near the surface of the oceans the water is saturated with both gases, but their concentration and relative proportions vary with depth. As the surface water circulates downward through the first few scores of feet, intense plant activity depletes the supply of carbon dioxide. At the same time, oxygen is given off by the plants. Consequently, the near-surface zone is deficient in carbon dioxide and tends to be oversaturated with oxygen. Were it not for the slow circulation of sea water through the ocean basins, water at the greatest depths would be devoid of oxygen. Actually, at the bottom of some ocean basins, circulation of water is so slow that almost no oxygen is present and the water has become stagnant. Along with vertical differences, oxygen characteristically varies diurnally and seasonally within estuaries. The ranges of such variations differ, depending upon the nature of the freshwater source, the morphology of the basin, and effects of tides.

BIOLOGICAL ASPECTS

The environment of the seas is divided ecologically according to depth, distance from land and degree of light penetration and, in general, characteristic types of organisms occur in these various environmental divisions. The primary division is overlying water (pelagic) and bottom water (benthic). The pelagic realm is divided into neritic, or nearshore, and oceanic (the blue water of the open ocean). The pelagic regions are inhabited by floating (planktonic) or swimming (nektonic) organisms, and the benthic regions by sedentary, crawling or creeping organisms; among the animals, the benthos is further subdivided into those that live within the sediment (infauna) and those that are on the surface or attached to rocks, etc. (epifauna). Many organisms in or on the bottom, however, have larval stages which are planktonic, especially in the nearshore or neritic regions of the sea. Many benthic organisms feed on planktonic life or detritus derived from overlying waters, and fish whose young stages live near the surface feed as adults on bottom organisms. In the deep parts of the sea there is little interchange between the upper levels, and the benthos is ultimately dependent upon what may descend from the surface layers. Just as land plants depend on minerals in the soil for their growth, every marine plant is dependent upon the nutrient salt minerals in the sea water (Fairbridge, 1966).

A cupful of water may contain millions of diatoms, tiny plant cells, each of them far too small to be seen by the human eye; or it may swarm with an infinitude of animal creatures, none larger than dust which live on plant cells still smaller than themselves. The activities of the microscopic vegetables of the sea of which the diatoms are most important, make the mineral wealth of the water available to the animals. Feeding directly on the diatoms and other groups of minute unicellular algae are the marine protozoa, many crustaceans, the young of crabs, barnacles, sea worms, and fishes. Since they drift where the currents carry them, with no power of will to oppose that of the sea, this community of creatures, and the marine plants that sustain them, are called plankton. From the plankton the food chains lead on, to the schools of plankton-feeding fishes like the herring, menhaden, and mackerel; to the fish-eating fishes like the bluefish and tuna and sharks; to the pelagic squids that prey on fishes; to the whales that may live on fishes, on shrimps, or on some of the smallest of the plankton creatures (Carson, 1961).

Fishes and plankton, whales and squids, birds and sea turtles, are linked by ties to certain kinds of water, to warm water or cold water, to clear or turbid water, to water rich in phosphates or in silicates. For the animals higher in the food chains the ties are less direct; they are bound to water where their food is plentiful, and the food animals are there because the water conditions are right. Many plankton creatures make regular vertical migrations of hundreds of feet, rising toward the surface at night, sinking down below the zone of light penetration early in the morning. The tropical and subtropical areas are scantily inhabited by living organisms, whereas the polar waters, especially those of the Antarctic are characterized by a great abundance of floral and faunal organisms, in contrast to the conditions in the continents. For the same reason the largest animals, the whales, are found in the polar waters of the world ocean, which are rich in nutrients. Although the production processes in the ocean are equivalent to those on the land, attempts have been made to compare the results of observations about the rate of effective production, obtained indirectly in different oceanic areas, with the yields known in agriculture. These comparisons show that, at least, the orders of magnitude of the production in the ocean and on the land are approximately the same.

The dependence of plants on the sun's radiation leads to several peculiarities in their habits. Their environment in the ocean is restricted to the top layers, those penetrated by light.

Under natural conditions, this limit is attained between a few centimeters and 656-foot depth. In the open Atlantic Ocean, the limit is found at approximately 131 feet, in the North and Baltic seas between 66 and 98 feet. In the upper light-penetrated water layers under otherwise optimum living conditions, the assimilation activity and the rate of production of phytoplankton (plant portion of plankton) are approximately proportional to their exposure to light. However, in general, too much radiation again has an adverse effect. The maximum phytoplankton production is usually encountered a few feet below the surface.

An important condition that influences the living conditions of phytoplankton is their dependence on nutrient distribution. Nutrient is defined as all those salt-like substances that are needed by plants for building their organism and for the maintenance of life processes. Phosphorus, nitrogen, and potassium are recognized as the minimum substances in agricultural practice. The corresponding elements in the ocean are phosphorus, nitrogen, and silicon. In sea water, these three elements are present in the form of compounds, as well as nitrates, nitrites, ammonia, and as organically bound nitrogen. Abundant flora and, therefore, fauna can be expected in oceanic areas where there is sufficient radiation and where the water is furnished with great amounts of nutrients. The situation is quite different for the larger animal life of the ocean. Animals depend primarily on food produced by phytoplankton.

The influence of the tide over the affairs of sea creatures as well as men may be seen all over the world. The billions of sessile animals, like oysters, mussels, and barnacles, owe their existence to the sweep of the tides, which brings them the food which they are unable to go in search of. The most curious and incredibly delicate adaptations, however, are the ones by which the breeding rhythm of certain marine animals is timed to coincide with the phases of the moon and the stages of the tide (Carson, 1961).

Immense pressure is one of the governing conditions of life in the deep sea; darkness is another. The darkness of the deep waters has produced weird modifications of the abyssal fauna. The colors of marine animals tend to be related to the zone in which they live. At depths greater than 1,500 feet, all the fishes are black, deep violet, or brown, but the prawns

Oceans

wear amazing hues of red, scarlet, and purple. The phenomenon of luminescence is displayed by many fishes that live in dimly lit or darkened waters, and the eyes of fishes become enlarged at great depths.

There is little similarity between the chemical composition of river water and that of sea water. The various elements are present in entirely different proportions. The rivers bring in four times as much calcium as chloride yet in the ocean the proportions are strongly reversed. An important reason for the difference is that immense amounts of calcium salts are constantly being withdrawn from the sea water by marine animals and are used for building shells and skeletons, for the microscopic shells that house the foraminifera, for the massive structures of the coral reefs, and for the shells of oysters and clams and other mollusks. Another reason is the precipitation of calcium from sea water. There is a striking difference, too, in the silicon content of river and sea water, about 500 percent greater in rivers than in the sea. The silica is required by diatoms to make their shells, and immense quantities brought in by rivers are largely utilized by these plants of the sea. Because of the enormous chemical requirements of the fauna and flora of the sea, only a small part of the salts annually brought in by rivers goes to increasing the quantity of dissolved minerals in the water.

Life in the sea varies with the temperature of the water. There is a variety of tropical life, yet, in any species there are far fewer individuals than in the colder zones, where the mineral content of the water is richer. In the tropics the sea birds do not compare in abundance with the birds seen over far northern or far southern fishing grounds. In the tropics sea life is intense, vivid, and infinitely varied. In cold seas it proceeds at a pace slowed by the icy water in which it exists, but the mineral richness of these waters overturns and makes possible the enormous abundance of the forms that inhabit them. In certain tropical and subtropical waters, there are areas where the sheer abundance of life rivals the Grand Banks or the Barents Sea or any Antarctic whaling grounds. Examples are the Humboldt Current, off the west coast of South America, and Benguela Current, off the west coast of Africa. In both currents, upwelling of cold, mineral-laden water from deeper layers of the sea provides the fertilizing elements to sustain life (Carson, 1961).

Coral reefs are essentially tropical, the reef-building organisms will not grow in waters where the temperature falls much below 70°F. Growing reefs are found outside the tropics in a few places. In such places warm currents bring tropical waters into higher latitudes. Within the tropics, coral reefs are rare on the Pacific coast of America and the Atlantic coast of Africa, because of cold currents. The richest reef developments are in the western Pacific, the Indian Ocean and the Caribbean. Many kinds of corals, like the precious coral of the Mediterranean, grow in colder water, but they do not form reefs. The corals themselves are animals, tiny polyps ranging from the size of a pinhead to that of a pea, according to the species, living as immense colonies in the limestone skeletons that they have jointly built. The shape and sculpturing of the skeleton depends on the particular species of coral. Some species form smoothly rounded masses, with a surface molded like that of the human brain, hence they are called brain corals. Others form branches of various sizes and shapes, like fingers or, in the staghorn corals, like the antlers of deer. The coral animals are nocturnal, extending their tentacles to filter their food from the microscopic life of the water only at night. The basic plant life of the reef or of any marine situation is the invisible algae in the floating plankton (Carson, 1961).

One of the most significant features of estuaries is the oyster reef. This assemblage of organisms is usually found near the mouth of the estuary in a zone of moderate wave action, salt content, and turbidity. Because of its location, depth, and areal dimensions, an oyster reef is often a salient factor in modifying estuarine current systems and sedimentation. The form and position of the reefs vary depending upon the nature of the substrate, currents, and salinity. The reef may occur as an elongate island or peninsula oriented across the main current, or it may develop parallel to the direction of the current. In shallow coastal areas, reefs may grow as islands, often exposed for considerable periods of time during low tides. Biologically, the oyster reef is a unique and interesting community of various mollusks and other organisms.

The mid-ocean regions, bounded by the currents that sweep

around the ocean basins, are in general the deserts of the sea. There are few birds and few surface-feeding fishes, and there is little surface plankton to attract them. The life of these regions is largely confined to deep water. The Sargasso Sea is an exception. A line drawn from the mouth of Chesapeake Bay to Gibraltar would skirt its northern border; another from Haiti to Dakar would mark its southern boundary. It surrounds Bermuda and extends more than halfway across the Atlantic, its entire area being roughly as large as the United States. The Sargasso is a creation of the great currents of the North Atlantic that encircle it and bring into it millions of tons of floating sargassum weed from which the place derives its name, and all the weird assemblage of animals that live in the weed. Its waters are warm and heavy with salt. The sargassum weeds are brown algae belonging to several species (Carson, 1961).

Man has harvested fish from the seas and inland waters for centuries. Fish was important food long before the birth of Christ, and the movement of man across the land during his life as a hunter often depended upon the abundant fish and shellfish, found along the edge of the sea. Asiatic tribes from Siberia found food plentiful and available as they wandered down the west coast of North America, closely following the shores of the sea, and along inland waterways where fish and shellfish (clams and oysters) were abundant. Fish is a highly nutritious food. Its protein content compares favorably with that of meat, milk, or eggs. In addition to the value of fish as a protein food, fish oils recently have been found to contain relatively large quantities of unsaturated fats.

The important fishing areas are a very small part of the ocean. Between 1955 and 1959, approximately 75 percent of the world catch of fish came from the continental shelf of the Northern Hemisphere. The best-known and most heavily fished areas of the oceans of the world are those within which there is a large, shallow shelf. Such rich fishing areas are the Grand Banks of the northwest Atlantic, the North Sea of the northeastern Atlantic, and the Sea of Japan and the East China Sea of the eastern Pacific. As much as 25 percent of the world fish catch in the form of fish such as flounders, cod, and perchlike ocean fish, and significant amounts of the world catch of herring-like fish, come from these areas. A close interrelation exists between the abundance of nutrients and the presence of dense fish populations. Areas rich in nutrients at the sea surface are always abundant in fish. While certain traditional fishing areas of the world ocean have produced a great part of the world fish catch, new and highly productive areas of the ocean have recently been found which are contributing an increasing proportion of the world fish catch (Long, 1964).

Present-day fishing methods are mainly two: either netting fish which are closely gathered in schools, or hooking them with bait. Fishing methods in most parts of the world are primitive. Even the most sophisticated nets now in use tend to be rather simple modifications of very primitive fishing gear, in use for centuries. Many of the most widely used methods of fishing involve primitive boats and small crews, perhaps only a single man. Others, such as purse seines and trawlers, require up to fifteen or twenty men for efficient operation.

Some new methods of capturing fish and other living resources, such as plankton, have been explored; but few of these are in wide use today. Electricity is being used to a very limited extent, in various parts of the world, mostly to concentrate the fish, once they have been enclosed in a net, for more rapid pumping or bailing into the hold of the boat. Scientists have found that an air curtain of bubbles rising from the bottom in relatively shallow water forms an impenetrable barrier to small herring off the coast of Maine. The schools have been concentrated by means of the air curtain and made available to the fishermen. There has been considerable progress recently in the use of certain sound-ranging methods to locate and identify fish schools. The most important sense a fish has is its chemical sense, and this may be exploited in two ways: by ringing a school with a repellent to concentrate it, and then luring the school to an attracting chemical; or it might be rendered senseless by another chemical, and swept from the surface of the sea.

The total volume of plankton in the sea is much greater than the volume of fish. A practical method of concentrating and utilizing plankton, therefore, would be of great value. Scientists have been experimenting recently with using low-operating-cost energy and large nets with which to capture plankton in large quantities. With these tools, the world ocean can provide several times its present yield of food for future generations (Long, 1964).

The total world catch of fish has almost doubled in the past ten years, from 22·8 million tons, in 1951, to 41·2 million tons, in 1961. Practically nowhere in the sea are the fish being fully utilized, even in such heavily fished grounds as the Grand Banks and the North Sea. Perhaps the seas immediately off Japan are the closest to producing their maximum. Fishermen are highly selective about species, and often avoid the most abundant crop of fish. Unfished stocks of fish are known to be present off both coasts of South America and Africa, and in the Indian Ocean. The present trend to fish production could well lead to a doubling of the world fish catch before the turn of the century.

Increasing biological knowledge of fish and shellfish will provide the basis for farming and artificial culture at the edge of the sea. Enormous, shallow, inshore areas in the sea along the edges of all continents can be turned over to fish farming. Relatively little aquaculture is practiced anywhere in the world today except in Japan and Southeast Asia. New knowledge of the food of fish and new methods of rearing larvae of clams and oysters are now available, and should bring about an increase in shellfish farming. New products are needed which will more efficiently utilize a greater proportion of the catch. Current developments in the manufacture of fish protein concentrate in the form of a fine powder, with and without odor and taste, has great potential for using all of the catch and producing a product highly nutritious and capable of storage under adverse conditions for long periods of time.

OCEANOGRAPHIC INSTRUMENTATION

Eight areas of investigation present themselves to oceanographic instruments: the observation of ocean waves, in particular the distinction between the long-term water level fluctuations and the rapidly changing surface waves; depth soundings; temperature measurements; density determinations, which replace pressure observation since these are not sufficiently accurate for many purposes (the pressure is then computed from the density); salinity determination; current measurements; determination of the content of suspended particles, and determination of the content of dissolved substances. For investigations of simple phenomena and processes, at the sea surface, an expensive aid, namely a seaworthy vessel, is necessary for offshore investigations. Depending on the kind of problems as well as the operational area, specifications for a research vessel differ. In coastal areas and in protected waters, simple and small vessels can be used profitably. However, this does not hold true for problems in the open sea. More rigid requirements are posed concerning seaworthiness, good manoeuverability, and radius of action. A low freeboard is important to facilitate the handling of instruments as near to the sea surface as possible. Deck space is required for accommodation of winches and equipment; a sufficient power supply must be available for the winches as well as adequate laboratory space in the quietest part of the ship.

In general, scientists on research vessels have not been able to manage with less than two laboratories, one on deck serving as working space near the hydrographic winch, and a chemical laboratory for those investigations which must be performed immediately after the water samples have been taken. For problems of a marine biological nature, additional laboratories are needed. Because, for in situ observations, methods which transmit data (current, temperature, depth, and marine optical measurements) on the indicators or recorders have been used more and more, the necessity for a third oceanographic laboratory, i.e., a recording center, has recently arisen. Sea and swell exert considerable wave resistance to moving vessels, and designers try to keep this hindrance to a minimum by suitable methods of ship construction (Long, 1964).

Perhaps the most fascinating trend in oceanography today is the use of an increasing number of underwater vehicles. The largest group of underwater vehicles is composed of full-scale submarines. Some of these have been specially instrumented to make oceanographic measurements. There are a number of other smaller submarines which have been built for oceanographic research. The Perry Submarine is a two-man vehicle 20 feet long $3\frac{1}{2}$ feet wide, and capable of diving to 600 feet. The Aluminaut was the first all-aluminum submarine.

Oceans

It is 51 feet long, 10 feet wide and is capable of diving to 15,000 feet. Other submersibles include the bathyscaphe Trieste, a ballast tank to which is attached a 6-foot diameter sphere capable of operating at depths of over 35,000 feet; the RUM (remote underwater manipulator), which is an unmanned, Army tanklike device; and the Deepstar, a flying-saucer-shaped vehicle capable of operating at 1,000 feet.

In contrast to cruising research vessels that travel the oceans, other vehicles for oceanographic and related research are designed to remain in a fixed position through anchoring or, in shallow water, through rigid attachment to the sea floor. These are called fixed platforms. A network of such stations, comprised of unmanned anchored buoys with suspended sensing instruments, provides a synoptic coverage of oceanographic variables at less expense than ships. Anchored buoys of varying geometric form have been used in recent years for the deployment of oceanographic instruments, mainly current meters and temperature-measuring devices. Several types are designed for meteorological observations.

Scuba (self contained underwater breathing apparatus) permits the formerly land or deck-bound scientist to personally enter the kingdom of the sea. For centuries, man has waded the tidal pools and shallows. He has sailed the surface. He had probed into the water, raking, scratching, netting, and dredging up samples of underwater life and bottom. More recently he has invaded this domain in diving bells, suit and helmet rigs and underwater vehicles. None of these have permitted man to comfortably study the underwater ecology with an appreciable degree of ease or continuity.

For each oceanographic observation, a geographic position at sea must be determined. In most cases, the astronomical methods of position determination and dead reckoning are sufficient. Sextant and chronometer, compass, and log are indispensable instruments.

Direct and indirect methods are used for the determination of the topography of the ocean floor. Direct soundings are performed by using sounding leads at the shallow depths (to about 328 feet), or sounding machines can be used at greater depths. The indirect methods utilize three principles: the determination of the hydrostatic pressure and the thermometric depth determination; the determination of the time a plummet needs to sink to the bottom; and the measurement of the travel time of sound by means of the echo sounder. At present, thermometric depth determination and the echo sounder are widely used. The development of echo-location techniques (sonar) during World War II proved to be a great help to oceanography. Rapid progress is being made in mapping the topography of the ocean floors by echo-location.

It has long been understood that a knowledge of sea levels and their variations with time is of great importance to the practical aspects of coastal engineering, shipping, land and sea survey, oceanography, and others. Many gages, adapted to particular problems, are now available. According to the purpose they serve, they are: coastal gages and high-sea gages. Three different types are used for coastal gages: lath gages, float gages (with direct mechanical registration and with electrical remote transmission of the data), and air pressure gages. High-sea gages are employed to obtain records of water-level changes in the open sea, especially records of tides. The principle, however, has been limited until recently, to water less than 984 feet deep. Without exception, high-sea gages are automatically registering pressure gages which record pressure fluctuation in the sea bottom. The pressure variations are obtained either through the determination of volume changes of an enclosed air volume or by the determination of the elastic deformation of a hollow container (Long, 1964).

The determination of water motions in the ocean is one of the main tasks of oceanography. The methods for the determination of water motion are:

Indirect methods, by which the currents are computed on the basis of hydrodynamic laws. Either the pressure distribution in the ocean, the measured surface inclination, or the distribution of hydrographic properties (mainly temperature and salinity) serves as a base for the indirect methods.

Drift measurements, which consists of following the trajectory described by a float.

Current measurements at a fixed point.

Numerous types of oceanographic instruments are in use for measuring waves. Measuring elements are located either above or below the water, or at the sea surface, and the wave motion is indicated and recorded by acoustical, electrical, optical, and mechanical means. The following five quantities of waves have to be measured: height, period, length, propagation velocity, and propagation direction. All methods register heights and wave periods; only photographic methods register the wave length, and no method determines the velocity and direction of the waves. However, velocity measurements are not essential since they can be computed from the wave period if the water depth is known. The determination of the direction, however, must always be supplemented by visual observations.

The determination of the spatial distribution and the time changes of oceanic temperatures involves: temperature measurement at the sea surface, determination of the vertical temperature distribution, and observation of the time changes in particular places at certain levels. Instruments have been adapted to these requirements. According to the applied method, a distinction is made between fluid thermometers, deformation thermometers, electrical resistance thermometers, and thermoelements, all of which can be used as indicators as well as for the registration of temperatures.

Several types of water samplers have been developed which differ in the methods for closing the sampler at a desired depth as well as in the closing design itself. The closing is obtained by one of the following methods: by a propeller which coasts during the lowering of the sampler and which activates the closing valve as soon as the hoisting starts; by a messenger, which is released to board and travels along the wire to which the sampler is attached, thus activating the closing valve after contact with the sampler; and by hydrostatic pressure which activates the closing valve when a certain pressure value is reached, that is, at a certain depth.

Chapter 4

Ice Caps and Glaciers

About 80 percent of all the fresh water in the world is in the form of glacier ice. Most of the world's ice remains in storage from year to year, responding only to long-term climatic fluctuations. The amount released seasonally is, however, significant in many civilized lands. Permanent or perennial ice occurs as the great continental ice sheets of Antarctica and Greenland; as the many cirque, valley, and ice-cap glaciers of the high altitudes and high latitudes; as ground ice in the permafrost regions; and as floating ice shelves attached to Antarctica, the Canadian Arctic islands, and Greenland. The amount of water stored in the continental ice sheets is huge; latest results from International Geophysical Year Studies in Antarctica indicate that this single body of ice has a volume of about 7×10^6 cubic miles. The water equivalent of this volume is equal to the precipitation during the last 60 years over the whole earth.

The area of Antarctica is more than seven times that of the Greenland ice sheet and is $1\frac{1}{2}$ times that of the continental USA. The ice reaches a maximum thickness of nearly 3 miles (Hatherton, 1965). Along the coast it may extend more than 5,000 feet below the level of the sea. In the interior great mountain peaks, called nunataks, project through the ice at heights of 17,000 feet above sea level. The earth's South Pole lies under the Antarctic glacier at a point where the ice is about 8,000 feet thick. The Greenland glacier is about 650,000 square miles in area and thousands of feet in average thickness. It covers all of Greenland except a small coastal strip (Ordway, 1966; Namowitz and Stone, 1965).

During the last million years the world has experienced four major glaciations. For much of this time large portions of the earth's surface were covered by ice sheets, but only those of Greenland and Antarctica persist at the present day. All existing glaciers either occupy or originate in highland areas of the earth's surface. A highly elevated land mass of continental dimensions, centrally located over the South Pole, and completely surrounded by water, would thus represent the ideal combination of conditions under which an ice sheet might be expected to form. These are the conditions that exist in Antarctica today, and which have obviously proved favorable to the growth and maintenance of a very large ice sheet. These conditions have most likely prevailed for millions of years, and it seems just as likely that the ice sheet itself was established some millions of years prior to the onset of world-wide Pleistocene glaciation approximately a million years ago (Leet and Judson, 1954).

A glacier is a mass of ice that has formed from compacted, recrystallized snow and refrozen meltwater, which is moving or has moved, and which lies entirely or partly on land. A valley glacier moves down a channel previously eroded by a stream. It may be wide and thick and tens of miles long, with numerous tributary glaciers, or it may be quite narrow and short. Commonly the ice fills the entire lower part of a valley from wall to wall. In contrast, an ice sheet is a very extensive mass of ice that spreads radially outward from a central area and rests like a blanket upon the surface; it is not confined to a single channel. Continental ice sheets may be a mile or more thick and completely bury billions of square miles of the earth's surface. Small ice sheets called ice caps exist in Iceland, Baffin Land, Spitzbergen, and other large islands of the Arctic Ocean. An ice cap may have a diameter of about 100 miles and an area of several thousand square miles. A piedmont glacier is graduational between a valley glacier and an ice sheet and forms along the base of a mountain by the coalescence of a number of valley glaciers. If growth continues, both areally and vertically, and if a number of piedmont glaciers coalesce, an ice sheet may eventually be formed (Chow, 1964).

Glacier ice consists of a mass of interlocking grains which can flow under pressure, by more or less continuous changes in the individual particles. The rate of flow of glacier ice varies from a maximum measured rate of over 100 feet to a day, to a general average of a few feet per day. The surface of a valley glacier moves more rapidly in the center than along its sides because less friction occurs there.

The snow line is highest near the equator and lowest near the poles. As climates become colder with increasing latitude, less altitude is needed to reach a snow line. The position of the snow line also varies with such factors as the total yearly snowfall and the amount of exposure to the sun. From the equator through Central America, South America, and North America to the North Pole, the snow line drops with increasing latitude approximately as follows: Andes Mountains at the equator, 18,000 feet or $3\frac{1}{2}$ miles; Mexico, 15,000 feet; Sierra Nevada and Rocky Mountains in the United States, 13,000 to 9,000 feet; southern Greenland, 2,000 feet; and the North Pole, sea level.

In many parts of the world streamflow consists mainly of water released by the melting snow. The coming of spring exposes the snow to heat, causing a rapid melt and a short period of runoff. Since the water yielded by the melting of snow often appears in the natural stream channels out of phase with the demand for water for human endeavors, extensive water-resources engineering systems have been developed to store snowmelt runoff and make it available throughout the remainder of the year. In many parts of the world snow acquires a great importance in the occurrence of floods in the spring-time. Sudden outbursts of water from glaciers or from glacier-dammed lakes are of economic as well as scientific interest. The instability of snow in mountainous regions may lead to sudden downward movements of the snow known as snow avalanches.

SNOW AND ICE

A complete description of snow includes information on depth, surface conditions, surface features, density, hardness, and temperature as they may pertain to profiles of a snow layer. The ratio between the volume of meltwater derived from a sample of snow and the initial volume of the sample is known as the density of the snow. Uniform density in a snow-pack is rarely to be found. Snow at the time of fall may have a density as low as 0·01 to as high as 0·15, and the average density of snow is 0·10. Thus, a ten-inch snowfall is equivalent to one inch of water. The water equivalent is the depth of water which would result from the melting of the snow without regard to the density distribution (Chow, 1964).

Measurements of water equivalent of snow at time of fall are made with precipitation gages having designs of various types, including seasonal storage gages, snow boards, and snow stakes. Snow boards or snow markers at least 16 inches square are laid on the previous accumulation of snow. The freshly fallen snow can be readily identified, and snow samples can be cut from it. Wooden stakes, $1\frac{3}{4}$ inches square in cross section, provided with angle-iron supports and calibrated in inches, in a design resembling the markings of a stadia rod, are used to indicate the vertical depth of snow on the ground.

Many of the characteristics of the snowpack, such as the water equivalent, density, and depth, are determined in place by snow surveys. Snow surveying is performed by taking samples of the snowpack with suitable core cutting equipment. Since determination of water equivalent by melting is not practical in the snow fields, the water equivalent is customarily determined by weight of the snow at the time of sampling. A snow course consists of a series of sampling points. Access on foot to snow courses usually requires snowshoes or skis. On-foot cross-country travel in the mountains is hazardous, laborious, and time-consuming. Therefore, extensive effort has been expended on the development of over-snow vehicles. Over-snow vehicles apply their propelling force in various ways; they are air-driven vehicles, track-laying vehicles, and sliding vehicles. Aerial photographic snow-depth measurements are commonly made. The recent availability of radioactive isotopes of elements capable of yielding known intensities of electromagnetic radiation has made possible the development of a snow-water equivalent gage based upon the absorption of gamma radiation by water substance.

Computations and forecasts of runoff from snowmelt are performed for a number of objectives, among which are seasonal water-yield forecasting and rate-of-stream runoff forecasting. Both of these objectives may require snowmelt computations either for the operation of existing projects or for use in designing future projects. Snow- and icemelt computations are pertinent to the hydrologic operations in drainage basins partly fed by water yielded from glaciers. Irrigators are dependent on seasonal water-yield forecasting for planning their crop programs. Hydro-electric generating systems are concerned with seasonal water-yield forecasting to assist in securing the most efficient management with the highest overall income. Flood control, navigation and municipal and industrial water supply make use of seasonal water-yield forecasting.

A major problem in river regulation, forecasting, and operations is the river ice. Under turbulent-flow conditions, needle-like frazil ice may be formed. Deposition of frazil ice on banks, rocks, or engineering structures may take place at rapid rates and possess sufficient mechanical strength to impede or stop the flow of water. When a flowing stream becomes loaded with a sufficiently heavy amount of frazil particles, it is not uncommon to freeze the flow rapidly and solidly to a depth of several feet. Anchor ice is another source of trouble in river regulation and power-plant operation. This is a type of ice formed on underwater rocks or engineering structures.

Frost in the ground is important to hydrologists because it affects stream runoff and infiltration, and to engineers because it may damage ground surface structures such as highways, airfield pavements, and canals. The occurrence of frost in the ground depends on many factors, including air temperature, soil condition, moisture content, vegetal cover, and snow on the ground. The ground perennially below the freezing temperature is known as permafrost. The thickness of the permafrost varies roughly with annual mean temperature. It varies from a maximum of about 2,000 feet reported at Nordvik in Siberia to about 920 and 170 feet at Umiat and Northway, respectively, in Alaska. Experience of building foundations in permafrost regions has shown the necessity of keeping the permafrost in a perpetually frozen condition. Any local disturbance may cause instability, such as sudden outpours of water, with subsequent freezing. Presence of subsurface groundwater channels may cause thawing, with resulting progressive differential settlement in summer and excessive heave in winter (Chow, 1964).

GLACIATION

The Ice Age may have begun approximately $\frac{1}{2}$ to $1\frac{1}{2}$ million years ago. During the Ice Age, great changes took place above, at, and below the earth's surface both in the glaciated areas and outside them. The changes involved climates, animals and plants, crustal movements, sea water, erosion, and deposition. Because a large ice sheet requires many years to disappear, a glacial age can be said to end at different times in different places; the North American ice sheet retreated northward from the Great Lakes region about 10,000 to 11,000 years ago. Glaciers have shrunk the most or disappeared entirely in the upper middle latitudes, especially in the Northern Hemisphere (Leet and Judson, 1954).

Because the total amount of water at the earth's surface in the ice age probably remained about constant, the volume of ocean water was reduced by the amount that became frozen on the lands as ice. Thus, the sea level fluctuated as the volume of land ice fluctuated, and it may have been 300 to 500 feet below its present level during the maximum extent of the glaciers. The earth's crust sagged beneath the tremendous weight of an ice sheet. As the ice sheet melted, the crust warped upward, and rock material at depth returned slowly under the glaciated areas. Similar warping of the crust was associated with each advance and retreat of the ice sheets. Because the ice retreated only recently in terms of geologic time, the earth's surface is still rising slowly in areas.

Climatic changes also occurred during the Pleistocene in nonglaciated areas because climatic belts were shifted equatorward and narrowed. Present-day lakes were much larger during the glacial ages, and lakes existed in basins that are now dry; sediments of these now vanished lakes can be observed; such lakes are called pluvial lakes. As the Pleistocene ice sheets gradually advanced, animals and plants apparently migrated to warmer climates, each generation inhabiting an area a little nearer to the equator than its predecessor. Conclusions concerning the migrations of flowering plants and climatic changes can be drawn from a study of fossil pollen grains and other spores (palynology).

The rock-studded bottom of a glacier is an effective file or rasp and polishes, scratches, and abrades the surfaces over which it moves. A glacier gathers debris from the mantle or bedrock in its path and from rock materials that slide upon it from valley walls, a process that is less important for ice sheets. Glaciers also pluck out blocks of bedrock loosened by the freezing and thawing of water in fractures beneath the ice. Like a plow, a glacier pushes and shoves loosened debris ahead of it.

Glaciation of a region usually results in the formation of many new basins or depressions in the land surface. If these basins are permanently filled with water, they form lakes, ponds, or swamps, depending on how large and deep they are. Three important types of lakes resulting from glaciation are cirque lakes, kettle lakes, and moraine-dammed lakes. Cirque-lakes are formed when water fills the rock-floored cirque basins left by alpine glaciers that have disappeared. Alpine glaciers may scoop out additional rock basins in soft rock areas below the cirques. Lakes in such basins are called rock-basin lakes. Cirque lakes and rock-basin lakes are also called tarns. Kettle lakes form in large numbers in the kettle holes of moraines and outwash plains. Small kettle holes may contain ponds or swamps. Moraine-dammed lakes are formed where river valleys are blocked by glacial moraines that prevent the flow of the river. In rising to the height of the moraine dam, the river floods its valley to form a long, usually narrow lake (Leet and Judson, 1954).

When a glacier melts, it leaves its moraines in nearly the same positions as they occupied in the glacier. Ground moraine forms a thin, fairly even deposit over the entire area occupied by the ice. Lateral and medial moraines form ridges running approximately in the direction of glacial movement. The terminal moraine, usually the thickest and most conspicuous of the moraines, forms a ridge all along the ice front, marking the farthest position reached by the advance of the glacier. The longer the ice front stays in one place, the larger the terminal moraine becomes. When a receding ice front stops in new positions for any length of time, new terminal moraines are formed behind the principal one. These moraines are called recessional moraines. Drumlins are long, smooth, oval-shaped hills composed of till. They usually occur in groups in which all the drumlins are more or less parallel to each other and pointing in the direction of glacier movement. Drumlins usually range in length from a quarter-mile to a half-mile, and in height from 50 to 100 feet.

Ice Caps and Glaciers

The water from the melted ice of a glacier pours out at the ice front, over and through the terminal moraine, in streams filled with rock flour, sand, and gravel. Dropping the coarse gravels and sands first, while carrying the finer silts and clays much farther, these streams form gently sloping deposits that may extend for miles beyond the terminal moraine. The deposits resemble alluvial fans, and in front of large glaciers they merge to form broad, relatively flat areas called outwash plains. Like terminal moraines, outwash plains may parallel the ice front for hundreds of miles. Much of the water of a melting glacier falls to the bottom of the ice through crevasses, forming subglacial streams which run in tunnels beneath the ice until they emerge at the ice front. The winding tunnels of these streams become partly filled with layers of roughly stratified sands and gravel. When the glacier disappears, the deposits slump down on the sides and are left as winding sand-gravel ridges called eskers.

Kames are small cone-shaped hills of stratified sand and gravel. They are formed when streams from the surface of the glacier deposit their sediments in heaps at the ice-front margins of the glacier or at the bottom of circular depressions in the glacier itself. Kames may occur as parts of terminal moraines or in the areas between the moraines and the level outwash plains. Where kames occur in groups, the depressions between them are called kettles. The term kettle, or kettle hole, is also applied to circular depressions found on terminal moraines and pitted outwash plains. Kettles are formed when moraine or outwash deposits surround and bury large blocks of ice left by slight glacial recession. When the blocks melt, they leave the kettle holes. Long, narrow kamelike deposits sometimes form terraces between the side of a glacier and the valley wall. These are called kame terraces. When glacial streams empty into lakes at or beyond the ice front, deltas are formed. These consist largely of layers of gravel and coarse sands. Fine sands and clays may be spread evenly over the entire lake floor (Leet and Judson, 1954).

In order to qualify as a glacier, an ice mass must have an area where snow or ice usually accumulates in excess of melting and another area where the wastage of snow or ice usually exceeds the accumulation, and there must be a slow transfer of ice mass by creep from the first region to the second. Glaciers exist in a wide variety of forms and characteristics. Some are active ice streams in areas of very high precipitation and have large amounts of meltwater runoff, whereas others occur in such cold desert environments where yearly snowfall is negligible (Chow, 1964).

Continental glaciers such as Antarctica and Greenland, glacier caps of more limited extent such as the many in the Canadian Arctic Archipelago, and highland glacier systems such as the Juneau Ice Field in southeastern Alaska extend in continuous sheets, the ice moving outward in all directions. The valley glaciers of the Cascade Range, cirque glaciers, which are the most common type of glacier in the American Rocky Mountains, and many less common types of glaciers are confined to a more or less marked path.

There are transection glaciers, in which a whole valley system is filled by ice, wall-sided glaciers, summit glaciers, hanging glaciers, ice aprons, cliff glaciers, crater glaciers, regenerated or reconstituted glaciers, and glacier tongues afloat. Piedmont glaciers, such as the huge Malaspina and Bering Glaciers of southeastern Alaska; foot glaciers; and shelf-ice, such as that which occurs along the northern portion of Ellesmere Island in Canada, spread in large or small cakelike sheets over the ground.

Throughout temperate glaciers the ice temperatures correspond to the melting point of ice, except in the wintertime, when the top layer is frozen to a depth not exceeding several tens of feet. The Alps fall into this group. In high-polar glaciers the ice temperature is below the freezing point to a considerable depth, and even in summer the temperature is so low that there is no melting. Most of Antarctica falls into this group. In subpolar glaciers, the summer temperatures allow surface melting and the formation of liquid water, but the main mass of ice at depth is below the freezing temperature. The Greenland Icecap at lower elevations, and especially its southern parts, is a subpolar glacier.

The activity of a glacier depends upon its depth, speed of flow, and material balance. The rate of movement of an active glacier is generally high because it must transport a large amount of precipitation from one area to another where the amount of melting is likewise high. An inactive glacier has sluggish movement because the accumulation of snow on its surface and the wastage are both small. In general, active glaciers occur in maritime environments at relatively low latitudes, and inactive glaciers occur in high latitudes and very continental environments (Chow, 1964).

Glaciers grow and shrink according to changes in snowfalls and melting during the different seasons. In order for a glacier to remain at a constant size, there must be a balance between the accumulation and loss of mass. The balance is referred to as the glacier's mass budget. If snow accumulation exceeds wastage or ablation, the glacier grows, and if wastage exceeds accumulation, the glacier shrinks. In general, glaciers strive to maintain a balanced budget. The snow accumulation from a given winter is transformed from snow to firn and finally to ice. This transition results in an increase in grain size and density and a partial or complete homogenization of the contrasts in grain size and density between individual years. In temperate glaciers melting is the dominant process and normally accounts for all but a few percent of the removal of ice. Glaciers which terminate in lakes or oceans lose mass by the calving of icebergs. In some high arctic environments, appreciable snow and ice are removed by wind erosion; in some unusual cases, glaciers lose mass by the breaking off of avalanches. In many temperate glaciers melting at the surface exceeds 10 or 20 feet per year. The highest level on a glacier to which the winter snow cover retreats during an ablation season is normally called the firn limit. The firn limit corresponds to the elevation at which the accumulation equals the wastage in temperate glaciers.

In late spring, glaciers are covered entirely by a thick snowpack at the melting temperature. Meltwater and liquid precipitation must travel through the snowpack by slow percolation until reaching meltwater channels in the solid ice below. In summer, the snowpack becomes thinner and drainage paths within the snow become more defined. Some bare ice is exposed, and on this there may be surface drainage. Thus, meltwater can be transmitted through the glacier more rapidly than in the spring. In fall, a thin, dense snow layer covers only part of the glacier and bare ice is exposed over the rest of the glacier. Meltwater travels quickly from the surface to the outflow stream. In winter, snow accumulates and the surface layer freezes. The movement of surface meltwater and precipitation stops. Rain which falls on the frozen surface refreezes to join the ice reservoir. A small amount of water deep within the glacier slowly drains out during the winter. In early spring, the surface begins to thaw. The daily fluctuation of meltwater discharge from a glacier in midsummer is pronounced. Glaciers carry large amounts of debris, as evidenced by their massive moraines. It has been found in central Alaska that as one traces a river back toward its source in a glacier, the suspended-sediment concentration increases (Chow, 1964).

Prolonged changes in the mean annual or mean summer temperature of less than one degree may instigate glacier advances or retreats amounting to hundreds, or even thousands of feet. Glaciers exist according to a delicate balance between accumulation and wastage and a slight disturbance in this balance results in an appreciable reaction. Glaciers provide indirect evidence of climatic variations because they advance or retreat in response to very small changes in climate, and these advances and retreats leave a stamp on the landscape in the form of moraines, terraces, or changes in vegetation. Frequently these advances or retreats can be precisely dated. Glacier data indicate a warm-dry interval from 3,000 to 7,000 years ago. A major readvance of the ice took place at the beginning of the sixteenth century; most glaciers seen today are products of this 'Little Ice Age.' This cool-wet period persisted until the beginning of the twentieth century. At least in northwestern United States, the climate became warmer and drier until about 1945, when it rather abruptly changed back to cool and wet (Chow, 1964).

ANTARCTICA

The ice sheet lies wholly within the Antarctic Circle and extends below sea level at many points. The load of the ice sheet has caused considerable depression of the Antarctic land mass. In the event of complete melting of the ice sheet the land mass would recover by an amount equal to one-third of the thickness of the ice. Nevertheless, much of Antarctica would remain below sea level (Hatherton, 1965). Geographically Antarctica can be divided into two distinctive regions: West Antarctica lying south of the Americas, and East Antarctica bounded by the Atlantic and Indian Oceans, and separated from West Antarctica by a line linking the southern extremities of the Ross and Filchner Ice Shelves.

The land margins of Antarctica are fringed with a continental shelf that is everywhere narrow except in the two large embayments occupied by the Weddell and Ross Seas and their associated ice shelves. The Antarctic continental shelf is notable for the great depth at which the break in slope lies. With small exceptions, the continental slope descends to depths of at least 10,000 feet all round Antarctica. North of the escarpment of the continental slope the Antarctica sea floor is of two types, either broad ridge or deep basin. The most extensive features are the basins.

The Pacific-Antarctic Basin trends eastward as an elongated triangular area bordering the Antarctic continent and extending to southern Chile. In the north it is bounded by the Pacific-Antarctic Ridge and the South-eastern Pacific Plateau. Its central area, 1,000 miles long, is more than 16,400 feet deep and a maximum sounding of 21,300 feet has been reported at the western end. Two further large basins border the Antarctic continent. The Eastern Indian-Antarctic Basin extends from the Scott Island-Balleny Islands area west to the Kerguelen Ridge, its greatest depth is 18,000 feet. West from the Kerguelen Ridge the largest of the three basins, the Atlantic-Indian-Antarctic Basin, encircles the remainder of the Antarctic Continent. Its greatest depth is 19,200 feet.

Three major ridges form the northern limits to the basins. The Atlantic-Antarctic Ridge extends from mid-Atlantic toward the Kerguelen Ridge. The Indian-Antarctic Ridge extends from the mid-Indian Ocean to the Balleny Islands area. Finally the Pacific-Antarctic Ridge extends from the vicinity of Scott Island north and east towards Easter Island. Three north-trending ridges separate the three major basins, Scotia Ridge in the Atlantic sector, Kerguelen Ridge in the Indian Ocean sector and Macquarie Ridge in the Pacific sector, the last linking the Balleny Islands area with New Zealand (Hatherton, 1965).

The World of Water

The land beneath the ice

Including its continental shelf, Antarctica is a roughly circular land mass about 2,800 miles in diameter; its coast is broken by the narrow curving peninsula of Graham Land, and by two deep embayments, the Ross and Weddell Seas. East Antarctica (that part of the continent, chiefly in latitudes east of Greenwich, that lies south and west of the Ross Sea and south and east of the Weddell Sea) is a high ice plateau making up about three quarters of the total area of Antarctica. Unlike the simple dome-like surface of the Greenland ice sheet, that of East Antarctica is deeply embayed south of the Indian Ocean by the huge Lambert Glacier, whose drainage system extends 620 miles inland towards the Weddell Sea. The pattern of ice flow outward is greatly affected by an immense mountain range, the Trans-Antarctic Mountains, which border the ice sheet along its Ross Sea-Weddell Sea edge. This range stretches for 1,370 miles from near Cape Adare in Victoria Land, through the Queen Maud Range to the Horlick and Thiel Mountains, with summit heights of 10,000 to 13,000 feet. The thresholds of the narrow outlet glaciers that flow through this mountain chain are seldom below 6,560 feet above sea level in the Ross Sea area, and the range as a consequence presents an almost complete barrier to the movement of ice outward from the continental ice sheet. Only two other major mountain systems project through the East Antarctic ice cap, that near the Dronning Maud Land coast that stretches intermittently in an arc from near the Weddell Sea coast to the neighborhood of Lutzow-Holmbukta, and the granges that flank the Lambert Glacier. In most other places, the ice sheet extends to sea level, unbroken except for local nunataks near the coast. Much of the central area of West Antarctica is occupied by a deep basin (the Byrd Basin) with depths as much as 8,200 feet below sea level.

No sub-sea level through joins the Ross and Weddell Seas. A deep channel has been recognized however, in several places immediately east of the mountains bordering the western side of the Ross Ice Shelf, and a long and narrow sub-sea level channel runs south-west from the eastern part of the Weddell Sea toward the Ross-Weddell divide, north of the Thiel Mountains (Hatherton, 1965).

Ice Caps and Glaciers

The East Antarctic continental mass has a simple structure of broad basins and swells. For the most part the rock surface is at an altitude of zero to 6,560 feet, rising to dome-like elevations of 10,000 to 13,000 feet. There are several long shallow depressions lying immediately west of, and parallel to, the Ross Sea section of the Trans-Antarctic Mountains in which the rock surface is slightly below present sea level.

Almost all the land is covered by the great ice cap; only toward the margins of the continent do mountains project above the ice. As the coast is approached, more and more of these rocky mountain summits appear, finally merging into more or less continuous valley walls, between which outlet glaciers flow seaward. In some parts of Antarctica, between the nunataks and the coast, lofty ice-free walls rise above glaciated valleys, but the glaciers which once flowed through these valleys and eroded them have largely disappeared and no large masses of ice remain. These are the Antarctic 'Oases' which display outcrops of bedrock.

Ice surface, shelves, and sheet
The topography of the ice surface of the major part of East Antarctica is fairly simple. An irregular elliptical dome, with a maximum elevation slightly over 13,000 feet, is centered slightly to the east of the Pole of Inaccessibility (the point farthest from the sea). The shape of this high central dome is largely independent of rock topography with one major exception, the 400-mile indentation of the Amery Ice Shelf-Lambert Glacier region. The effect of the barricade formed by the Trans-Antarctic Mountains is apparent in the ice divide between the mountains and the South Pole. Obstruction to the free flow of ice into the Ross Ice Shelf has resulted in an asymmetric drainage pattern with major flow towards the Weddell Sea. Between the Thiel Mountains and the Rensacola Range there is a conspicuous valley in the ice surface which appears to be a reflection of the deep sub-glacial valley directly beneath it (Hatherton, 1965). In West Antarctica the ice topography is strongly controlled by the shape of the underlying bedrock. In the mountainous area of Marie Byrd Land and south of the Ellsworth Mountains are two high regions forming the horns of a saddle-shaped configuration. The flanks of the saddle reflect the un-

The World of Water

obstructed flow of ice into the Ross Ice Shelf and the Amundsen Sea.

The surface of the Antarctic Ice Sheet possesses a great variety of surface relief forms which may be subdivided into micro-scale features formed at the surface as a direct result of wind, and macro-scale surface structures related to irregularities in the subglacial topography and to ice movement. The micro-relief includes primary accumulation features such as snowdrifts and dunes that are laid down during snowstorms. The most conspicuous features of the macro-relief are crevasses, open cracks that form wherever the ice sheet is stretched or sheared beyond its breaking point. They are particularly common in areas of relatively thin and highly deformed ice near the coast.

More than one third of the coast line of Antarctica is fringed by ice shelves. The ice shelves are floating ice sheets. They have a level or gently undulating surface and flow under their own weight. Ice shelves cover more than 535,000 square miles in the Antarctic; the Ross Ice Shelf, covering 202,000 square miles, and the Filchner Ice Shelf covering 153,000 square miles, being the two largest. Ice thickness varies from about 656 feet at the ice front to as much as 4,270 feet at the junction with land ice.

Nourished by abundant snowfall and free to creep under its own weight in any direction, an ice shelf would probably maintain an equilibrium thickness of around 656 feet. Except at the ice front, ice shelves are generally confined by a flanking arm of the inland ice sheet or of land. Free to move in one direction only, their thickness increases with distance from the ice front and varies with the configuration of the ice shelf boundaries. In places where the ice is forced to converge in order to pass through a strait, it may reach a thickness of up to 4,270 feet (Hatherton, 1965).

The ice shelf forms a sheer cliff from 165 feet in height. Ice shelves are made of snow, firn, and ice and contain rock material derived from nunataks and from land over which the ice moves before it reaches the sea. The temperatures of ice shelves lie close to the mean annual air temperatures near the surface and the freezing point of sea water at the icewater interface.

The ice shelves are nourished by the accumulation of snow

on their surface, by ice discharged from land glaciers, by the products of sublimation and in some places by the freezing of sea water. Accumulation of snow is probably the principal source of nourishment of the ice shelves. Loss by calving accounts for by far the greatest discharge to the ocean; it is followed in descending order of importance by bottom melting, the blowing of snow into the sea and evaporation.

The Antarctic Ice Sheet covers approximately 98 percent of the land mass of Antarctica. It is seven times as extensive as the Greenland Ice Sheet and is at least comparable in size to the Laurentide Ice Sheet that covered a large part of North America less than 20,000 years ago. The area of the ice sheet is estimated to be almost 5,150,000 square miles, and has a maximum diameter of about 2,800 miles. Its marginal length is in excess of 12,400 miles. The Antarctic Ice Sheet is veneered by a relatively thin blanket of snow that is slowly transformed into ice at depth. Approximately 95 percent by volume of the ice sheet is glacier ice.

The ice sheet probably originated by the coalescence of two ice sheets in the East and West Antarctica which were themselves formed by merging of several highland icecaps. Although this ice sheet welds East and West Antarctica together, it can be readily subdivided into a vast interior portion, the inland ice, and a variety of marginal components which include the ice shelves, valley glaciers and ice streams, and their seaward extensions, the ice tongues. The inland ice, up to 13,000 feet thick in some places, is usually thick enough to completely submerge the underlying land mass (Hatherton, 1965).

In East Antarctica much of the inland ice discharges directly into the sea along a broad front of heavily crevassed terraced sheets. Channelling of the ice into valleys and depressions leads to the formation of relatively fast-moving ice streams and outlet glaciers which may extend some distance into the sea as ice tongues. In West Antarctica a large portion of the inland ice is fed into large floating ice shelves. These include the Ross and Filchner Ice Shelves, which occupy the two large embayments of the Ross and Weddell Seas, respectively. The trans-Antarctic Mountains effectively block any massive flow of ice from the South Polar Plateau. The mean elevation of Antarctica is approximately 6,560 feet which makes it the loftiest continent on earth. Although this great average elevation is due in large part to the ice sheet itself, ice thickness measurements in East Antarctica show that the high point of the ice sheet corresponds to the maximum elevation of the land mass beneath the ice.

The average snow fall on the Antarctic Ice Sheet, about half that of Greenland, is five to six inches of water per year, which is comparable to the rainfall of the semi-arid regions of the Earth. Antarctica is a very cold desert; sub-freezing temperatures persist all year around over 95 percent of its surface. Mean annual temperatures in East Antarctica are generally very much cooler than those of areas of comparable latitude or distance from the coast in West Antarctica (Hatherton, 1965).

Organisms

The dominant constituents of the phytoplankton in Antarctic seas are the diatoms. The bottom fauna is essentially a deep water fauna. Littoral faunas on the Antarctic Continent are almost non-existent. Sponges make up a very substantial proportion of the benthic biomass. Four families, the Antarctic cods, Antarctic dragon fishes, ice fishes and plunder fishes include over 95 percent of the total shore fish fauna. The Antarctic cods comprise over 50 percent of the total shore fish fauna. The world's greatest seals and sea birds are found in Antarctic waters, and the Blue Whale, the largest animal the world has ever known, grows fat on the summer abundance of food in southern waters. Marine birds and mammals make only sparing use of the Antarctic continent; with few exceptions they spend more of their time at sea than on land, and feed entirely in the water.

The rocks and ice blanket offer bare hospitality to animal and plant life. Land vegetation is sparse, restricted by cold, aridity, and lack of soil to a meager assembly of small plants. Algae, mosses, and lichens are the characteristic plants of Antarctica; only two genera of flowering plant are known. Land animals are limited in species to a few invertebrates of soil, vegetation and fresh water; protozoa, mites, tardigrades, nematodes, rotifers, and primitive insects are the only creatures which have so far been found on the continent itself (Hatherton, 1965).

Forty-three species of birds and six species of seals breed in the Antarctic region. To take advantage of food resources in cold water, warm-blooded animals need the means of reducing heat losses between their bodies and the sea. The dense, water-repelling plumage of the penguin and petrel, the thick, tough skin of whale and seal, the fur borne by some of the seals of temperate and low-Antarctic latitudes, the sub-cutaneous fat or blubber common to all warm-blooded marine vertebrates, are devices for reducing the flow of heat between warm animal and cold sea. Compactness and size are further adaptations in the same cause. The extremities of seals and penguins are generally short and bony; muscles are concentrated in the body mass, so that little blood need circulate in the periphery. Largeness is itself an asset, for large animals have a low ratio of surface to volume and can therefore conserve heat more efficiently than smaller animals. Some animals, notably the whales, have a heat exchange system in the blood vessels of the skin, whereby cooled blood flowing inward from the skin is warmed by arterial blood flowing outward. The warm-blooded animals of Antarctica seldom experience extreme cold. Most of them keep away from the continent during the coldest months; only the Emperor Penguin remains to breed in the depths of winter.

Land mammals are present in Antarctica; both reindeer and brown rats flourish where they were introduced by whalers and sealers. Rats and mice were from time to time reported at occupied land whaling stations, but did not survive after the stations were abandoned. There are no land birds in Antarctica. Amphibians, reptiles and freshwater fish are totally lacking on Antarctica. Among the arthropods, or jointed-legged animals, the terrestial crustaceans, scorpions, centipedes, millipedes and spiders are absent. Only tardigrades, mites, ticks and five orders of true insect are present.

ARCTIC BASIN

The total ice area for the whole Arctic Ocean in winter reaches 4,100,000 square miles. By the end of summer, an average of 570,000 square miles of ice melts in the Arctic Basin, about 36,000 square miles in the White Sea, and around 95,000 square miles in the Barents. Over 470,000 square miles of ice

The World of Water

is carried off annually from the Arctic Basin into the Greenland Sea where it melts. By the end of the polar summer, the ice area of the Arctic Ocean decreases to 3,050,000 square miles, due to melting.

The main difference between the arctic and the antarctic is the fact that in the center of the latter, a high continent is located; in the middle of the arctic there is located a deep basin, more than 13,000 feet deep. The main mass of the ice cover in the arctic is sea ice and in the antarctic is glacial ice (Zubov, 1943).

The main glacier in the arctic is in Greenland, where 90 percent of glacier ice in the Northern Hemisphere is concentrated. It occupies an area of 0·7 million square miles; the overall area of Greenland is 0·8 million square miles. The sea ice of the Northern Hemisphere at its greatest development occupies an area of about 450 million square miles.

In the Northern Hemisphere, aside from Greenland, land ice reaching sea level is located on the outer shores of Baffin Bay. The Vatna Glacier of Iceland is a small ice sheet measuring about 75 miles by 100 miles and 750 feet in thickness. Smaller, isolated glaciers are found in the American sector of the arctic on Prince Patrick and Melville Islands. In the Eurasian sector of the arctic, glaciers are located on the islands of the Spitsbergen archipelago, on White and Victorian Islands (between Spitsbergen and Franz Joseph Land), on the islands of Franz Joseph Land, on Novaya Zemlya, on Ulsakov and Schmidt Islands (between Franz Joseph Land and Severnaya Zemlya), and on Severnaya Zemlya.

The more northerly parts of Greenland and Ellesmere Land; Labrador, having a very low summer temperature, and also being located in the path of summer cyclones; and the entire northern shore of Spitsbergen are almost completely free of glaciers. High geographic latitudes and low summer temperatures are not enough for the formation of glaciers. Altitude above sea level is also not enough, nor are large horizontal distances. For instance, the very small Victoria Island (about 3·1 miles long), located between Spitsbergen and Franz Joseph Land, is almost completely covered by glacier ice, whereas higher and larger islands, located further to the north along the northern shores of Spitsbergen, do not have an ice cover. The most important reason for the formation of glaciers, other factors being equal, is the amount of precipitation. In Iceland, along the drier northern side, the snow line is located at 3,280 to 4,300 feet above sea level, while on the southern, moister side, it decreases to 2,000 to 2,600 feet. On the western side of Greenland, the snow line passes approximately 56 miles from the shore and divides the ice dome into two parts, accumulating and wastage. The accumulating part annually receives 14 inches of precipitation. The thickness of the wastage part decreases from 6 feet at the edge to 0 feet at the snow line and averages 37 inches. Of these 37 inches about 75 percent is wasted in melting and evaporation and about 25 percent in the formation of icebergs along a 56 mile belt (Zubov, 1943).

The icecap of Greenland consists of two domes: the northern, having its center near 75° north, and the southern, having its center near 65° north, with corresponding heights of 10,700 and 9,600 feet. The thickness of the ice in the western part of the glacier attains 1·2 to 1·9 miles. Greenland is divided by a deep valley; the ice flows into this valley along the slopes of both domes and along the valley into the sea, mainly on the side of the Baffin Gulf.

Icecap islands can be roughly divided into two types. In the first type are Bruce and Evaliv Islands in the Franz Joseph Archipelago, and also Ushakov and Schmidt Islands, located between Franz Joseph Land and Severnaya Zemlya. These islands are completely buried under an ice cover. White and Victoria Islands, located between Spitsbergen and Franz Joseph Land, belong to the second type. These islands have only small and low spits (with a developed shore ridge) which project from the precipitous ice wall. The precipitous ice walls are particularly high on White and Victoria Islands, where in some places, in spite of the small size, they reach 40 to 50 feet. The main difference in ice cover on the icecap islands from the usual glaciers is almost a complete lack of fissures and variations on their upper surface. Icecap islands are located in the middle of, or not far from, islands of the same size and height, and even larger, which have no great accumulations of snow or ice.

All the Greenland glaciers which descend into Northeast Bay and Disko Bay, have been receding since approximately the beginning of the present century. In particular the Jakobshavn glacier recorded about 66 feet during the period 1880 to 1902.

Receding of glaciers during recent years has been observed on Spitzbergen, Franz Joseph Land, and Novaya Zemlya (Zubov, 1943).

The quantity of ice cover in the sea depends on the area occupied by ice and ice thickness and solidity. Seas are classified by the origin of the ice encountered in them, and by the length of time in which ice is found in the given region. In respect to origin of ice, the individual ice regions of the World Ocean can be divided into the following groups: regions where the ice is entirely or predominantly of local origin, for example, the Barents, Kara and White Seas; and regions where the ice is entirely or predominantly not of local origin, but is carried in by winds and currents from other regions, for example the region south of Newfoundland where icebergs are constantly being carried which originated along the shores of Baffin Bay and which have consequently completed a journey of 1,200 to 1,900 miles.

In respect to time during which ice is found, the ocean ice regions can be divided into ice regions, freezing regions, and ice-free regions. Ice regions are in turn subdivided into polar and subpolar regions. In both of these the ice usually remains throughout the entire year. In the polar regions, open water never exceeds in areas the sea area covered by ice. In the subpolar regions the quantity of ice decreases considerably in the summer season and in the most favorable years it disappears completely. Freezing regions are completely cleared of ice in the summer season. Ice in the White Sea is found during more than half of the year. The Gulf of Finland, Sea of Azov, and the northern part of the Caspian Sea, have lesser ice abundance. The relatively great ice accumulations (ice massifs) in the northwestern parts of the Greenland and Barents Seas, and the more or less broad expanses of clear water in the southeastern parts are characteristic of the adjacent seas of the northern hemisphere. These ice massifs are due not only to the warm Atlantic water pouring into these basins from the south, as occurs in the Greenland and Barents Seas, but also to the fact that in the southern parts of the adjacent seas the melting of ice and heating of water is more intensive. Due to the effect of sea currents, ice-free regions may sometimes be located at higher latitudes than ice regions.

Chapter 5

Subsurface Water

Subsurface water is an important source of water supply throughout the world. Its use in irrigation, industries, municipalities, and rural homes continues to increase. The world's groundwater reservoirs are functional components in nature's system for draining the land. They are recharged by water which infiltrates into the land surface. They store and convey water by slow movement. They discharge water through springs and seep into the streams to sustain the flow of streams when no rain falls. Our knowledge of subsurface water is not proportional to its importance in our civilization. This lack of knowledge results largely from the fact that the paths of movement of subsurface water cannot be watched, as can be those of surface water. Yet, hydrologists with such tools as water well records and water well tests are able in a sense to look below the surface and measure subsurface resources with a reasonable degree of accuracy.

Most rocks contain numerous open spaces, called interstices, in which water may be stored and through which water can move by percolating from one interstice to another. Water that exists in interstices of rocks is called subsurface water; that part of subsurface water in interstices completely saturated with water is called groundwater. Subsurface water in interstices above the zone of saturation in the zone of aeration where interstices are only partially saturated with water is called vadose water. The zone of aeration is subdivided into the soil water zone, intermediate zone, and the capillary zone. The soil water zone consists of soil and other materials near the surface which discharge water into the atmosphere by evapotranspiration. The capillary zone (capillary fringe) extends immediately above the zone of saturation to the limit of capillary rise of water. The

133

intermediate zone lies between the soil water and capillary zone (Meinzer, 1923).

GROUNDWATER

An aquifer is a saturated bed, formation, or group of formations which yields water in sufficient quantity to be of consequence as a source of supply. An aquitard is a saturated bed, formation, or group of formations which yields inappreciable quantities of water to drains, wells, and springs compared to an aquifer but through which appreciable leakage of water is possible. An aquiclude is a saturated bed, formation, or group of formations which yields inappreciable quantities of water to drains, wells, and springs and through which there is inappreciable leakage. A formation may be classified as an aquifer in one area but only as an aquitard in a different area depending upon the availability of groundwater.

An aquifer serves as a transmission conduit and storage reservoir. It transports water from recharge areas to surface bodies of water, wetlands, springs, areas of evapotranspiration, and wells and other water collecting devices. As a storage reservoir, an aquifer provides reserve water for use during periods when withdrawals exceed recharge. The quantities of water available in storage in the most productive aquifers are so great that in some places large withdrawals over a long period of years fail to produce marked evidence of depletion.

Geologic aspects

Differences in the number, size, shape, interconnection, and arrangement of the interstices of aquifers, aquitards and aquicludes result from the great diversity of geologic processes by which rocks were produced and later modified. Most interstices are small and interconnected; some are cavernous in size while others are small and largely isolated so that there is little opportunity for movement of water from one interstice to another. The nature of interstices is determined by the geologic framework of rocks and an orderly description of the geology and geologic history of an area is essential for an understanding of groundwater conditions.

The interstices of rocks may be divided into two groups,

Subsurface Water

original and secondary. Original interstices came into existence when the rocks were formed and can be subdivided into those of sedimentary origin and those of igneous origin. Secondary interstices are the result of processes by which rocks were modified after coming into existence and largely comprise joints and other fracture and solution openings. Original interstices consist of the spaces between adjacent fragments of sedimentary rock; small cavities or inclusions, within crystals and small intercrystal spaces developed in igneous rocks during their congealing. Most consolidated rocks are broken by joints cutting the rocks in various

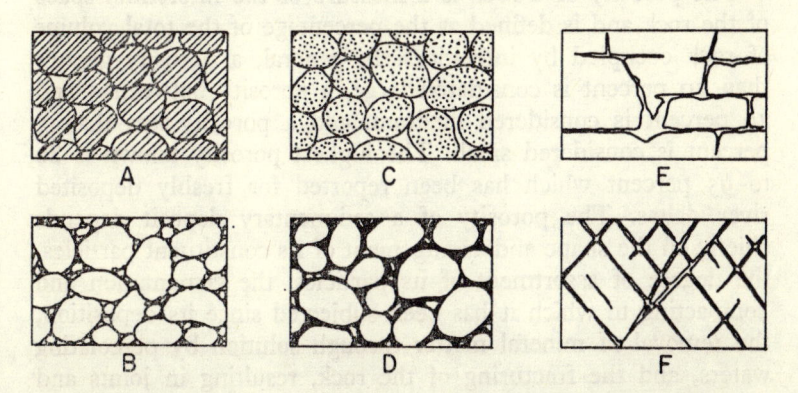

Diagram showing several types of rock interstices and the relation of rock texture to porosity: A, well-sorted sedimentary deposit having high porosity; B, poorly-sorted sedimentary deposit having low porosity; C, well-sorted sedimentary deposit consisting of pebbles that are themselves porous, so that the deposit as a whole has a very high porosity; D, well-sorted sedimentary deposit whose porosity has been diminished by the rock deposition of mineral matter in the interstices; E, rock rendered porous by solution; F, rock rendered porous by fracturing (Meinzer, 1923)

directions and extending to varying distances and depths. These secondary interstices, produced chiefly by shrinkage, pressure and deformation of rocks, commonly vary in number and size. Joints often intersect one another, frequently have no regularity of spacing, and tend to become tighter and spaced farther apart with depth. Secondary interstices are also produced by the chemical decomposition of rocks and the solution and subsequent removal of the soluble products or by the solution and removal of soluble rocks. The removal of the calcareous cement from the original interstices of a sandstone or the removal of soluble material such as limestone results in abundant secondary openings on many areas. In some consolidated sedimentary rocks the original interstitial space has been reduced by deposition of cement in the interstices. In consolidated rocks interstitial space is likely to decrease with depth; most deep wells have encountered few interstices below a depth of a mile. In many consolidated rocks most interstices are found within a few hundred feet of the surface (Meinzer, 1923).

The porosity of a rock is a measure of the interstitial space of the rock and is defined as the percentage of the total volume of rock occupied by interstices. In general, a porosity greater than 20 percent is considered large, a porosity between 5 and 20 percent is considered medium, and a porosity less than 5 percent is considered small. The highest porosity known is 80 to 95 percent which has been reported for freshly deposited river deltas. The porosity of a sedimentary deposit depends chiefly on the shape and arrangement of its constituent particles, the degree of assortment of its particles, the cementation and compacting to which it has been subjected since its deposition, the removal of mineral matter through solution by percolating waters, and the fracturing of the rock, resulting in joints and other interstices. In well sorted and rounded deposits the size of grains has no influence on porosity; thus, a deposit of boulders may have the same porosity as a deposit of clay. The porosity of many deposits is increased by the irregular angular shapes of its constituent grains. Porosity decreases with increases in the variety of size of grains; small grains fill interstices between large grains.

Not all of the water in the interstices of a saturated rock can be withdrawn through wells, drains, springs, or seeps. A part of the water is retained in interstices largely by the forces of molecular attraction and adhesion. The amount of water retained varies directly as the aggregate surface of the interstices and indirectly as the size of grain; thus, retention is greatest in rocks having small interstices. The amount of water retained in interstices also depends on the time of drainage, the temperature and mineral composition of ground water which affects its surface tension, viscosity, and specific gravity, and on various physical relations of the rock. The specific yield of a rock is a measure of the water-yielding capacity of the rock and is expressed as the percentage of the total volume of rock occupied by groundwater that ultimately will drain under the force of gravity. In general, a specific yield greater than 20 percent is considered large, a specific yield between 1 and 10 percent is considered medium, and a specific yield less than 1 percent is considered small. For most rocks gravity drainage of interstices in not instantaneous and the water-yielding capacity increases at a diminishing rate as the time of drainage increases, gradually approaching the specific yield.

A study of the surface and subsurface distribution of rocks and of their character, thickness, and depth below land surface is prerequisite to an understanding of the occurrence and movement of groundwater at any locality. The earth's crust consists of layers of rocks laid down in succession one upon another underlain or intersected at places by massive bodies that were intruded into or extruded through the stratified rocks. Rock formations, distinct units of the earth's crust consisting of rocks of one or more kinds, may range from a few feet to thousands of feet in thickness and may occur at the surface or be buried beneath other rocks. Formations may extend over thousands of square miles or may be limited in areal extent to less than a square mile. There may be important differences in the same formation at different horizons and in different localities.

Water wells penetrate formations deposited in a region during the geologic ages of the past; generally the youngest formation is encountered first and then successively older formations are passed through. At places, because of the occurrence of intrusive rocks, folds, faults and thrusts older formations may rest upon the younger. In most places the lowest known rocks are crystalline igneous or metamorphic rocks (basement complex) which have an eroded upper surface and are overlain by younger formations. There is great variety in the succession of beds overlying the basal complex; commonly a coarse-grained formation rests unconformably on older rocks. Generally, beds of a sedimentary series become increasingly fine-grained and calcareous from the bottom upward. The thickness of most sedimentary formations consisting of layers of rock is very small in comparison with the areal extent of the formations (Meinzer, 1923).

Most formations are stratified. Beds of formations may differ in thickness, composition, and compactness; aquifers may be interbedded with aquitards or aquicludes. Due to differences in the conditions under which deposition occurred, a stratified formation changes gradually in thickness and character from place to place. As a rule, formations are found to become thinner and finer grained at increasing distances from the source of the sediments. Lateral gradations are of great significance with respect to the occurrence and movement of groundwater.

There is often a rapid lateral gradation in unconsolidated deposits; lenses, layers and stringers of sand and gravel occur irregularly and give way abruptly to clays. Radical changes in thickness and character are to be expected from place to place. Extreme local variations in glacial deposits and river alluvial deposits are in striking contrast to the relatively uniform conditions of some sedimentary bedrock aquifers. Glacial till has a very chaotic structure and consists of clayey materials with highly irregular interbedded lenses or layers of sand and gravel. Outwash deposits of sand and gravel made by streams that flowed from melting glacial ice, often persist over large areas and sometimes change gradually in thickness and character from place to place. Alluvium tends to be irregular in structure but often has fewer local irregularities than glacial till. Lake deposits are better stratified than either glacial drift or alluvium. The composition of glacial deposits, alluvium and lake deposits depends largely upon the nature of the rocks which were eroded to supply the material out of which they were formed (Meinzer, 1923).

Rock formations are rarely horizontal; dips may be due to deposition in a sloping position or to deformation after deposition. Alluvium generally dips downstream, lake deposits dip away from shore, and lava beds dip away from vents. Because of deformation, formations may have slight inclination, or they may turn into a vertical position or overturn. Knowledge of the dip of the formation underlying a region is necessary for the determination of the distribution of the aquifers and aquitards and for the forecasts of the depths to aquifers. The determination of the distribution and depth of aquifers would be relatively simple if formations everywhere had the same angle and direction of dip. However, many formations have been warped, forming folds including anticlines, synclines, simple tilts or mono-

Subsurface Water

clines or irregular flexures. Anticlines may form ridges or structural domes; synclines may be troughs or structural basins. Formations dip in all directions away from a common center in a structure dome and from all directions toward a common center in a structural basin.

Fractures result chiefly from compression during earth movements and from rock shrinkage due to drying of sediments or cooling of igneous rocks. A joint is a natural rock fracture; if blocks of rock on opposite sides of a fracture are dislocated with reference to each other, the fracture is called a fault. Faults are of two kinds, normal and thrust. They differ greatly in their lateral extent, in depth and in amount of displacement. Large faults may affect the distribution and position of aquifers, act as subsurface dams or as conduits through which deep-seated waters may escape. At places there is a fault zone called fault breccia containing many small parallel faults or masses of broken rock. The raised side of a fault may produce an escarpment with great differences in the altitude and topography of the surface on opposite sides of the fault. Deposition of coarse materials may result in the downthrown side from rapid erosion of the exposed rocks on the raised side. So much erosion may occur with the lapse of geologic ages that the escarpment is obliterated. A fault may displace alternating permeable and impermeable beds so that the impermeable beds face permeable beds. There may be clayey gouge along the fault plane. The opposite sides of many faults are not everywhere pressed together; few faults are single, clear-cut breaks (Meinzer, 1923).

The geologist utilizes petrography, stratigraphy, structural geology, and geomorphology in the search for groundwater. Logs of wells and excavations, either artificial or natural give geologic sections of the earth's crust. Successive deposits are examined as they exist in place in natural outcrops. Vertical sections are used to show the positions of aquifers, aquitards, and aquicludes. Areal geologic maps showing areas in which various formations occur at the bedrock surface, and structure-contour maps showing successive contours of the upper or lower surface of a formation are also useful. A map shows conditions throughout a region whereas a cross section shows conditions along a certain line. However, a section shows geologic structure more directly. A map and a series of cross sections are often prepared. The correlation of formations depends on either tracing beds from place to place or identifying the same beds in different localities. Identification can often be made by studying characteristic physical properties. Determination of the relative age of formations in different localities is sometimes made with radioactive dating methods. Correlation on the basis of characteristic physical properties is often impossible or at least uncertain, because of the lateral changes in formations and the similarity of different beds. Fossils can be used to correlate widely separated sections. The method most commonly used to correlate aquifers and aquitards is based on a study of well records and examination of samples of drilling cuttings (Davis and DeWiest, 1966).

In outcrop areas, boundaries of formations can be mapped from field observations; where formations are concealed by other rocks this is impossible and the boundary must be inferred from data on the dip of the formation and the altitude of the land surface. Dips of rocks are often determined by correlating the formations in outcrops and well sections. Unconformities are characterized by great irregularities; it is possible to construct a rough approximation of the contour map of a buried unconformity from observation of natural and artificial exposures and from well logs. By well construction, mining, tunneling, and other excavations, man had added hundreds of thousands of places where he can collect data concerning aquifers beneath the land surface. Although these potential observation points are numerous, they represent in the aggregate a negligible proportion of the total volume of rock materials through which groundwater moves, and in large areas concepts of the occurrence of subsurface water are based on inferences. Nevertheless, the collected data form the basis for a good working knowledge of the physical principles governing the movements of groundwater.

In recent years there have been many applications of geophysical methods in geologic correlation. The success of geophysical work depends on simple but distinct variations of density, electrical conductivity, magnetic susceptibility, electrical potential, elasticity, and other measurable physical properties of the earth. Surface and subsurface geophysical methods of investigation that yield data interpretable in terms of aquifer

Subsurface Water

depth, thickness, continuity, areal extent, structure, porosity, permeability, and degree of saturation and on the chemical quality of the contained water are now in general use.

An electric log is a record of the resistance or apparent resistivity and spontaneous potential of the formation penetrated by a drill hole. Resistance and resistivity are determined by sending an electric current into the wall of the hole and measuring the potential drop, for resistance between the point of current emission in the hole and a point on the land surface. This method is also used for apparent resistivity between two points at a fixed separation and at some distance from the point of current emission in the drilled hole, or between a point in the bore-hole some distance from the point of current emission and a point at the land surface. The equipment used in making these measurements consists of an electrode or system of electrodes which is lowered into the hole, a single or multiconductor cable spooled on a winch which raises or lowers the electrode system, a measuring sheave which records the depth of the electrode system, electrical measuring instruments and a source of electromotive force on the land surface connected to the electrode system by a cable, and a plotting mechanism which records measured values on film or paper.

Differences in the intensity of natural radioactivity emitted by rocks of the earth's crust make possible the use of radiation measurements for well logging. The radioactivity of rocks other than those containing radioactive ores is extremely small, and highly sensitive instruments are required for its measurement. Gamma rays have high penetration power and can easily pass through steel casings; they are useful in well logging to indicate the radioactivity of rocks. Because neutrons are largely affected only by material containing hydrogen, for example water, a measure of the dissipation of neutron energy in the material adjacent to a borehole constitutes the basis of a useful well logging method. The basic instrument used in radioactive logging consists of a detecting unit, which may be one of the following: ionization chamber, Geiger-Mueller counter, scintillation counter, or neutron detector (Davis and DeWiest, 1966).

The thermal gradient of groundwater with depth in any locality is mainly a function of the thermal conductivity of the rocks that underlie it. The reference temperature at shallow depth (50 to 100 feet) is approximately the average annual air temperature. The temperature change with depth below the land surface and the zone of seasonal fluctuation is generally expressed in terms of the reciprocal gradient, that is, depth per degree of temperature change. Reciprocal gradients in the crust within 20,000 feet of the surface generally range from 50 to 100 feet per degree F. Inasmuch as the thermal gradient is in part a function of the textural properties of rocks, temperature logs provide information on the lithologic units penetrated by a well. A temperature log is a record of the apparent temperature of the rocks penetrated by a borehole. Temperature logging is readily accomplished by adapting conventional electric-logging circuits to measure change of resistance of a temperature-sensitive metallic conductor lowered into the hole on the logging cable (Todd, 1959). Measurements of the temperature of water from a flowing or pumped well are used to estimate the depth of the aquifer tapped. If a well taps two aquifers, the temperature of the water pumped from the well may be used to estimate the relative rate of withdrawal from each aquifer.

A flow-meter log is a record of the magnitude of the velocity and direction and movement of water in a well at all depths. The flow-meter log serves to identify and evaluate the aquifers tapped by a cased well having multiple screens, leaks in cased wells, and permeable zones penetrated by uncased wells. Flow-meter logging requires the use of a velocity-sensitive instrument, a system of cables and conductors for lowering the device into a well, a depth-measuring device by which the position of the flow-meter can be determined at all times, a cable reel and well-head equipment for lowering or raising the instrument and a recording device at the land surface.

Different types of rock may produce similar patterns of diameter change when drilled under analogous conditions. However, there generally is sufficient variation among rock types so that, with a general knowledge of the sequence to be expected, certain identifications are possible. The rocks that form the walls of a borehole are worn away as the hole is deepened, partly by abrasion from drilling tools and partly by erosion and hydration effects of the drilling mud. The extent of diameter variation with depth depends upon the action of the drilling tools; the relative hardness, competence, and fluid content and permeability of the rock formations penetrated, and the degree to which the rocks dissolve to become hydrated by the drilling mud. The variation of borehole diameter with depth is measured mechanically and recorded electrically by making a traverse of the hole with a caliper or section gage on the end of an insulated cable.

A fluid-conductivity log is a record of the electrical conductivity or conductance of the borehole fluid at all depths. It is useful in determining the depth of salt-water leaks in cased artesian wells, and the depth and relative artesian head of salt-water aquifers penetrated by uncased wells. It is useful also in the interpretation of the spontaneous-potential curve of electric logs.

A useful surface geophysical method is the seismic method. The seismic method measures the reaction of formations to artificially induced vibrations. The vibrations are detected at various distances and directions from the source of energy by means of small seismometers which are commonly called geophones or detectors. The vibrations created by explosives are recorded on photographic paper or on magnetic tape. In the electrical surface geophysical methods, two types of electrical potentials are measured: the natural electrical potential that exists between two electrodes placed in the ground, and an artificial potential created by passing electricity through the ground (Davis and DeWiest, 1966). Several electrode arrangements are possible.

By introducing a tracer substance into groundwater at an upstream location and observing the time required for it to appear at a downstream point, estimates of groundwater velocity can be obtained. This information, together with the existing hydraulic gradient, provides a measure of the permeability of an aquifer. Measurements with tracers in the field usually have been limited to distances of a few feet, and results obtained are approximate only. In essence, the concept of a tracer to follow the movement of groundwater is very simple. Such methods, using dyes and salts, have been employed for many years.

Tracers may be classified as to method of detection—colorimetry, chemical determination, electrical conductivity, nuclear radiation, mass spectrography, and flame spectrophotometry. Organic dyes, such as sodium fluorescein, may be detected in very low concentration; however, they may be absorbed by clay fractions present in natural media. The chloride ion, used in low concentrations, has proved to be a satisfactory tracer. Radioactive substances provide a convenient and very sensitive means of detection. They do not modify the flow properties of porous media, but are affected by base exchange and absorption phenomena. Certain radioisotopes, tritium in particular, can be used as a field tracer without danger of contamination, but others must be carefully controlled or restricted to laboratory studies because of dangerous radiation levels.

Tritium is produced in the atmosphere by cosmic radiation (and thermo-nuclear explosions), and its abundance in rain varies roughly with the distance ocean water vapor must travel before precipitation. After rainfall infiltrates into the ground, no further additions of tritium occur; moreover, a predictable exponential diminution of the radioactive isotope concentration occurs. Thus, from well samples of groundwater, estimates of time which the water has been underground can be obtained. The method is most feasible in confined aquifers recharged from a single recharge area. From several samples taken from wells scattered over a basin, the direction and rate of movement sometimes may be calculated.

Water levels

An unconfined aquifer is one in which groundwater possesses a free surface open to the atmosphere. The upper surface of the zone of saturation is called the water table. Changes in the stage of the water table correspond to changes in the thickness of the zone of saturation. When the water table declines gravity drainage of interstices occurs. An artesian aquifer is one in which groundwater is confined under pressure by overlying and underlying aquitards or aquicludes and water levels in wells rise above the tops of the aquifer. Artesian aquifers are classified as leaky or nonleaky depending upon whether the aquifer is overlain by an aquitard or an aquiclude. Water levels in wells tapping artesian aquifers sometimes rise above the surface to cause wells to flow. Rises and falls in the water levels in wells tapping artesian aquifers correspond to changes in the pressure of the water. The imaginary surface to which water rises in wells tapping artesian aquifers is called the piezometric surface. When

Subsurface Water

the piezometric surface is lowered, water is released from storage by the compaction of the aquifer and its associated beds and by expansion of the water itself, while the interstices remain saturated. An artesian aquifer becomes an unconfined aquifer when the piezometric surface declines below the top or below the water table depending upon whether the vertical movement of water is from or into the aquifer.

Water levels measured in wells are conveniently studied by means of maps and graphs. Most frequently used are water-level contour maps, water-level change maps, depth-to-water maps, water-level profiles, and well hydrographs. Water-level change maps are constructed by plotting the change of water levels in wells during a given span of time. The water-level change map may be used to calculate the changes in the volume of the saturated part of an aquifer. Water-level change maps are also useful in measuring the local effects of recharge or discharge. Hydrographs of water levels in wells can be constructed from data obtained from measurements by chalked tape, electric probes, air lines, or the reflection of sound. Continuous records can be obtained by mechanical or electrical devices. Some of the automatic recordings are adapted to direct use of high-speed data-processing equipment.

Water-level fluctuations in wells are caused by surface-water body changes in stage, changes in atmospheric pressure, earth tides, earthquakes, trains, earth moving equipment, explosions, and pumping. Any phenomenon which produces a change in pressure on the groundwater will cause the groundwater level to change. Alternating series of wet and dry years in which the rainfall is above or below the mean, produce long-period variations of groundwater levels. Many groundwater levels show a seasonal pattern of fluctuation resulting from influences such as recharge from rainfall and withdrawals. Unconfined aquifers with water tables near ground surface frequently exhibit diurnal fluctuations which can be ascribed to evaporation and/or transpiration. Minor fluctuations of water levels are caused by wind blowing over the tops of wells. In coastal aquifers in contact with the ocean, sinusoidal fluctuations of groundwater levels occur in response to tides. Regular semidiurnal fluctuations of small magnitude have been attributed to earth tides, resulting from the attraction exerted on the earth's crust by the moon and, to a lesser extent, the sun. The elastic property of artesian aquifers results in changes in hydrostatic pressure when changes in loading occur.

The water table is located by measuring the depth of water in shallow boreholes or in wells. The water table is a subdued replica of surface topography. In most places there is only one water table, but in some localities because of the presence of aquitards or aquicludes, there may be perched aquifers with additional water tables. The water table map delimits the surface areas subject to influent and effluent seepage. Influent seepage occurs where the water table is below ground surface and stream influent seepages takes place where the water table is below the level of streambeds. Effluent seepage starts at the intersection of the water table with the ground surface and continues throughout the area in which the water table is at the surface. Contour maps of the water table are graphic representations of the hydraulic slopes of the water table and are the basis for studies of the direction and rate of motion of groundwater, of drainage of groundwater by pumping or drainage ditches and natural streams, and recharge of groundwater from all sources (Tolman, 1937).

Hydraulic characteristics

Water in the saturated interstices of permeable rocks, as a rule, moves very slowly and steadily. This movement is called laminar flow, and is governed by a law which states that the flow rate through porous rocks is proportional to the head loss and inversely proportional to the length of the flow path. The range in groundwater velocities is great. Under heavy pumping conditions, except in the immediate vicinity of a pumped well, velocities are generally less than 100 feet per day. Under natural conditions, rates of more than a few feet per day or less than a few feet per year are exceptional. As the water moves, energy is expanded in overcoming friction and is converted into heat or some other form of energy. Hydraulic gradients are three-dimensional, water moves not only horizontally but also vertically to depths below the water table and generally upward again to the surface. In aquifers, the head at some depth is likely to be lower than the water table if it is in a recharge area and higher if it is in a discharge area.

Subsurface Water

Permeability is a measure of the ease of flow of groundwater through aquifers and aquitards. The rate of vertical leakage of groundwater through an aquitard is dependent upon the vertical permeability of the aquitard. The storage characteristics of rocks are expressed by the coefficient of storage. Unconsolidated sand and gravel deposits commonly have permeabilities 100 times as great as the permeabilities of sandstones. Some clayey materials have vertical permeabilities 1,000 times as great as the permeabilities of shales but 1/100 as great as the permeabilities of sandstones. The storage coefficient under water-table conditions may be 1,000 times as great as the storage coefficient under artesian conditions.

Much work has been done in developing accurate methods for measuring the permeability and storage characteristics of rocks. Field-discharge methods involving pumped wells are most widely used. The permeability and storage characteristics of aquifers and aquitards are commonly determined by means of aquifer tests, wherein the effect of pumping a well at a known constant rate is measured in the pumped well and in nearby observation wells penetrating the aquifer. Graphs of water-level decline versus time after pumping starts, and/or of water-level decline versus distance from the pumped well, are used to solve equations which express the relation between the permeability and storage characteristics of an aquifer and its aquitard, if present, and the lowering of water levels in the vicinity of the pumped well.

Water levels are lowered around a pumped well in the form of an inverted cone and hydraulic gradients are established from all directions toward the well. Water is first withdrawn from storage within the aquifer in the immediate vicinity of the well. The cone continues to spread, drawing water from storage within an increasing area of influence. The cone may eventually extend to the limits of the aquifer. Water levels continue to decline until hydraulic gradients are established from recharge areas sufficient to divert to the pumped well the quantity of water discharged. Cones of depression may extend to distances of tens and hundreds of miles from the pumped well over a long period of time and intersect aquifer boundaries.

Equations describing water-level declines in artesian aquifers having leaky roofs and in water-table aquifers with fully or partially penetrating wells have been developed. The permeability and storage characteristics of aquifers and aquitards are also estimated with maps of the water table or piezometric surface. The quantity of water percolating through a given cross-section of an aquifer can be computed by multiplying the permeability by the hydraulic gradient of the water table and this product by the cross-sectional area through which flow occurs.

Recharge

If there were no recharge aquifers would soon dry up. But groundwater reservoirs are a part of the hydrologic cycle and periodically part of precipitation percolates to the water table. Whenever and wherever recharge occurs water goes into storage in an aquifer, the water table rises, the vertical head is increased, new energy is supplied, and ground water movement both horizontally and vertically is increased. The major sources of recharge to aquifers are direct precipitation on intake areas and downward percolation of stream runoff. Recharge from precipitation on intake areas is irregularly distributed in time and place. Most recharge occurs during wet months when the ground is not frozen, evapotranspiration is small, and soil moisture is maintained at or above field capacity by frequent rains. At many places during summer and early fall months evapotranspiration and soil-moisture requirements are so great that little precipitation percolates to the water table except during periods of excessive rainfall. Recharge during winter months in places where the ground is frozen is negligible.

Only a small fraction of the annual precipitation percolates downward to the water table. A large proportion of precipitation runs overland to streams or is discharged to the atmosphere by the process of evapotranspiration before it reaches aquifers. The amount of precipitation that reaches the zone of saturation depends upon several factors. Among these are: the character and thickness of the soil and other deposits above and below the water table; the topography; vegetal cover; land use; soil-moisture content; the depth to the water table; the intensity, duration, and seasonal distribution of rainfall; the occurrence of precipitation as rain or snow; and the air temperature.

Recharge to aquifers by induced infiltration of surface water occurs when the water table is below the surface of a stream and the streambed is permeable. The rate of induced infiltration depends upon several factors: the surface water temperature, the permeability of the streambed and the aquifer, the thickness of the streambed and aquifer, the position of the water table, and the depth of water in the stream. During flood periods, the water surface in the stream rises higher than the adjacent water table, thus creating a greater hydrostatic pressure in the stream than in the banks. Surface water then percolates into lowlands adjacent to the stream creating bank storage.

Recharge direct from precipitation and by induced infiltration of surface water involves the vertical movement of water under the influence of vertical head differentials. The quantity of vertical leakage varies from place to place and it is controlled by the vertical permeability and thickness of the deposits through which leakage occurs, the head differential between sources of water and the aquifer, and the area through which leakage occurs. At many places recharge directly from precipitation during a year of near normal precipitation exceeds ten percent of annual precipitation. Recharge rates are determined by analysis of water-table and piezometric maps and data on water-level declines and groundwater discharges. Other methods of determining recharge are based on the rise of water levels in wells.

In order to increase the natural supply of groundwater, man has artificially recharged groundwater reservoirs. A variety of methods have been developed, including water spreading, recharging through pits, excavations, wells, and shafts, and pumping to induce recharge from surface-water bodies. The choice of a particular method is governed by local topographic, geologic and soil conditions, the quantity of water to be recharged, and the ultimate water use. In special circumstances land value, water quality, or climate may be an important factor (Todd, 1959).

Discharge

Streamflow consists of surface runoff and groundwater runoff. Surface runoff may be defined as precipitation that finds its way into the stream channel without infiltrating into the soil. Groundwater runoff is precipitation that infiltrates into the soil or to the water table and then percolates into the stream channel.

Groundwater runoff includes bank storage during floods. Surface runoff reaches streams rapidly and is discharged from drainage basins within a few days. Groundwater percolates slowly towards and reaches streams gradually. Under natural conditions, groundwater continuously percolates towards streams; however, the roots of plants and soil capillaries intercept and discharge into the atmosphere some of the water which otherwise would become groundwater runoff.

Rating curves may be prepared to determine the relationship between mean groundwater stages and groundwater runoff. Averages of groundwater levels in drainage basins are determined for selected dates when streamflow consists entirely of groundwater runoff. Groundwater runoff into a stream channel ceases temporarily during periods of flood; however, groundwater continues to percolate towards the stream creating groundwater storage in the lowlands adjacent to the stream channel. As soon as the stream stage starts to fall, groundwater runoff is considerably increased not only because of the accumulated bank storage but also because of the accumulated groundwater storage. When bank and groundwater storage is drained out, groundwater runoff will generally be greater than before precipitation occurred because during most flood periods precipitation infiltrating into the groundwater reservoir causes the water table to rise and the hydraulic gradient toward the stream to increase.

Groundwater runoff is related to such drainage basin characteristics as geologic environment, topography, and land use. It is not uncommon for groundwater runoff to constitute more than 40 percent of streamflow. Analytical solutions for several important problems involving the flow of groundwater toward streams and drains have been devised. Equations have been developed for estimating the permeability and storage characteristics of aquifers based on groundwater contribution to streamflow.

Groundwater reservoirs lose water by spring flow or by dispersed seepage, or by evaporation and transpiration wherever the water table or its overlying capillary fringe is at the land surface or is within reach of the roots of water-hungry vegetation (phreatophytes). Springs occur in many forms. Volcanic springs are associated with volcanic rocks and fissure springs

Subsurface Water

result from fractures extending to great depths in the earth's crust. Such springs are usually thermal in that their water temperature exceeds that of the normal local groundwaters. Waters of thermal springs are usually highly mineralized. Gravity springs are formed where the land surface intersects the water table, are created by a permeable aquifer overlying an impermeable formation which intersects the water table, result from releases of water under pressure from artesian aquifers either at an outcrop of the aquifer or through an opening in the aquitard, and issue from openings in impermeable rocks connected to the surface.

Most springs fluctuate in their rate of discharge in response to fluctuations in recharge to aquifers. Fluctuations may be caused by variations in transpiration, by atmospheric changes, by tides, and by natural siphons acting in aquifers. A geyser is a periodic thermal spring resulting from the expansion force of superheated steam produced by water in contact with heated rock at great depths. Some large springs are fed by water from rivers or lakes which seep into permeable aquifers. Almost all large springs issue from lava, limestone, boulder, or gravel aquifers.

Phreatophytes are one of the most useful surface indicators of groundwater conditions. The total area of vegetation gives some rough indication of the total amount of water being discharged at the surface. Phreatophytes give some indication of depth to water. Grasses thrive where the water table is generally less than 10 feet below the surface, shrubs where the water table is less than 30 feet below the surface, and trees where the water table is less than 90 feet below the surface.

Chemical and biological aspects

The usefulness of groundwaters for domestic, industrial, and agricultural purposes is determined by their chemical and biological characteristics. The water that falls upon the earth as rain or snow contains only small quantities of dissolved mineral matter. As soon as it reaches the earth, however, it begins to react with the minerals of the soil and rocks with which it comes into contact. The amount and character of the mineral matter dissolved by meteoric waters depend upon the chemical composition and physical structure of the rocks with which they have been in contact, the temperature, the pressure, the duration of the contact, and the materials already in solution. The solvent action of the water is assisted by the presence in solution of carbon dioxide, derived from the atmosphere as the water fell as rain or from the soil through which it passes, where it is formed by organic processes. Natural waters range from less than 10 parts per million (ppm) of dissolved solids for rain and snow, to more than 300,000 ppm for some brines (Meinzer, 1942).

The mineral matter dissolved in a groundwater is not a collection of random quantities of different constituents. The quantities of the basic constituents (calcium, magnesium, sodium, and potassium) dissolved in a water are together chemically equivalent to the sum of the acidic constituents (bicarbonate, sulphate, chloride, and nitrate). In addition to these constituents that are in chemical equilibrium with each other, all groundwaters contain iron, aluminum, and silica, which are generally supposed to be present in the colloidal state as oxides. The waters from some formations show a family likeness to one another; they are similar in mineral content and in chemical character. Waters from other formations differ greatly in mineral content and chemical composition. These differences are usually due to local variations in the mineral composition of the rock materials, except where the composition of the waters has been altered through contamination by salt water or pollution by domestic or commercial wastes. Some waters pass through several formations or are composites of waters from different sources and are not representative of any particular formation.

The number of major dissolved constituents in groundwater is quite limited. In most natural waters, silica is usually only the fourth or fifth most abundant dissolved constituent. Most groundwaters contain between 5 and 40 ppm silica. The concentration of iron in solution ranges between 1 and 10 ppm if the pH is between 6 and 8 and the bicarbonate concentration is low. Concentrations of calcium in normal potable groundwater generally range between 10 and 100 ppm. Common concentrations of magnesium range from about 1 to 40 ppm. Areas of igneous and metamorphic rocks that are also in regions of moderate to high rainfall have waters with 1 to 20 ppm of sodium. Waters with total dissolved solids ranging from 1,000 to 5,000 ppm generally have more than 100 ppm of potassium. Concentrations of bicarbonate range between 50 and 400 ppm. Groundwater from igneous and metamorphic rocks, or from sediments derived from them, generally contains less than 100 ppm of bicarbonate. Shallow groundwater in regions of heavy precipitation generally contains less than 30 ppm of chloride. Concentrations of 1,000 ppm or more are common in groundwater from arid regions. Normal groundwater contains only from 0·1 to 10 ppm nitrate.

Besides the more abundant elements already discussed, there are a number of additional minor and secondary elements of considerable importance. Most water contains about 1 ppm bromide for each 300 ppm of chloride. The natural concentration of fluoride appears to be limited to about 9 ppm in pure water. Normal groundwater concentrations of boron range from 0·01 to 1·0 ppm.

The heavy isotope of hydrogen, H^3 or tritium, is produced continuously by cosmic-ray activation of nitrogen. Before 1952, the tritium content of most rain ranged from about 1 to 10 tritium units. Testing of thermonuclear devices since 1952 has greatly increased the H^3 content of rain water. Tritium can be used both to date and to trace groundwater. Sometimes groundwater can be identified as water which has recently originated from rain or water which has resided out of contact with the atmosphere for more than a decade or so. Artificial tritium is an ideal groundwater tracer. Future work may find that water related to the period of testing of thermonuclear devices can be detected as it moves in the subsurface.

The safe disposal of wastes from reactor operations and fuel reprocessing is one of the major problems in the widespread utilization of nuclear power. Large volumes of low-level wastes have been disposed of through injection wells in unused aquifers or under groundwater conditions where the wastes will not contaminate existing or future water supplies.

Several types of bacteria may thrive inside wells and in the surrounding aquifer. Pathogenic organisms, fortunately, are rarely found in groundwater. Cases of contamination are caused by poor well construction or large aquifer openings connected to polluted surface water. Diseases which have been known to be spread through groundwater are typhoid, cholera, amoebic dysentery and infectious hepatitis.

Coastal aquifers come in contact with the ocean at or seaward of the coastline and here, under natural conditions, fresh groundwater is discharged into the ocean. With increased demands for groundwater in many coastal areas, however, the seaward flow of groundwater has been decreased or even reversed causing sea water to enter and to penetrate inland in aquifers. This phenomenon is called sea-water intrusion. Sea-water intrusion also can develop or be accentuated wherever a direct artificial access exists between sea water and groundwater. Sea level canals provide a means of ingress at places. Most small oceanic islands are relatively permeable, consisting of sand, lava, coral, or limestone, so that sea water is in contact with groundwater on all sides. Because fresh groundwater is supplied entirely by rainfall, only a limited amount is available.

The density difference between sea water and fresh water is only about one-fortieth of the density of fresh water; for this reason the fresh-water body has a thickness below sea level of about 40 feet for each foot of elevation of the water table above sea level. Near the seashore, however, dynamic factors become significant. If static conditions alone were to prevail here, the fresh-water body would taper to a knife edge at the beach and there would be no way for the freshwater to escape. When the dynamic factors are considered, it is found that the fresh water flows through a narrow gap between a fresh water-salt water interface and the water-table outcrop at the beach. Under steady-flow conditions the fresh water-salt interface would be sharply defined, but tidal action and the rise and fall of the water table maintain a zone of diffusion between the fresh water and salt water. Where a zone of diffusion exists, the salt water is not static but flows perpetually in a cycle from the floor of the sea into the zone of diffusion and back to the sea. This flow tends to lessen the extent to which the salt water occupies the aquifer. The salts are transported largely by a flow of the salt water with a consequent loss of head in the salt-water environment. The zone of diffusion can have a thickness exceeding 1,000 feet. Sea water and fresh water become intimately mixed in the zone of diffusion by the mechanism that creates this zone. Both convection and molecular diffusion are important parts of the dispersion process, convection in producing large transfers, and molecular diffusion in completing the blending.

In the interpretation of water-quality data, the analyses must be correlated with one another and with related information. The techniques for accomplishing this range from brief inspection to careful statistical analysis of the data, and can include preparation of maps and graphs and other techniques to relate the chemical-quality data to other hydrologic factors. Water analyses can be studied in various ways to demonstrate similarities and differences of composition. Trilinear diagrams constitute a very useful tool in water analysis interpretation. By use of the diagrams the chemical relationships among waters may be brought out in more definite terms than is possible with any other plotting procedures. Chemical data may be shown to be related to the hydrologic factors by such means as direct plotting of chemical properties against groundwater pumpage or water levels. The technique of mapping water quality characteristics by drawing lines of equal concentration of dissolved solids or single ions has been used for many years. In many studies, the hydrologic relationship of surface waters to groundwaters is important. The comparison of chemical analyses of waters from both surface and groundwater sources often aids in establishing the existence and extent of such relationships (Davis and DeWiest, 1966).

Whether a groundwater of a given quality is suitable for a particular purpose depends on the criteria or standards of acceptable quality for that use. Quality limits of water supplies for drinking water, industrial purposes, and irrigation apply to groundwater because of its extensive development for these purposes. The quality requirements for waters used in different industrial processes vary widely. Thus, make-up water for high pressure boilers must meet extremely exacting criteria whereas water of as low a quality as sea water can be satisfactorily employed for cooling of condensers.

The suitability of a groundwater for irrigation is contingent upon the effects of the mineral constituents of the water on both the plant and the soil. Salts may harm plant growth physically by limiting the uptake of water through modification of osmotic processes, or chemically by metabolic reactions such as caused by toxic constituents. Effects of salts on soils, causing changes in soil structure, permeability and aeration, indirectly affect plant growth. Specific limits of permissible salt concentrations for irrigation water cannot be stated because of the wide variations in salinity tolerance among different plants; however, field-plot studies of crops grown on soils that are artificially adjusted to various salinity levels provide valuable information relating to salt tolerance.

An important factor allied to the relation of crop growth to water quality is drainage. If a soil is open and well-drained, crops may be grown on it with the application of generous amounts of saline water; but, on the other hand, a poorly drained area combined with application of good-quality water may fail to produce as satisfactory a crop. Poor drainage permits concentrations in the root zone to build up to toxic proportions. Adequate drainage is necessary to maintain a favorable salt balance, where the total dissolved solids brought to the land annually by irrigation water is less than the total solids carried away annually by drainage water. Limits of salinity for water quality are commonly expressed by classes of relative suitability. The suitability of a water for irrigation, assuming soil character and drainage to be favorable, can usually be determined if the following chemical factors are known: the concentration of dissolved solids, the percent sodium, the residual sodium carbonate, and the concentration of boron.

Well drilling

Before drilling a water well in a new area it is common practice to put down a test hole. The purpose of a test hole is to determine depths to groundwater, quality of water, and physical character and thickness of aquifers without the expense of a regular well which might prove to be unsuccessful. Most test holes and large, deep high-capacity wells are constructed by drilling. Three basic methods of construction are employed: cable tool, hydraulic rotary, and reverse rotary. Well drilling involves intensive mechanical abrasion of the bottom of the hole and accompanying rapid movements of fluid outward and upward from the face of the cutting tool, the 'bit.' The drilling fluid suspends the cuttings and is the medium for their removal from the hole. As a general rule cable tools are employed in areas underlain by consolidated rock (sandstone, limestone, shale, etc.); both cable and hydraulic-rotary tools are used in areas underlain by unconsolidated rock (sand, gravel, clay, etc.), the latter to an increasing degree (Bennison, 1947).

Cable tool drilling is accomplished by crushing the rock with hammer-like blows delivered by a heavy (several hundred pounds) chisel-shaped bit suspended on a cable. The bit rises and falls freely in the hole, the spring-like action of the cable causing it to deliver a sharp quick blow; and the lay of the cable gives a twist on each fall that turns the bit a few degrees. When water-yielding zones are penetrated they must be cased off or sealed with cement if the hole is to be deepened. As drilling continues, the action of the bit is impeded by the accumulation of cuttings beneath it. The bit is periodically removed from the hole and a bailer (a cylindrical device with a flap valve in the bottom) is run in. The bailer is allowed to fall to the bottom of the hole where it strikes the water, causing a rapid surge of water and cuttings upward within it. The bailer is surged (rapidly raised and lowered) a few times and withdrawn from the hole with the cuttings.

Hydraulic-rotary drilling is accomplished by the combined effect of a rotating bit on the lower end of a hollow forged-steel drill pipe and high velocity jet streams of drilling fluid directed downward and outward through holes in the face of the bit. The annular space between the drill collar (a length of very heavy drill pipe immediately above the bit) and the borehole is so narrow that there is a violent upward flow of drilling fluid laden with cuttings. The rotation of the bit further increases the lateral component of mud-fluid energy, tending to cause enlargement of the hole diameter. Above the drill collar the annular space between the drill pipe and hole wall generally is larger, and accordingly the drilling fluid rises more slowly to the land surface where the drill cuttings settle out in a pit. Freed of its load, the mud fluid is then recirculated.

The reverse rotary equipment draws the fluid upward through the drill pipe. The fluid is discharged into a mud pit through special pumps with open-blade rotors which allow large gravel to be passed. The walls of the hole during drilling are supported by hydrostatic pressure acting against a film of fine-grained material deposited on the walls by the drilling water.

After a deep well has been drilled it must be completed. In consolidated formations, where the material surrounding the well is stable, groundwater enters directly into the uncased well. Original well yields can be increased by surging the well, by using acid to enlarge openings in carbonate rocks, by fracturing the rock with explosives or with fluid pumped into the well under high pressure, and by various combinations of these methods. In unconsolidated deposits, a screen or perforated casing is required to hold back sediment and allow water to flow into the well without excessive head loss or the passage of fine materials during pumping. There are two types of screened wells: natural pack and artificial pack. Materials surrounding the well are developed in place in the case of the natural pack well; materials having a coarser uniform grain size than the natural formation are artificially placed around the well in the case of the artificial pack well. In the natural pack case, development removes the finer material from the aquifer so that only coarser material surrounds the screen. The materials around the well are made more uniform in grain size and the sand and gravel is graded in such a way that fine deposits from the aquifer cannot clog the natural pack. Other sections of the well contain blank casing and are sealed by puddled clay or cement grout to prevent vertical water movement along the exterior of the casing. Casing may be constructed from standard pipe or from well casing of corrosion resistant steel with individual sections connected by threaded or welded joints. In drilling any deep well it is important that proper alignment be maintained so as not to interfere with pump installation and operation (Bennison, 1947).

Following completion, a new deep well is developed to increase its yield. Development is accomplished by pumping, surging, injection of compressed air, backwashing, and addition of solid carbon dioxide. An effective method for developing a well is surging, created by the rapid up-and-down motion of a bailer or circular surge block.

Following development of a new well, it is tested to determine its yield and drawdown. This information provides a basis for determining the water supply available from the well, for selecting the type of pump, and for estimating the cost of pumping. Several types of pumps are suitable for deep well operation:

plunger, deep well turbine, displacement, air lift, submersible, and jet.

Many wells yield decreasing quantities of water with time because of corrosion or incrustation of screens and perforated casings. The effects of corrosion are minimized by selecting well screens of corrosion-resistant metal (such as nickel, copper, or stainless steel). Incrustation is commonly removed by adding hydrochloric acid to the well, followed by agitation and surging.

In many places in Europe and the United States, groundwater is pumped from collector wells. A collector well consists of a vertical concrete caisson about 13 feet in diameter and horizontal laterals. The laterals are jacked hydraulically into the aquifer and are commonly perforated pipes 6 to 8 inches in diameter and more than 200 feet long. Infiltration galleries (horizontal permeable conduits) are sometimes used for collecting groundwater by gravity flow.

Resource measurement

The groundwater hydrologist is concerned with the quantitative description of aquifers and their physical parameters and with the response of aquifers to development. It is his responsibility to evaluate groundwater resources and to forecast the consequences of the utilization of aquifers. Proper planning of groundwater development requires testing of all possible schemes and appraising of the relative merits of various alternatives. Thus, the groundwater hydrologist must consider many choices of development and describe their effects. Groundwater resource development and management personnel are concerned with the sustained yields of wells and aquifers, interference between wells and well fields, and the interrelation between surface water and groundwater. Questions pertaining to the use of groundwater resources require that pumping be related to water-level change with reference to time and space. The groundwater hydrologist must then determine the change in water levels due to the withdrawal of water from aquifers. The two factors to be considered are the cause and effect—pumpage and changes in water level. The hydraulic characteristics and dimensions of the aquifer, and existing aquitards, and the boundaries of the aquifer are of utmost importance in relating cause and effect.

Changes in water levels can be evaluated only if the widths, lengths, and thicknesses of the aquifer and the aquitards are known. Boundaries, such as folds, faults, or relatively impervious layers of shale or clay, and beds of rivers, lakes and other bodies of surface water, influence the response of an aquifer to pumping. Thus, cause cannot be related to effect until maps are available, which describe the following factors: hydraulic characteristics of the aquifer; areas of the aquifer; saturated thickness of the aquifer; coefficients of vertical permeability of existing aquitards; saturated thicknesses of existing aquitards; and location, extent, and nature of the aquifer and the aquitard boundaries. These prescribed maps must encompass all nonhomogeneous and irregular groundwater conditions.

The response of an aquifer to pumping cannot be predicted with great precision unless the basic definition of the groundwater conditions of the aquifer is precise. However, the task of defining the groundwater conditions of the aquifer is difficult, because available data are seldom sufficient to permit rigorous descriptions of aquifers, and economic limitations often prohibit the collection of extensive and detailed information concerning the complexities of these aquifers. Insufficient basic data require much interpretation, extrapolation, and application of geologic principles together with intuition in the preparation of requisite quantitative groundwater maps.

In applying analytical methods to well and aquifer evaluation problems, the boundaries of the aquifer evident from areal studies must be idealized to fit comparatively elementary geometric forms such as wedges and infinite, or semi-infinite, rectilinear strips. Boundaries are assumed to be straightline demarcations and are given mathematical expression. The hydraulic characteristics of the aquifer and aquitard and recharge are considered mathematically by using appropriate groundwater formulas. Actual groundwater conditions are simulated with model aquifers which have straightline boundaries, and an effective width, length, and thickness. The aquifer is sometimes overlain by an aquitard which has an effective thickness. Mathematical models are based on the hydraulic characteristics of model aquifers and groundwater formulas. Problems associated with boundaries are simplified to consideration of an infinite aquifer in which real and image wells operate simultaneously. The effects of real and image wells are computed with appro-

Evaporation Station at Jefferson City, Tennessee, U.S.A. At several locations in the Tennessee Valley, continuous measurements are made of evaporation and the meteorological conditions which affect it. This station is equipped with a standard evaporation pan, maximum and minimum thermometers for both air and water, nonrecording rain gage, hygrothermograph, and anemometer with recorder. The trash can at left is used for storing water so that it will be at the surrounding temperature when poured into the pan. (TVA photo)

Continuous plankton recorder silk showing zooplankters

Continuous plankton recorder

A scene in Antarctica

Large springs discharging from a basalt aquifer into a river

Water well-drilling rig

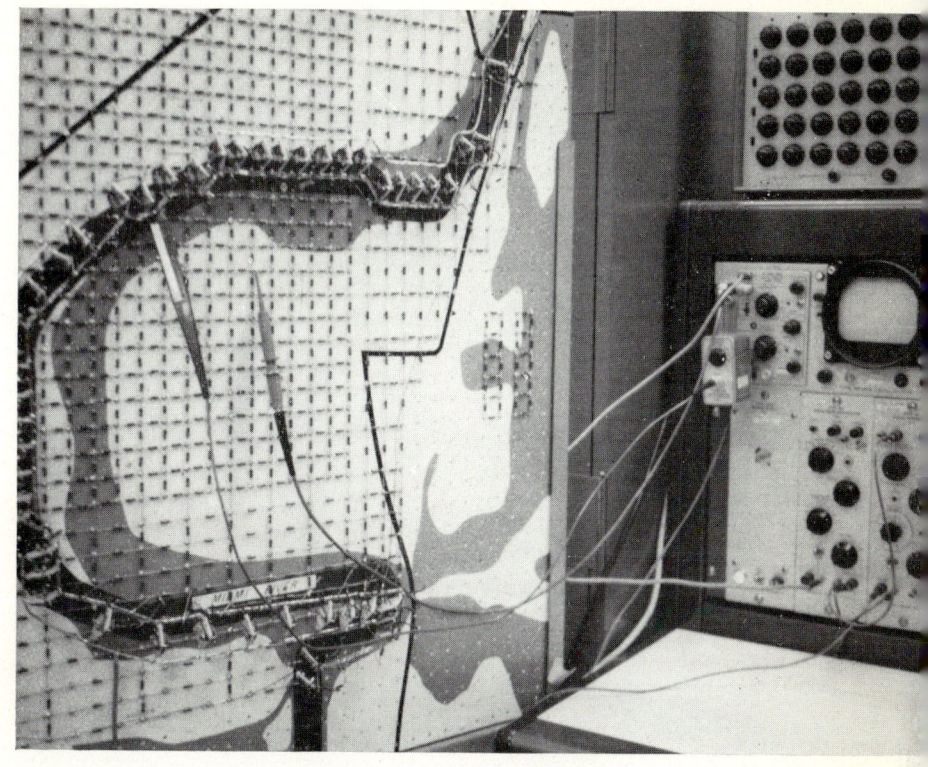

Electric analog computer for studying groundwater problems

A stream in a plateau terrain

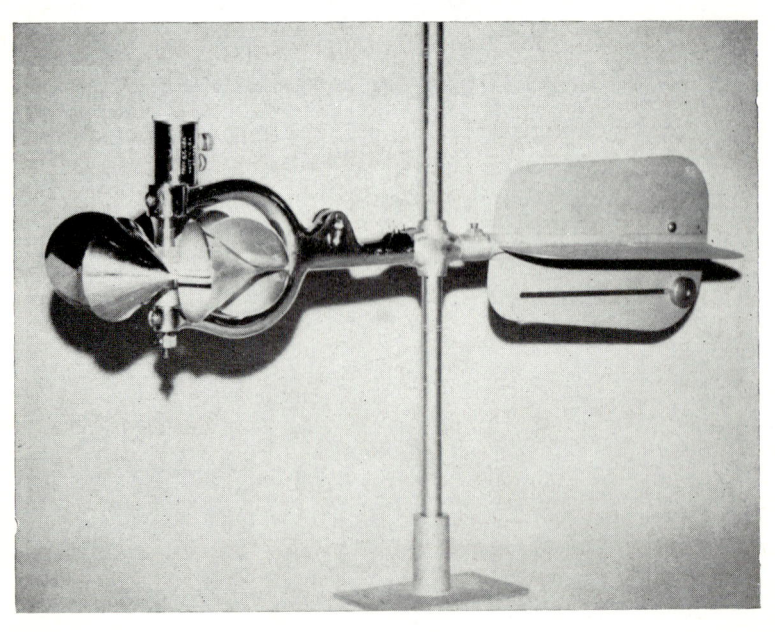

Current meter for measuring streamflow

Soil erosion

Erosion on a large scale

Flooding (above) of urban areas; (below) of rural areas

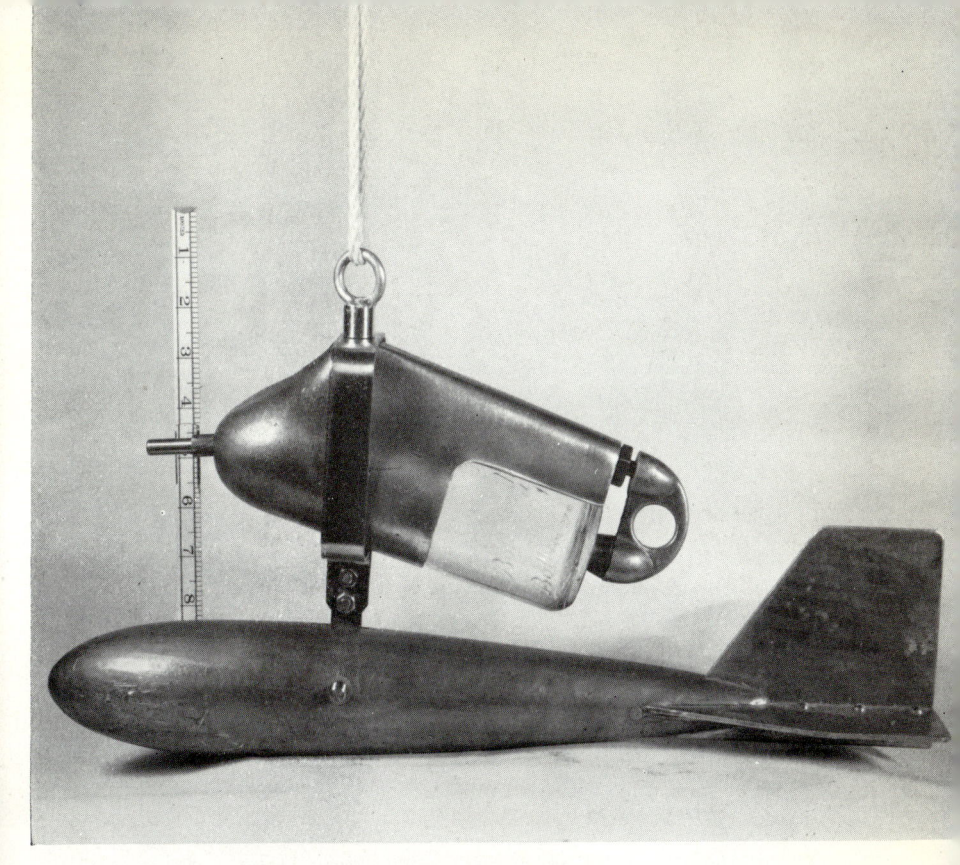

Depth-Integrating Sampler for Suspended Sediment.
This sampler is designed for use in streams too deep for sampling with a wading rod but not great enough to justify the transportation of the 50-pound equipment necessary for sampling major rivers under flood conditions. The equipment can be lowered and raised with a handline as shown. The sampler is moved at a uniform rate to the bottom and instantly raised at the same rate. The water flows into the sample bottle through a tube which remains horizontal throughout the operation. (TVA photo)

Navigation dam and lock

Model for studying a dam structure (above); barge on inland waterway (below)

Above: Fontana Dam on Little Tennessee River in North Carolina, U.S.A.
This is one of the major tributary storage reservoirs in the TVA multiple-purpose water control system. Controlling 1,571 square miles of drainage area, it has 1,157,000 acre-feet of useful storage, of which at least 771,000 acre-feet are reserved for flood control by January 1 each year. Its maximum height of 480 feet makes Fontana Dam the highest dam in the United States east of the Rocky Mountains. (TVA photo)

Below: Hydroelectric dam and power plant

Ice fishing (above); trout fishing (right)

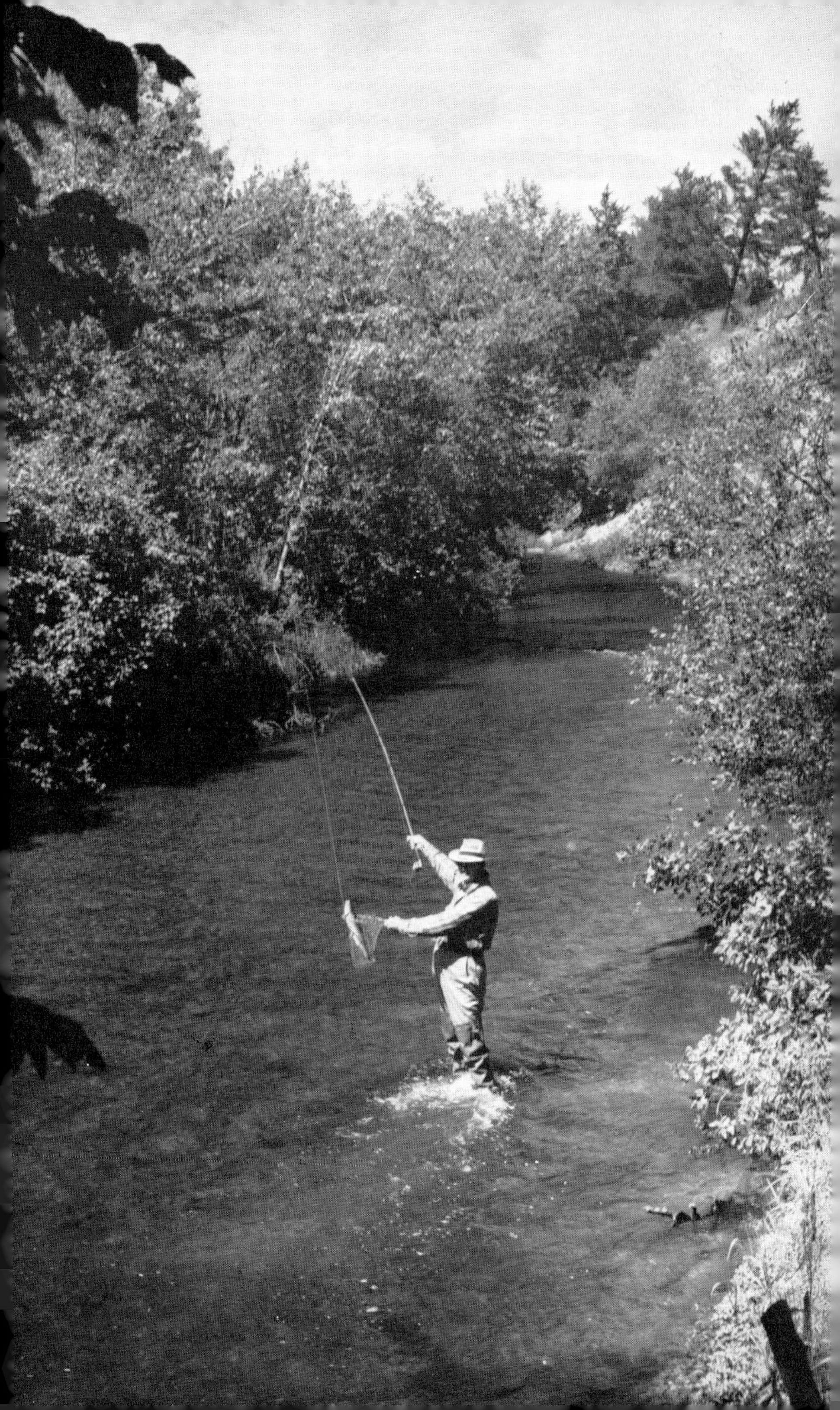

Water-oriented recreation (above); wetlands and waterfowl (right)

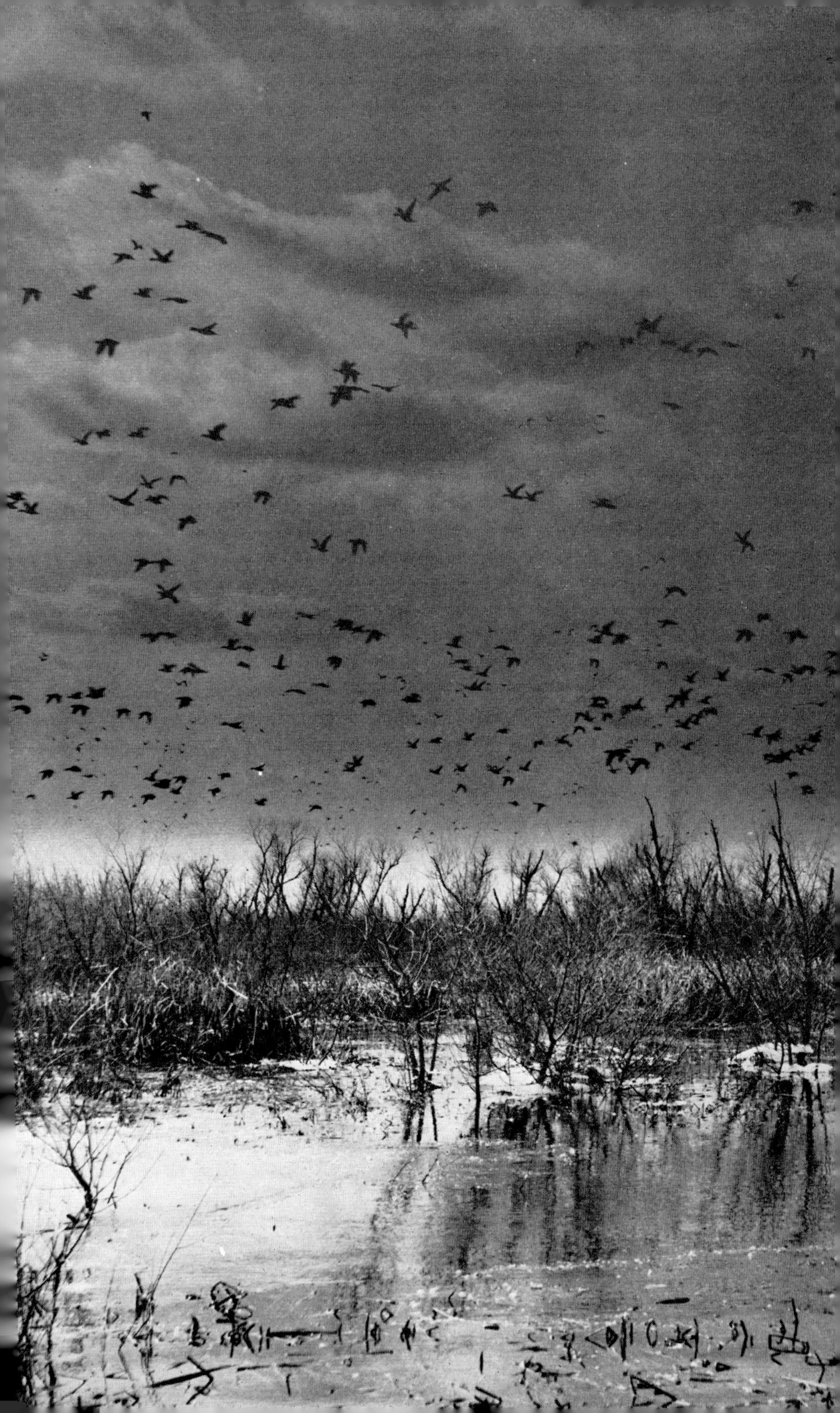

Soil conservation (above); dead waterfowl caused by accidental oil spill and associated pollution (below)

priate groundwater formulas. Mathematical models have been formulated for the flow of groundwater towards drains or infiltration galleries. The water-logging of lands has been investigated. There are solutions for flow towards canals and seepage under dams. Digital computers are often used in mathematical model computations.

For many field problems the boundary conditions are too complex to permit analytical expression of the particular solution. Under these conditions recourse to methods of relaxation and iteration often provide answers. For field problems where analytic solutions are impossible and finite difference equations or other mathematical methods become too laborious, if not impractical, there are available the analog models. Investigators have used mechanical (elastic), hydraulic, and electric analogs in the solution of groundwater problems. The mechanical models consist of a rubber membrane stretched and supported along the edges of a frame. A load applied at a point displaces the membrane surface in a shape corresponding to the cone of depression about a pumped well. The hydraulic model is either a sand-filled tank or an arrangement using a glass plate and tank in which the flow passes between the plate and the wall of the tank. In wet electrical models, a tank of electrolyte and an appropriate potentiometric circuit are used to map the flow pattern for different conditions of well and aquifer distribution. In the dry type of electrical models a sheet of graphite or a graphite-impregnated material is used in lieu of the electrolyte.

Electric analog computers play an important role in the forecast of the consequences of developing nonhomogeneous aquifers having irregular shapes and boundaries and a variety of head and discharge controls. Analog computers are versatile and simple and of low to moderate cost. The use of analog computers enables groundwater development schemes to be tested rapidly and accurately, thus permitting the appraisal of the relative merits of alternate choices of development. The electric analog computer consists of an analog model and excitation-response apparatus, i.e., power supply, waveform generator, pulse generator, and oscilloscope. The analog model is a regular array of resistors and capacitors, and is a scaled-down version of the aquifer. Resistors are inversely proportional to the hydraulic conductivity of the aquifer, and capacitors store electrostatic energy in a manner analogous to the storage of water in an aquifer. The behavior of the electrical network is described by an equation that has the same form as the finite-difference equation for nonsteady state, three-dimensional flow of groundwater. Electrical units (voltage, coulombs, amperes, and seconds) and corresponding hydraulic units (feet, gallons, gallons per day and days) are connected by four scale factors. Excitation-response equipment forces electrical energy in the proper time phase into the analog model and measures energy levels within the energy-dissipative resistor-capacitor network. Oscilloscope traces, i.e., time-voltage graphs, are analogous to time-drawdown graphs that would result after a step function-type change in discharge or head. A catalog of time-voltage graphs provides data for construction of a series of water-level change maps.

Aquifer conditions
Unconsolidated deposits of sand and gravel are the most important aquifers; in many countries probably more than 90 percent of all water pumped comes from sand and gravel. The types of occurrence of these aquifers may be grouped as: watercourses, abandoned or buried valleys, and plains and intermontane valleys. Watercourses consist of a stream channel together with the groundwater in alluvium that underlies the channel and forms the bordering flood plains. Wells in watercourses are readily recharged by infiltration of water in the stream channel. In recent years, groundwater supplies recharged by induced infiltration of surface water have been extensively developed. Where the alluvium has a high permeability watercourses offer excellent opportunities for large groundwater supplies, whereas at places where the alluvium is predominantly of fine texture watercourses will yield only meager supplies. The distribution of clay, silt, sand, and gravel within river valleys is exceedingly complex in detail. The relative thickness of the coarse and fine units depends on the type of sediments carried by the river and the geologic history of the river at the point of interest (Thomas, 1951).

Abandoned or buried valleys are no longer occupied by the stream that formed them. Some alluvium deposits have thicknesses and areal extents much greater than existing stream

Subsurface Water

valleys. Some valley deposits are buried and do not form a part of the present drainage system. Although the permeability of materials in abandoned or buried valleys is as high as that in watercourses, the recharge is generally much less than recharge to watercourses. Many valleys were buried or abandoned during the Pleistocene ice age. Buried and abandoned valleys are numerous in glaciated areas and in valleys of streams that drained ice sheets.

Great plains flank highlands or mountains that were the source of the sediments. Stream-deposited sand and gravel occur beneath the plains in broad belts. Sand and gravel underlie parts of coastal plains where strata are partly marine and partly fluviatile in origin. Aquifers of these plains are recharged directly from precipitation and from streams. Many stratigraphic units along coastal plains grade oceanward from partly alluvial deposits into entirely marine units. This gradation is accompanied by a tendency for the sediments to become progressively finer grained. The bulk of the sediments are clays and silts. Coastal plains vary in size from small isolated valley deposits that grade inland into normal stream deposits to vast, almost featureless plains that fringe hundreds of miles of coasts.

In basins bordered by mountain ranges occur tremendous volumes of unconsolidated deposits including sand and gravel. The sand and gravel derived by erosion of mountains underlying intermontane valleys yield more than half of all the water pumped from wells in many countries. There is some recharge directly from precipitation, but generally most recharge is by seepage from streams into the alluvial fans lying beneath the base of mountains and the basin floors. Subsurface flow through the walls of the mountains into intermontane valley deposits is very large in comparison to annual recharge in arid regions.

About 30 percent of the land surface of the earth has been covered by glacial ice during the past million years. At present, 10 percent of the land surface is covered. Glacial till covers several million square miles of the earth's surface, yet relatively few water wells draw their supplies directly from the till. Of the wells drawing water from clayey till, most of them probably obtain their water from joints or small sand lenses within the till. A number of wells in mountain valleys probably draw water from coarse-grained till.

Eolian deposits (formed by the wind) are far less abundant than either stream or glacial deposits. Many parts of the world such as southern Ukraine, Nebraska, and southeastern Saudi Arabia, however, are blanketed by eolian deposits. Eolian deposits can be divided into two types, loess and dune sand. Loess is not commonly an aquifer because of its low permeability and where its permeability is the highest it is usually in high topographic positions where subsurface drainage is efficient. If loess overlies impermeable soils or consolidated rocks, stock or farm wells can be developed that will give good service except during long periods of dry weather. Aquifers of dune sand are not widely utilized because wells that prevent entrance of the loose sand are difficult to construct by standard practices and active dune areas are not favorable for habitation. Despite these drawbacks, some dune areas are favorable for water development because of high recharge rates, good water quality, and moderately high permeabilities.

Limestones and dolomites, constituting between 5 and 10 percent of all sedimentary rocks, vary widely in permeability. The most important aquifers are those in which secondary solution openings occur. In regions where limestone forms the land surface and extends to considerable depth, groundwater dissolves the rock and waters are hard because of this dissolved mineral matter. The ultimate development of limestone terrains is a karst region with such features as sinkholes, lost rivers, large springs and subsurface drainage. Solution openings are irregularly distributed both horizontally and vertically in limestones. Some wells may penetrate deep into limestone without yielding appreciable quantities of water; nearby wells may have large yields. Gypsum is sufficiently soluble to develop a high permeability. Water hard and high in sulfate is pumped from gypsum in places.

The porosity of sandstone and conglomerate is generally much less than that of their equivalents, sand and gravel, because of the presence of cementing materials between grains. The interstices of quartzites have been almost completely closed by cementation and the rock yields water from joints or other secondary openings. Many sandstones are only partly cemented and yield most water from the original interstices between grains. Sandstone wells seldom have yields as high as the yields of wells in unconsolidated sand and gravel. Cementation makes a sandstone coherent and less likely to cave into wells.

Shale, silt, clay, glacial till, weathered residual rocks and poorly sorted alluvium often have high porosities but retain much water by molecular attraction and have a low permeability. They furnish small supplies to domestic wells at many places. Siliceous shale and some claystones will develop closely spaced joints of the rocks near the surface. Also, if these rocks are involved in faulting, fractures that stay open at considerable depths may develop. The joints and fractures may yield a few gallons of water per minute to wells. Most commonly, however, the fine-grained rocks will be barriers to the movement of water.

The volcanic rock basalt has about the same range of permeability as limestone. Permeable zones include flow breccias, porous zones between successive lava beds, lava tubes and cracks and joints. Although porosity may be quite high, the permeability is largely a function of other primary and secondary structures within the rock. Joints caused by cooling, lava tubes, vesicles that intersect, tree molds, fractures caused by buckling of partly congealed lava, and voids left between successive flows are some of the features that give basalt its high permeability. Sediments interbedded with the lava will greatly increase the average porosity of large volumes of rocks that are predominantly volcanic. Both the permeability and porosity of volcanic rock tend to decrease slowly with geologic time. Pyroclastic rocks associated with lava flows are generally porous but not very permeable. Exceptions are blocky, coarse material near volcanic vents and tuffs which have been reworked by water (Meinzer, 1923).

Crystalline and metamorphic rocks, commonly occurring in mountainous areas, are poor aquifers especially in areas where these rocks are buried beneath other rocks. Where crystalline and metamorphic rocks are the uppermost bedrock they yield small but reliable amounts of water to wells in the upper decayed portions of these rocks extending to depths up to 100 feet. Some water occurs at depths up to 300 feet in joints or shear planes. Most wells in crystalline and metamorphic rocks yield supplies sufficient only for domestic use. Igneous and metamorphic rocks are at or near the surface in more than 20 percent of the land surface of the world. In northern Europe and North America the bedrock is mantled with a variable thickness of glacial deposits whose aquifers yield most of the groundwater used in these regions. Large parts of most other continents, however, must rely more heavily on small supplies of water from igneous and metamorphic rocks. Even in these regions groundwater development is commonly confined to alluvium within small valleys. The average permeability of metamorphic and igneous rocks decreases rapidly with depth.

The presence of permafrost, even though it may not be continuous, affects the circulation of groundwater, and in extreme cases makes the recovery of groundwater virtually impossible. Large springs and lakes deeper than about 10 feet afford the only common year-long sources of water, other than well water, that persist throughout the winter. Suitable springs are not common in the arctic, and lakes are subject to contamination. Wells, if they can be developed, are the best sources of potable water. The search for groundwater in arctic regions is essentially a search for permeable and unfrozen zones that are saturated with potable water.

Desert conditions profoundly affect the type of sedimentation, which, in turn, controls the type of aquifers that are found in deposits underlying deserts. Fresh water and suitable aquifers are only found along the margins of such basins or in deeper aquifers not affected by present arid conditions. Stream-channel deposits form the most important aquifers deposited under desert conditions. The relatively small amounts of recharge in desert regions is reflected in the great depths to water in upland areas and the exceptionally flat hydraulic gradients that are commonly encountered. Aquifers that antedate the formation of deserts are not greatly affected by increasing aridity.

Development problems
Groundwater is generally a renewable resource. Precipitation periodically replenishes aquifers which supply wells and springs. However, the natural supply of groundwater is usually limited as to time and place. In recent years man's use of this limited supply has grown enormously. Because of this growth, many startling news reports have appeared in the press and on the radio about the groundwater situation in certain cities and other areas. In some parts of the world, the water-level trend

in most wells has been downward for several years. These areas are sufficiently numerous and so widely scattered over the world that they have given rise to statements that our groundwater resources are being depleted quite generally and may be exhausted within the lifetime of the present generation. However, in many localities groundwater supplies are as abundant today as in the past. The popular notion is that there has been a general and progressive decline of water tables. There are enough records to show also that this condition is not universal, for water tables in many areas are higher today than in past decades and in some instances higher than at any time in history (Thomas, 1951).

It is true that in many areas water is pumped from wells faster than it is replaced by nature. Such overdevelopment affects the considerable part of the population dependent upon groundwater for agricultural, industrial, and municipal uses, but the aggregate of these areas is only a few percent of the world. In a much larger proportion of the world groundwater levels are not declining progressively, and in some areas groundwater storage has increased appreciably in past decades.

Throughout most of the world there has been little development of groundwater. There are extensive areas where adequate supplies of good groundwater can be obtained from wells. Because we are deficient in technical knowledge, the effective use and conservation of groundwaters has been hampered.

The difficulties created by pumping from wells are of several types. Some problems pertain to entire groundwater reservoirs where the rate of replenishment is inadequate to meet the continuing demand. Other problems pertain to the inability of groundwater to move rapidly enough through aquifers to supply the demand.

The most serious problems of groundwater shortage are in areas where water is pumped out faster than the entire groundwater reservoir is replenished. Under these conditions the reservoir is being emptied of water that may have taken decades or centuries to accumulate and there is no possibility of a continuous supply unless present conditions are changed. Even more serious is the condition where salty or otherwise unusable water flows into a groundwater reservoir as the good water is pumped out, for these reservoirs may be ruined before they are

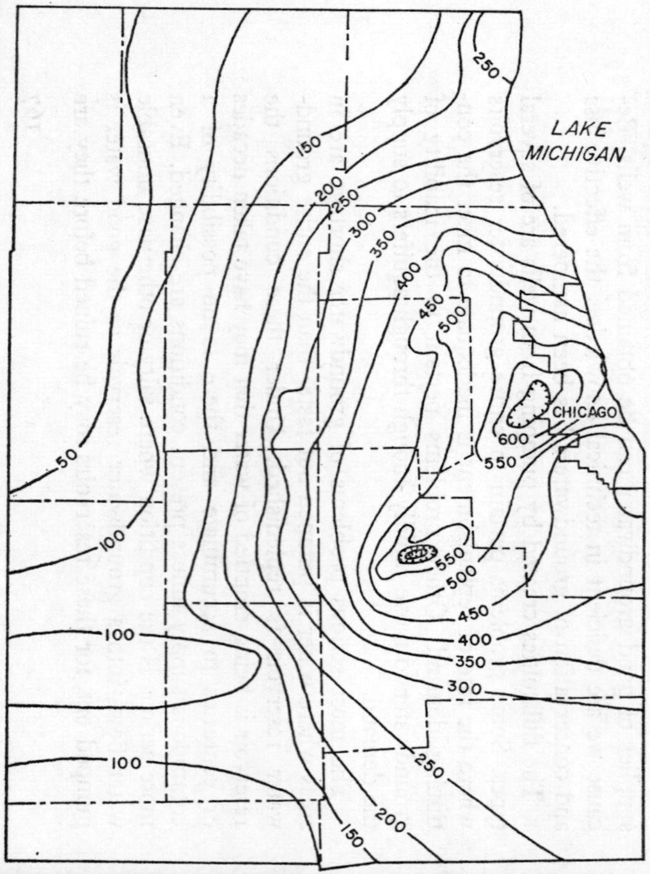
LAKE MICHIGAN
CHICAGO
50
100
150
200
250
300
350
400
450
500
550
600

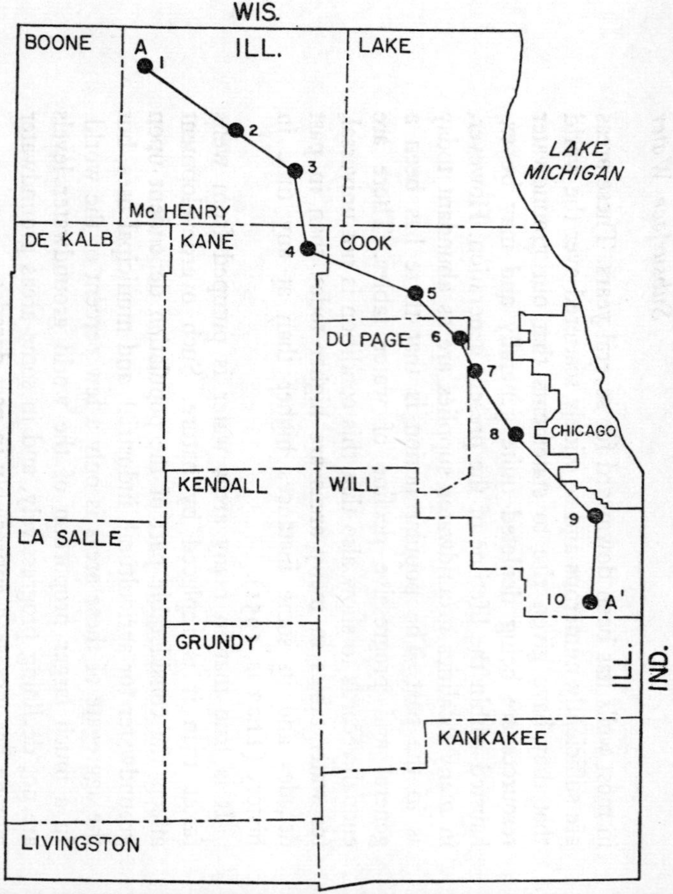
WIS.
ILL.
BOONE
LAKE
Mc HENRY
DE KALB
KANE
COOK
DU PAGE
KENDALL
WILL
LA SALLE
GRUNDY
LIVINGSTON
KANKAKEE
LAKE MICHIGAN
CHICAGO
ILL.
IND.
A
A'
1
2
3
4
5
6
7
8
9
10

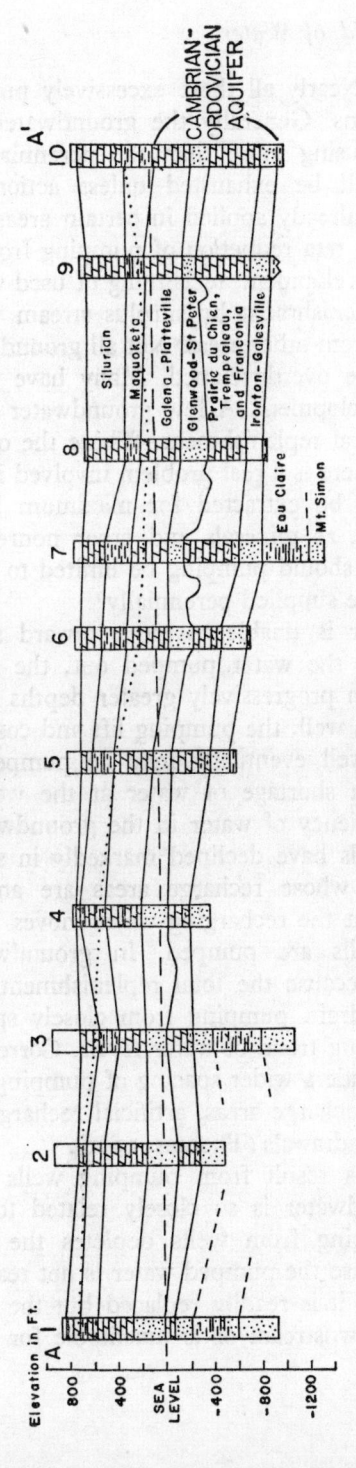

Cross sections of the structure and stratigraphy of the bedrock and piezometric profiles of the Cambrian-Ordovician aquifer in the Chicago region, U.S.A., and decline of artesian pressure, 1864–1958

emptied. Nearly all these excessively pumped reservoirs are in arid regions. Generally the groundwater users are aware that they are using more than the perennial supply and that the supply will be exhausted unless action is taken. Corrective measures already applied in certain areas include prevention of waste, pro rata reduction of pumping from wells, prohibition of further development, reclaiming of used water, artificial groundwater replenishment by surplus stream water, and importation of water from other areas. Not all groundwater reservoirs in arid regions are overdeveloped. Many have potentialities for additional development. A few groundwater reservoirs receive very little natural replenishment. Where the quantity stored in them is large, there is a real problem involved in development: should the water be extracted for maximum benefit of the present generation, as minerals and other nonrenewable resources are mined, or should pumping be limited to the negligible quantity that can be supplied perennially?

If water is unable to move toward a well rapidly enough to replace the water pumped out, the pump inevitably takes water from progressively greater depths in the immediate vicinity of the well, the pumping lift and cost of pumping increase, and the well eventually may be pumped dry. This certainly indicates a shortage of water at the well but not necessarily an insufficiency of water in the groundwater reservoir. Indeed, water levels have declined markedly in small portions of some reservoirs whose recharge areas are annually filled to overflowing but the recharging water moves too slowly to the areas where wells are pumped. In groundwater reservoirs being emptied because the total replenishment of the aquifer is less than the draft, pumping from closely spaced wells accelerates the declining trend of water levels. Corrective measures already taken include a wider spacing of pumping centers, moving wells closer to recharge areas, artificial recharge practices and reduction of withdrawals (Thomas, 1951).

Problems result from pumping wells along streams, where the groundwater is so closely related to water in the stream that pumping from wells depletes the streamflow. Problems arise because the pumped water is not readily replaced from the streams or it is readily replaced but the stream water is either needed downstream or is unsuitable for use. Some wells close to streams produce water free from harmful bacteria even though the stream is highly polluted.

Many activities unrelated to pumping of groundwater have modified the storage of water below the land surface. Drainage projects and irrigation projects have proved that it is possible to manipulate the storage in groundwater reservoirs. Unfortunately, groundwater storage has been increased by irrigation in some places until good agricultural lands have been water-logged and abandoned; and it has been decreased in other localities by drainage to the detriment of agricultural use of land or municipal use. Man has changed the quantity of water stored underground by his structures for storage of surface water or for protection against floods, by improving channels for navigation, and by building cities and providing them with storm sewers. He has damaged some water supplies by discharging contaminated water into the ground or into streams from which it enters groundwater reservoirs; and also by puncturing protective layers, thus permitting entry of sea water or other mineralized water into aquifers.

The reduction of artesian pressure in thick valley deposits has induced compaction of aquifers and adjacent silts and clays. Many areas of subsidence due to groundwater pumping are known in the United States as well as in Japan, Mexico, and England. The most spectacular subsidence areas, those of the southern Great Valley of California and the Mexico City area, are in large valleys of tectonic origin. In both areas the maximum subsidence has probably exceeded 15 feet and most certainly has exceeded 10 feet over relatively large areas. Extensive problems can be caused by subsidence. Groundwater storage capacity is permanently destroyed. Elevations determined by expensive surveys must be reestablished periodically. Topographic maps must be redrawn. Water flow in canals and rivers may become sluggish because of the reduction of the already low gradients by subsidence. If wells extend below major zones of subsidence, the bottoms of casings will remain stationary while the overlying material settles downward and exerts a drag along the casing. The resulting stress transmitted to the casing will commonly collapse the casing. Piles for buildings and other structures may also extend into or below zones of subsidence. The structures then tend to remain stationary as the ground surface subsides.

Any connections with the ground such as ramps and stairs will fail if they are not flexible (Thomas, 1951).

Groundwater problems in Sweden are described by Erickson, Gustafsson and Nilsson (1968).

SOIL MOISTURE

The part of the solid earth lying above the zone of saturation is called the zone of aeration because its interstices are largely filled with atmospheric gases. The zone of aeration varies in thickness from place to place according to the depth of the water table. In swampy tracts it is virtually absent, in mountains it may be more than 1,000 feet thick. Commonly it is less than 100 feet thick. The zone of aeration may be divided into three belts, the belt of soil water, the intermediate belt, and the capillary fringe. The belt of soil water consists of soil and other materials that lie near enough to the surface to discharge water into the atmosphere in perceptible quantities by the action of plants or by soil evaporation and convection. Where the water table is so far below the surface that the belt of soil water does not extend down to the capillary fringe there is an intermediate belt. Water may be present in the zone of aeration in three different conditions. It may be moving in the large soil pore spaces against gravitational forces; or it may be retained about individual soil particles by molecular attraction (hygroscopic water). Gravity water represents a transient state which exists after a rain or application of irrigation water until the water drains to the water table or is taken up as capillary or hygroscopic water. The capillary water can be removed from soil only by applying a force sufficient to overcome the capillary forces, while hygroscopic moisture can be removed only by heating (Meinzer, 1923).

In fine-grained material the earth is invariably moist for a distance of several feet above the water table. This moist belt above the water table is called the capillary fringe. Its water contents are likely to increase downward. The thickness of the capillary fringe varies inversely with the size of interstices. The fringe is relatively thick in rock or soil that has small interstices, such as silt or clay loam and relatively thin in substances that have larger interstices such as coarse sand. The capillary fringe often is several feet in thickness. If the capillary fringe is near enough to the surface to lose water by evaporation or by the absorption of the roots of plants there is a continuous movement of water from the water table upward through the capillary interstices.

The depths to which the roots of plants go for water varies greatly with different kinds of plants and with different kinds of soil and moisture conditions. Ordinary grasses and field crops do not draw from depths of more than a few feet. Large trees and certain types of deep-rooted desert plants draw water from considerable depths, several tens of feet below the surface.

The space between the lower limit of the soil belt and the upper limit of the capillary fringe forms an intermediate belt that is thick where the depth to the water table is great but thin where the water table is near the surface. Some water is held in the intermediate zone by molecular attraction. Materials of the intermediate belt are generally somewhat moist but do not contain as much water as they are capable of holding by molecular attraction.

Soil water is of great importance to the agriculturist because it is the water on which the crops depend and which in large measure determines their yield. Elaborate investigations have been made of the content of water in the soil, the conditions and rate of its discharge into the atmosphere, its consumption of plants, its upward and downward migration, the depth from which it is absorbed by different kinds of cultivated plants, and the behavior of different kinds of soil in all these respects. Soil moisture near the surface is subject to considerable seasonal variations due to evaporation and the withdrawal of water through the roots of plants and to rainfall.

The root system of an ordinary plant includes a large number of fine rootlets that penetrate all parts of the soil from which the plant draws its water supply and dissolved mineral matter. These rootlets have the power of absorbing much but not all of the water that is retained in soil pores against the pull of gravity by molecular attraction. To a great extent plants send their rootlets to portions of the soil where water is available rather than wait for the water to migrate to the roots by capillary. A part of the water that plants are unable to utilize for growth can be removed by evaporation, but some water remains in a soil even after it has been fully exposed to evaporation. The field capacity is the moisture content of the soil after free drainage has removed most of the gravity water. Since drainage of water will continue for some time after a soil is saturated, field capacity must be defined in terms of a specified drainage period, usually two to five days. The other end of the moisture scale from the agricultural viewpoint is the permanent wilting point. This represents the moisture content at which plants can no longer extract sufficient water from the soil for growth. The wilting point has been determined for many years by testing soil samples with young plants.

The oldest method of measuring soil moisture was to remove a sample of soil and determine its loss in weight when oven-dried. This loss expressed as a percentage of the weight of the dry soil is the moisture content of the soil. In-place measurements of soil moisture can be made by electrical-resistance methods. The most recent development for the measurement of soil moisture is the neutron scattering device. A fast neutron source is lowered into a prepared aluminum access tube in the soil. Fast neutrons lose much more energy when they collide with atoms of low atomic weight than when they collide with heavier atoms. The hydrogen in water is usually the only atom of low atomic weight in the soil. The fast neutrons which are slowed by collision with the hydrogen of the soil water are detected with a slow neutron counter which is part of the device lowered into the access hole. The higher the count the higher the hydrogen concentration and, hence, the higher the moisture content. Once a soil has been calibrated, time and depth variations in moisture content can easily be determined.

Chapter 6

Lakes, Swamps, and Reservoirs

The lakes, swamps, and reservoirs of the world provide such basic needs as food, primary water supply, and transportation routes. In addition, they provide energy to drive water-propelled turbines and make possible recreational activities of great variety. Only in rare instances have lakes been destroyed or severely modified by man because they obstructed the exploitation of a more valuable resource. Rabbit Lake in Minnesota, USA and Steep Rock Lake in Ontario, Canada were drained to obtain high-grade iron ore bodies which they covered.

A lake is generally defined as an inland basin filled or partially filled by a water body whose surface dimensions are sufficiently large to sustain waves capable of producing a barren wave-swept shore. Ponds are very small, very shallow, quiet bodies of water with extensive occupancy by higher aquatic plants. A swamp is a vegetated land area saturated with water. Quarries, pits, holes, and other excavations in the earth often become lakes. Large artificial lakes have been built by the construction of dams across river valleys to furnish water power for mills and other small industries, to hold public water supplies and irrigation reserves; for hydroelectric power, flood control, navigation purposes, fish and wildlife protection and propagation, and, more recently, recreation.

Inland lakes cover only a relatively small portion of the earth's surface, about 1·8 percent. The number of lakes, however, in several countries like Sweden and Finland is very large. The dimensions of most lakes are small; lakes with areas of more than 350 or even 35 square miles are exceptional. Only two lakes, Baikal in Siberia and Tanganyika in Africa, are known to have maximum depths over 3,280 feet and mean depths over 1,640 feet. At least nineteen lakes have maximum depths in excess of 1,300 feet. The Caspian Sea has the greatest area

(166,000 square miles) and volume of any body of water separated from the ocean. The St Lawrence Great Lakes of North America with an area of 92,000 square miles constitutes the largest mass of fresh water on the earth (Chow, 1964).

Lakes, swamps, and reservoirs are transitory features of the earth's surface. Usually the rim holding the lake starts to be destroyed as soon as it is formed. Meanwhile the lake's basin is continuously being filled with sediment from influent waters and by organic productivity.

Lakes are natural reservoirs in which water is temporarily stored during its passage to the sea, and they receive water as precipitation on their surfaces, from surface influents, and from groundwater entering as springs. Lakes from which water leaves only by evaporation are termed closed; those with any kind of effluent stream, open. Where the water passes out of a lake as groundwater discharge, the lake is said to be a seepage as opposed to a drainage lake. The rate of delivery of water into a lake and its loss by evaporation ordinarily varies with the seasons. The influents are usually high in rainy seasons or when ice is melting; the level of the lake tends to rise at such times. Shallow lakes may dry up completely during droughts, only to regain their former levels during subsequent wetter periods. The rate of change of water volume is controlled by the rate at which water enters the basin from all sources minus the rate at which water is lost by evaporation from its surface and discharges by surface and subsurface seepage.

Lakes, swamps, and reservoirs, whether a very dilute solution of a few fractions of a percent or one of high concentration, must serve as the nutrient media for the plants living in them which are not rooted in the bottom. Plants must be able to obtain in a usable form those elements they need for the formation of their tissues. Wherever plants grow, changes in the chemical state of the environment are caused by the withdrawal of nutrients on the one hand and by the release of the products of metabolism on the other. The life processes in the upper, well-lighted strata result in the removal of the dissolved nutrients; thus their effect is opposite to that of the processes at those depths of the lakes where the lack of light makes productive plant life impossible and where bacterial decomposition of the sinking organic substances predominates. There the substances built up in the bottom strata are broken down into their inorganic constituents, which again go into solution and increase the nutrient content of the bottom waters. Large amounts of organic wastes and materials added to waters act as fertilizers which encourage the growth of algae and micro-organisms. These may cause nuisance problems such as tastes and odors in water supplies, the clogging of filters in water treatment plants, growth on the surface and walls of storage reservoirs or in water distribution systems, and changes in color, pH, and other characteristics of the water.

ORIGIN OF LAKES

Eleven major genetic processes, which produce 76 different lake types have been recognized (Hutchinson, 1957). Submarine structural basins, or depressions, formed by differential marine sedimentation, when uplifted above sea level may become lakes, or broad upwarping of the earth's crust can form lake basins. Faulting is responsible for the origin of some basins, of which the graben (a depressed segment of the earth's crust bounded on at least two sides by faults) types are the best known; Lake Baikal lies in a multiple graben. Tectonic lake basins include: relict lakes cut off by gentle or epeirogenetic (the deformation of the earth's crust by which broader features of relief are formed) uplift of the sea bottom, the basin having an original structural identity retained from its marine period (Caspian Sea); new land lakes formed after epeirogenetic uplift of marine surfaces on which there were irregularities due to uneven sedimentation (Lake Okeechobee, Florida); lakes formed by movement reversing drainage patterns (Lake Kioga in central Africa); lakes formed by upwarping all around a basin (Lake Victoria in central Africa); lakes in areas of local subsidence due to earthquakes (Reelfoot Lake, Tennessee); lakes in basins formed by folding and by an upwarping of the earth's crust across its lower end (Fahlensee in Switzerland); lakes on old peneplain surfaces in intermontane basins (Lake Poso in Celebes); basins on tilted fault blocks (Albert Lake in Oregon); and basins in grabens between faults (Lake Baikal, Lake Tanganyika, and Pyramid Lake in Nevada.

The World of Water

Different kinds of basins are related to volcanic activity; lakes occupy volcanic craters or calderas. Craters are inverted conical depressions at the crest of a volcanic cone; calderas are much larger depressions resulting from collapse of the central part of a volcano after quantities of lava have been discharged from the underlying magmatic reservoir. Lakes originate when a lava flow dams a valley or the growth of a volcanic cone obstructs a pre-existing drainage system. Lake basins are sometimes formed when the solidified crust of a new lava flow collapses after the still-fluid lava beneath has drained away. Lake basins produced by volcanic activity include: lakes in relatively unmodified craters in cinder cones (Lake in Crater Butte, Mount Lassen National Park, California); lakes in basins formed by single explosive eruptions (the maars of the Eifel, Lake Evernus, and Lac d'Issarles in the Auvergne); crater lakes in stratovolcanoes modified during the terminal phases of eruption (Lac de la Gocivelle d'en Haut, the Auvergne and Lake Rotomahana, North Island, New Zealand); caldera lakes, in large basins due to collapse of the central part of a volcano after the ejection of magma (Crater Lake, Oregon and Toyako, Japan); lakes in large basins formed by slower collapse with step faulting over an emptied magma chamber (Lago do Bolsena, Italy); lakes between secondary peaks filling a caldera (Medicine Lake, California); lakes in volcano-tectonic basins comparable to calderas or conche but with the dimensions of the lake determined by pre-existing faults (Lake Toba, Sumatra); lakes on collapsed lava flows, (Myvatn, Iceland and Yellowstone Lake in Yellowstone National Park); lakes formed by a barrier constituted by a volcano or group of volcanoes (Lakes Kivu in central Africa and Niuafoou in the Pacific Ocean); lakes formed by damming of a valley (Snag Lake, Mount Lassen National Park) and lakes around Bandaisan, Japan (Hutchinson, 1957).

Landslides, initiated by events such as wave action, earthquakes, heavy rains, artificial excavations, etc., may result in lake basins as landslide debris dams a stream valley. The lake may drain suddenly when the water spills over the slide dam, producing disastrous floods downstream. A landslide lake will tend to fill rapidly with sediment because the inflowing stream has its sediment-carrying capacity lowered as it enters the newly formed lake. Lake basins produced by landsliding include:

Lakes, Swamps, and Reservoirs

lakes held by landslide dams (Lake Sarez in the Pamir Mountains, Lac des Chaillexon, Doubs, on the Franco-Swiss boundary, Lake San Cristobal on Lake Fork of Gunnision River, near Dunmore, County Galway, Ireland); lakes on the irregular surface of landslides (Lac de St Andre, Mount Granier); and lakes held by scree dams formed by prolonged rockfall (Goatswater and Hard Tarn in the English Lake District).

Glaciers have produced many lake basins. Lakes are formed by the damming action of glacier tongues across valleys and moraines. Valley glaciers and continental ice sheets erode the land surface and often scour or quarry basins in rocks. Lakes formed by glacial deposition are related to the collapse of outwash material surrounding masses of stagnant ice or are formed by differential deposition of glacial till and by dams of till or outwash. Lake basins produced by the action of glaciers include: lakes on or in ice, which are transitory but have occurred on alpine glaciers, on the surface of glaciers, within glaciers, and on ice sheets; lakes dammed by ice (Märjelensee, Switzerland, Gapshan or Shyok ice lake in south central Asia, lakes formerly associated with the Malaspins Glacier in Alaska); lakes held by the moraine of an existing glacier (Lake of Mattmark in Switzerland); ice scour lakes on shattered and jointed mature surfaces (in the Hebrides and western Scotland, in Norway, Finland, and northern Canada); cirque lakes, formed at about the snow line in glaciated valleys (Iceberg Lake, Glacier National Park, Watendlath Tarn, English Lake District, Tennesvatn, Moskenesoy, Lofoten Islands); valley rock basins formed below the snow line by glacial action (in Glacier National Park, the Nordfjord Lakes in western Norway, the larger lakes of the English Lake District and the Alps, and Great Slave Lake and the Laurentian Lakes); glint lakes or ice-cauldron lakes produced by glacial action in specific sites where the ice flow is impeded by the pre-existing topography (Tornetrask in Swedish Lapland); lakes dammed by terminal or recessional moraines (Quartz and Bowman Lakes in Glacier National Park, Lough Neagh in Northern Ireland, the Finger Lakes of New York State); lakes dammed by outwash filling a valley below the former glacier (Kintla and McDonald lakes in Glacier National Park); lakes formed in lateral valleys by terminal moraines (Lac de Clairvaux, Jura Mountains and Lac de Barterand, Jura

Mountains); lakes between parallel recessional moraines (Big Cedar Lake, Wisconsin, and Lilla Le Dalsland, Sweden); lakes in irregularities in ground moraine (Heron Lake, Jackson County, Minnesota); lakes in kettles or cavities left by melting of ice blocks in outwash discharged into a pre-existing valley (Barrett Lake and others in the Pomme de Terre Valley, Minnesota); lakes in kettles in drift-filled valleys, the drainage having no relationship to the pre-existing hydrography (numerous lakes in Martin County, Minnesota); lakes in kettles in pitted outwash plains (most of the lakes in Vilas County, Wisconsin); lakes in kettles in till of continental ice sheets (numerous but frequently not well-characterized examples on Minnesota); lakes in kettles in eskers (Hill and Pine Lakes, Minnesota); glacial tunnel lakes formed as plunge pools in ground moraine where water descends a crevasse to continue as a stream below the ice (Jelser Seen and other examples in northern Germany); thaw or thermokarst lakes in regions of permafrost, unoriented, initiated by local melting by water, or by destruction of plant cover (many lakes in eastern Alaska); and elliptical oriented thaw or thermokarst lakes in regions of permafrost, the form being primarily due to current pattern (many lakes in northern Alaska around Point Barrow) (Hutchinson, 1957).

Lakes in regions characterized by carbonate or evaporite rocks are associated with solution by groundwater and subsurface drainage channels. Rock basins are called sinks which generally are funnel-shaped in cross section. The water levels in solution lakes commonly fluctuate rapidly in response to changes in groundwater stages. Solution lakes include: lakes formed in depressions due to solution of limestone by water, by water draining along joints, etc. (Deep Lake, Collier County, Florida and Murrensee, Glarus, Switzerland); polje or tectono-karstic lakes, formed mainly by solution in large tectonically determined basins (Lake Scutari); lakes forming in caves by solution and deposition of calcareous sinter; lakes formed by subsidence after solution of underground soluble salts (Mansfelder See in southwest Saxony, Germany); and lakes formed by action of acid water on sediments containing ferric and aluminum hydroxide, apparently formerly and to some extent now occurring in the coastal plains of South Carolina.

Lakes are formed by stream deposition at the confluence of

Lakes, Swamps, and Reservoirs

a tributary and the main channel. Streams sometimes plunge as waterfalls to excavate basins. Lakes occur on floodplains of mature rivers in the forms of abandoned meander loops of a river and in saucer-shaped basins behind natural flood stage levees. Deltas contain closed basins formed by growth of bars and levees. Lake basins formed by fluviatile action include: plunge-pool lakes in basins excavated below waterfalls now dry (Falls Lake and Castle Lake in the Grand Coulee); fluviatile dams holding lakes, due to deposition by a lateral tributary, either temporarily or perennially, or more sediment than the main stream can remove (Lake Pepin, Minnesota-Wisconsin); fluviatile deposits of deltas dividing an original lake into two (Brienzersee and Thunersee in Switzerland and Derwentwater and Bassenthwaite in the English Lake District); strath lakes, formed between a growing delta and the adjacent margin of the lake (Loch Geal, cut off from the upper end of Loch Lomond); lateral lakes, formed when the sediments of the main stream, deposited as levees, back water up a tributary stream (Lake Tung-ting and other lakes on the Yang-tze kiang; deltaic levee lakes (Lake Ponchartrain, Lake St Catherine on the Mississippi Delta, and Etange de Vaccares on the Rhone Delta); meres formed behind levees built by sediment carried upstream by the tide (the former Red Mere in the English Fens); oxbows or isolated loops of meanders (numerous examples on the Mississippi); lakes in abandoned channels, common on most large flood plains but seldom important; and lateral level lakes lying between a levee and the scarp defining the flood plain (Catahoula Lake, Louisiana) (Hutchinson, 1957).

Wind produces closed depressions by the erosive process of deflation, by deposition of wind-borne sediment, or by combination of both. Lake basins formed by wind action are generally shallow and contain water only during certain seasons. Migration dunes sometimes obstruct natural drainage and form lakes. Lake basins formed by wind action include: basins dammed by wind-blown sand (Moses Lake, Washington); lakes between well-oriented sand dunes (examples in Cherry County, Nebraska and in the Basin of central Asia); and deflation basins formed by wind action under previously arid conditions, with or without some degree of erosion (numerous basins in northern Texas and New Mexico, South Africa, and parts of Australia).

Isolated basins may be created by formation of bars across openings of shores of inland lakes. Offshore islands are sometimes joined to mainlands by two bars and coastal lakes are formed. Lakes associated with shorelines include: maritime coastal lakes, ordinarily drowned estuaries (the lakes of the Landes area on the west coast of France); lakes enclosed by two tombolos or spits joining an island to the mainland (the Stagno di Orbetello); lakes cut off from larger lakes by a bar built across a bay (Buck Lake, Beltrami County, Minnesota and Lake Nabugabo on the northeast coast of Lake Victoria in central Africa); lakes divided by the meeting of two spits, (Marion Lake, Otter Tail County, Minnesota); and lakes formed behind cuspate spits or double tombolos (Gould Lake, Cass County, Minnesota) (Hutchinson, 1957).

Basin forming processes are associated with dead or living organisms. Large masses of plant debris may dam a stream or coral fragments in tropical and subtropical oceanic regions may accumulate and produce lakes. Lake basins formed by organic accumulation include: phytogenic dams, formed by dense growth of plants (Silver Lake, Halifax County, Nova Scotia); and lakes in slightly raised, completely closed coral atolls (the lake on Washington Island in the Central Pacific).

Lakes are formed by the impact of meteorites. The impact of meteorites produces explosion craters usually circular in plan view. Lakes produced by meteorite impact include: meteorite craters due to explosion on impact (Ungava or Chubb Lake, Ungava, Quebec and the bay lakes of southeastern North America).

LAKE FORMS

The three-dimensional form of a lake basin depends in part upon the origin of the lake, the topography in which the lake was formed, and condition and events since the lake was formed. The form of a lake as seen from above may be approximately circular, subcircular, elliptical, subrectangular-elongate, dendritic (branching), lunate (crescentic), triangular or irregular. The measurement of the form characteristics of lakes and lake basins is termed morphometry (Chow, 1964).

The form of a lake is expressed by a hydrographic chart.

It consists of an accurate depiction of the shoreline, a sufficient covering of the water area, with depth soundings accurately located, and depictions of islands, bars, shoals, etc. Lake outlines are usually delineated with aerial photographs. Shore outline measurements and depth soundings are made by applying the method of ordinary surveying at times when the lake is covered with ice. Under open-water conditions hydrographic charts are made by combining ordinary surveying, for shore outline, with lines of depth soundings made from a boat. For large lakes portable recording fathometers are used. A hydrographic chart with depth contours becomes a bathymetric map. From this map morphometric parameters are obtained which allow quantitative comparisons between lakes.

The majority of lakes have a ratio of mean depth to maximum depth which exceeds 0.33, approaching the value that a conical depression would have. With increasing age, this ratio tends to increase as maximum depths are filled in. Lakes in easily erodible rocks generally have ratios between 0.33 and 0.5. In the block-fault (graben) lakes, values of this ratio may exceed 0.5.

A newly formed lake has an irregular shoreline determined primarily by the adjacent terrain. The shoreline does not exhibit wave-cut notches or cliffs nor does it show the wave-deposited underwater shelf which terminates in a typical dropoff to the deep basin. Soon after the lake fills with water, erosional action of waves starts to cut a beach and to develop an underwater shelf, and along shore transport of sediments starts to smooth out indentations of the shoreline, Erosion of headlands provides the major portion of the sediments. Mature lakes exhibit wave-cut cliffs, beaches and underwater shelves terminating in dropoffs. Headlands are eroded, shorelines are smoothed, indentations of the shoreline tend to fill in or to be cut off by bars across their mouths, and downcutting of outlets occurs. A lake in early old age, as a result of further outlet erosion, demonstrates a shoreline of emergence with old raised wave-cut cliffs and beaches. Waves break well out from shore due to wide and shallow underwater shelves and aquatic plants start to invade from shores. Deep basin sediments contain appreciable amounts of organic materials and filling of the basin accelerates. Old lakes are commonly bordered by a band of swamp and are shallow and weedy. There is a high rate of production of new plant and animal material and organic materials fill the basins at increasing rates. Shorelines become progressively smooth and regular. The lake eventually becomes predominantly a swamp, usually with a stream running through its deepest parts. Outlets often become filled and lakes end as bogs (Chow, 1964).

A large number of lakes occupy basins of which the deepest point is below sea level. Such basins are said to be cryptodepressions. The deepest, that of Lake Baikal, has its bottom 4,200 feet below sea level. The majority of very deep cryptodepressions are graben lakes or fjord lakes.

Islands may be formed by faulting, as secondary volcanic cones, by cutting behind promontories, and by sedimentation away from the shore. Temporary anchored floating islands, formed when gas produced in the sediments buoys up a layer of the latter, are recorded in a few lakes. Deltas are formed where rivers enter lakes because the velocity and turbulence of the river is suddenly reduced, causing sedimentation to take place rapidly.

THERMAL PROPERTIES OF LAKES

The thermal conditions of any lake depend primarily on its geographical position and depth. In relatively deep lakes in temperate latitudes there are twice-yearly periods of uniform temperature when vertical circulation occurs. During autumn, surface waters are cooled and they sink from the surface and are replaced by warmer water from below. As cooling approaches 39°F the fall turnover occurs and the water becomes uniform in temperature as the result of convective circulation. At this time density differences from top to bottom are slight and turbulence from wind action provides mechanical mixing throughout the lake. Continued autumnal cooling lowers surface-water temperatures below 39°F, and an inverse temperature structure develops, with water at about 39°F on the bottom and colder, less dense water above. The formation of ice cover provides protection from wind action, and water temperatures during winter typically go from 32°F at the ice surface to about 39°F at the bottom. The ice cover is melted and surface water temperatures rise during the spring warming. When the surface temperature approaches 39°F, convective sinking, aided by the mechanical stirring of the wind, again produces a period of uniform vertical temperature and of vertical convective circulation. The spring turnover ends when the surface water is sufficiently warm and less dense so that wind can no longer destroy vertical density gradients (Hutchinson, 1957).

As the warm season progresses, heat is delivered to the lake at its surface, mainly as solar radiation which is rapidly absorbed by the water. An upper layer of epilimnion of relatively freely circulating water with a small variable temperature gradient occurs in which temperatures are relatively uniform and higher than those in the rest of the water. The epilimnion lies over a deep and more or less undisturbed cold layer of hypolimnion in which there is a gentle vertical fall in temperature. The zone in which the temperature falls most rapidly is called the thermocline, and the layers on either side of the thermocline, embracing the region of rapid fall in temperature with depth, are called collectively the metalimnion. When a lake has developed this type of temperature distribution it is said to exhibit direct or summer thermal stratification. The thermocline is poorly developed in spring, but becomes increasingly thin and sharp as summer goes on. The hypolimnion is largely cut off from the atmosphere and from wind action by the epilimnion and thermocline. The content of dissolved gases and chemicals in the hypolimnion may remain all summer much as it was left by the spring turnover if the lake is clean and deep, but it may suffer depletion of oxygen and accumulation of hydrogen sulfide (H_2S) and other chemicals if the bottom of the lake is dirty or shallow.

The conditions for ice formation, are, in general, air temperatures well below 32°F., water temperatures well below 39°F., clear skies, and low wind velocities. The conditions for the breakup of an ice cover are the reverse of those for its formation. The thermal contraction of ice, may cause cracks to develop. If the ice is less than about one foot thick, the expansion may produce buckling or pressure ridges. Rising temperatures may produce compression, which is relieved by fracturing when a small additional force is applied. The fracturing is usually accompanied by a loud sound.

Lake ice is now employed as roadways for vehicles and as

The World of Water

landing strips for aircraft. Ice also acts as a potent destructive agent on shore installations, both as a result of thermal contraction and expansion during the ice season and by shoreward movement under wind pressure during spring breakup. Ice is also a hazard to shipping in navigable waters.

Lakes belong thermally to the following types: amictic, sealed off by ice from most of the changes at the earth's surface, a very rare type known in the Antarctic and occasionally in high mountains; cold monomictic, with water temperatures never in excess of 39°F. at any depth, freely circulating in summer at or below 39°F., ice-covered with an inverse stratification in winter; dimictic, freely circulating twice a year in spring and autumn, inversely stratified in winter, directly in summer; warm monomictic, with the water never below 39°F. at any level, freely circulating in winter at or above 39°F., directly stratified in summer; oligomictic, in which the water is always well above 39°F., with rare circulation periods at irregular intervals; polymictic, continually circulating at low temperatures little above 39°F. whatever the depth. Most lakes at low altitudes in the humid tropic are ologomictic. The polymictic lakes are best known from the Andes. In tropical central Africa a great variety of intermediate types occurs. It is probable that all very deep tropical lakes are meromictic, having a chemically stabilized zone of dead water at the bottom (Hutchinson, 1957).

MOVEMENT OF WATER IN LAKES

Movement of water particles results in surface waves; the simplest water waves (progressive waves) are a train of alternate crests and troughs. Individual water particles move in vertical circular orbits and make only minor net forward progress. Standing waves occur when two or more progressive waves run in opposite directions. Usually numerous waves of various wave lengths, heights, and directions are seen in nature. Waves originate under the impetus of the wind; waves grow under wind pressure on the upwind sides of the crests, aided by reduced atmospheric pressure in the wind eddy behind each crest. Under strong winds the height of the highest waves is proportional to the square root of the fetch (over-water distance of wind action). The largest waves in lakes have a wave length to wave height ratio of about 10:1. Maximum waves seldom develop in lakes; whitecaps are generally the tops of high waves blown into instability. Waves approaching shore break in depth approximately equal to the wave height (Chow, 1964).

A seiche is an oscillation of a water surface; a natural seiche is a resonance phenomena of a lake basin and is determined by the dimensions of a lake basin. Forced seiches, for lack of resonance effects, are determined by the periodicity and energy of the seiche-producing force. Common seiche-producing forces are wind and barometric pressure. The lake surface undergoes a seesaw oscillation as surface water blown against the downward shore is released by a change of wind. The barometric seiche, or storm surge, results when the rate of passage of a barometric high or low across the lake is such as to reinforce one of the natural seiche periods of the basin. Barometric seiches are frequently destructive.

If a lake is stratified, the layers of various densities can oscillate relative to one another creating internal seiches. The most important internal seiche is that involving oscillation of the thermocline. Internal seiches are activated by the wind and barometric pressure. When wind setup occurs at one end of the lake, the thermocline at that end is depressed, and throughout the lake the thermocline is raised or depressed oppositely to the elevations of the surface. When the causative force releases and the surface seiche begins to operate, the internal seiche is also set in motion. Being confined between overlying water and the bottom, the internal seiche is subject to greater frictional affects than is the surface seiche and has a considerably longer period. In addition to its longer period, the internal seiche has a much greater amplitude than the surface seiche. The primary effect of an internal seiche is movement of the confined waters of the hypolimnion. This movement of colder water frequently brings water of unusually low temperature to water intakes in lakes (Chow, 1964).

Lakes with inlets and outlets have slope currents resulting from flow through; the slope currents are negligible in comparison with currents produced by the wind. Periodic current associated with seiches are usually reversing and they may have important local ventilative or mixing effects. Nonperiodic currents form as the result of transfer of wind-stress energy into the surface water and they play important parts in the lake-wide movement of water.

Surface currents produced by wind are usually found to have velocities between one and three percent of the wind velocity. Wind-produced surface currents flow in directions essentially downwind, but they also have components of direction due to the rotation of the earth. Theoretically, such currents in open deep lakes of the northern hemisphere should move at about 45° to the right of wind movement. Generally the Coriolis right deflection in shallow waters is small enough to be neglected.

The most accurate surface current tracers are discolorations of the water produced by dyes, water-base paints, and clay. Commonly, the direction of the along-shore current is downwind so long as the wind is within 45° of being parallel to the shore. The along-shore currents are primarily the result of the interaction of local topography and local winds; the effects of the earth's rotation are demonstrated only in occasional special aspects of the alongshore currents. Onshore winds tend to result in wind setup against the shore, with possibility of problems from high water levels. Onshore winds bring waves of maximum size and potential destructiveness, whose action reaches farther landward as water level rises with setup. Onshore winds, traveling over deep water before coming to shore, are most apt to have developed a visible Coriolis deflection in the currents they produce. On a west shore running north-south, onshore winds are from the quadrant between northeast and southeast. If a Coriolis deflection of about 40° right is present in the wind-driven water, a wind from the east moves water shoreward in about a west-northwest direction, and setup against shore probably occurs.

In open waters away from shore, the energy of wind stress is transferred downward into the surface water through a series of alternately clockwise and counterclockwise horizontal helices of water-particle motions. In a small circular shallow lake the current pattern is usually a central downward movement with associated upwind return currents around the sides of the lake. In lakes of moderate-to-large size and reasonable depth, the wind-induced current pattern usually takes the form of a main current accompanied by interlocked large and small eddies

Lakes, Swamps, and Reservoirs

whose pattern is determined by the interaction of flow-through earth-rotation effects, and local incidents of topography.

The primary relationship of wind and current is that in which the current and the axis of the slope of the water surface are both oriented to the right of the wind movement. Secondary relationships of wind and current occur in the presence of physical or hydrodynamic barriers, against which less dense water involved in the initial right deflected transport can pole up.

It may be expected that in every lake there is some maximum fetch of open water where the stress-energy input of the prevailing wind is greatest. A primary relationship of water current to wind may be expected to develop in this part of the lake, the remainder of the current pattern consisting of secondary currents and of interrelated eddies, which for the most part rotate like intermeshed gears. Currents have momentum, and upon the cessation of a wind, the current pattern will persist (with losses due to friction) until another wind enforces another current pattern. Effects of momentum bear heavily upon the events that follow a change of wind (Chow, 1964).

The movement of water in lakes is for the most part turbulent; at any point in addition to an average steady flow in a definite direction variable velocities in any direction may be observed. Turbulence permits the transfer of material and heat in any direction on the lake. In addition to the wind drift, current due to effluents can be important if the density of the incoming water differs from that of the bulk of the lake.

True tides can be detected only on the very largest lakes; in Lake Baikal and Lake Superior they have a maximum range of about 1·2 inches.

GASES AND INORGANIC CONTENT OF LAKES

During times of complete circulation, the oxygen concentration of a lake depends on the atmospheric pressure and therefore on the altitude. At any depth the quantity of oxygen that can remain in solution is determined by the pressure of the atmosphere and the layer of water above that depth. If oxygen is produced well below the surface, say in excess of 13 feet, the extra pressure of the water causes it to dissolve rather than to form bubbles, and supersaturation of several hundred percent relative to the lake surface pressure may thus be occasionally recorded. Surface waters in unproductive lakes are always more or less saturated with oxygen. In regions of high biological activity, supersaturation due to photosynthesis, or subsaturation due to respiration and oxidation of organic matter, are frequent. Dull, windless weather following the production of an algal bloom may cause catastrophic deoxygenation in shallow lakes. The majority of small productive lakes during summer stratification lose oxygen from the hypolimnion, the amount lost increasing in most cases with depth. In some lakes, very striking maxima in oxygen concentration develop in the metalimnion during stratification. Many lakes have a minima in the metalimnion. In shallow lakes that are frozen and are carrying a load of snow, loss of oxygen may be extremely serious, causing the death of much of the animal life (Hutchinson, 1957).

The quantity of carbon dioxide (CO_2) in solution in pure water under an atmosphere at sea level will depend on the quantity of the gas in the atmosphere and the temperature. Natural fresh waters are sometimes slightly undersaturated, as the result of photosynthesis, but more often a little supersaturated with CO_2 relative to the atmosphere. During summer stagnation the vertical distribution of carbon dioxide, including bicarbonate, is often roughly the inverse of the oxygen distribution. In the hypolimnetic mud of all lakes in which the oxygen of the deep water is exhausted during summer stagnation, some production of H_2S may be expected. A few cases are known in which appreciable quantities of free sulfuric acid occurs in lakes. Such acid, if not of industrial origin, is formed by the oxidation of volcanic sulfur or sedimentary pyrite.

The pH of lake waters varies from as low as 1·7 in some volcanic lakes containing free sulfuric acid, to 12·0 or more in some closed alkaline lakes rich in soda. The usual range for open lakes is between 6·0 and 9·0.

Molecular nitrogen may dissolve at the surface of the lake, and if the waters of the lake are being mixed the entire lake becomes saturated with respect to the surface temperature and pressure. During periods of stratification, ammonia accumulates in the hypolimnion.

In most lakes the mean cationic composition of the water is approximately that of the average river. Usually bicarbonate is the dominant anion in lakes. The main variations in anions are found in acid waters, in which sulfate is often dominant. The quantities present in surface waters range up at least to 77.5 ppm in open lakes, and in some cases silica is evidently more abundant than are the inorganic acids in solution. The development of diatom blooms constitutes the most important mechanism by which silica is removed from lake waters. Manganese is present in detectable quantities in nearly all surface water. Copper has almost always been detected wherever it has been sought. The quantities present range from an undetectable amount to several hundred milligrams per cubic meter. Zinc is probably present in lake waters in concentrations as great or greater than that of copper. Aluminium is normally present; the forms in lake waters are not known, though the very large amounts found in some shallow, closed alkaline lakes presumably represent aluminate ion. Gallium had been detected; it is likely to be universally present with aluminum, in small quantities. Molybdenum has also been detected in fresh water. The vertical distribution of iron is reflected in the vertical distribution or redox potentials. When the lower water is essentially free of oxygen, considerable amounts of ferrous iron usually accumulate in the deep water of the hypolimnion (Hutchinson, 1957).

Phosphorus is in many ways the element most important to the limnologist since it is more likely to be deficient; and therefore to limit the biological productivity in lakes than are the other major biological elements. The total quantity depends largely on geochemical considerations, usually being greater in waters derived from sedimentary rocks in lowlands regions than in waters draining the crystalline rock of mountain ranges. At the height of summer there may be a great increase in total phosphorus in the surface waters at times of algal blooms, though soluble phosphate is undetectable.

SOLAR RADIATION AND OPTICAL PROPERTIES OF LAKES

The total radiation falling on a lake surface during any day depends on geographical position, elevation, season, and the state of the atmosphere. At high altitudes the radiation received is greater than at sea level. Not all the radiation comes from the sun; the indirect solar radiation from the sky accounts for an appreciable though very variable fraction of the total flux, roughly on the order of 20 percent. In north temperate regions, at low or moderate altitudes, the period from April 1 to July 31 is generally the period when heating of lakes takes place. Part of the radiation delivered is reflected back from the lake surface and part scattered back from below the surface, into the atmosphere. The over-all reflection and backscattering vary in temperate latitudes from about ten percent in winter to seven percent in summer. The rest of the radiation is absorbed by the water, the solutes, and the suspended materials, and so directly or indirectly heats the lake (Hutchinson, 1957).

Solar radiation entering pure water is absorbed selectively, the minimum absorption being in the blue. Long-wave ultraviolet is absorbed a little more rapidly, but the main absorption by water is at the red end of the spectrum. Some of the light lost from a lake is scattered upward rather than absorbed. The color actually observed looking into a lake from above is that of the upward scattered light. This will depend partly on selective scattering, which gives pure water its blue color, and partly on absorption of the upward scattered light by the coloring matter of the water. A small amount of the latter produces a green lake; a larger amount, yellow or brown lakes. Certain optical phenomena of a striking nature may be observed at the surface of lakes. The sun or moon path, which is the reflection of the sun or moon drawn out into a band of light on disturbed water, depends on the distribution of reflecting surfaces on the waves. Very occasionally horizontal rainbows can be seen on lake surfaces. They are apparently formed in the same way as are ordinary rainbows, by refraction in droplets of mist stuck to the oil surfaces of lakes. Mirages have often been noted over lakes. Usually they are due to cold air lying over warmer water, which produces a more or less perfect inverted mirage of distant objects. When warm air lies over cold water, objects otherwise beyond the horizon may become visible.

BIOLOGICAL ASPECTS OF LAKES AND BOGS

The open water portion of a lake, the pelagial, is the habitat of the plankton which includes those organisms that float free

Lakes, Swamps, and Reservoirs

in the water involuntarily independent of the shore and the bottom of the lake. The prerequisite for the existence of plankton is the ability to remain suspended in water. The density of most organisms is somewhat greater than water. The turbulence of the water is the most important factor influencing flotation of plankton; flotation adaptations assume a supporting role. Floating ability is accomplished in part by reduction in weight of integuments and skeletal parts or by the secretion of light-weight material inside or outside the body; through organism movement; through gas bubbles contained within the body; through adaptations which increase the specific surface area of the body; by sticking elongations in a horizontal position; and by colony formation (Ruttner, 1963).

Species of plankton organisms are much smaller in number than of littoral (shoreward region of the lake) organisms in lakes. Tychoplankton consists of forms transported by currents from the littoral and effluents into the pelagial. Tripton consists of the dead organic and inorganic suspended matter in the water. The totality of living and non-living suspended matter (plankton+tychoplankton+tripton) is called seston.

The most predominant families of phytoplankton (the plant portion of plankton) are those in which the single-celled condition or the formation of small cell-aggregations (colonies) is the rule. The flagellated species of the Euglenophyceae, Chrysophyceae, Cryptophyceae, Xanthophyceae, Chlorophyceae, and Peridiniales are abundantly represented in many lakes, as well as the nonmotile, single-celled species of these groups, especially the Chlorococcales, Bacillariophyceae, Desmidiaceae, blue-green algae, and finally the bacteria. The zooplankton (the animal portion of the plankton) mostly consists of three phyla or animals: the Protozoa, including the Sarcodina, Flagellata and Ciliata; the rotifers; and the Crustacea, especially the Cladocera and Copepoda. Most of the animal representatives of the plankton in lakes are characterized by their small size: the protozoans and rotifers seldom exceed microscopic dimensions.

The plankton are composed of producers and consumers of organic matter. The producers are the autotrophic plants, which take up the sun's energy in the green and yellow chromotophores and use it for the assimilation of carbon (photosynthesis). First carbohydrate of fat is produced, and later the highly complex proteins and other proteins of the plant cell are synthesized. Each animal in the plankton community is directly or indirectly dependent upon this production by plants. Animals require special modifications for obtaining food. Some zooplankton in order to obtain necessary quantities of food must pass relatively large quantities of water through their food-catching devices. Some zooplankton capture their particles of food individually. Each physiological activity, such as assimilation of food, respiration, movement and reproduction, is affected by conditions of the environment, always by temperature, and frequently by light, oxygen content, and other physiochemical properties of water (Ruttner, 1963).

The vertical distribution of plankton is not uniform. The habitat of the plankton is bounded at the top by the water-air interface. Many organisms have established themselves at this transition between the two media. Plueston are driven over the water surface with the help of large gas bladders projecting out into the water. Nueston use the surface tension for stabilizing their position. The lower boundary of the vertical distribution of autotrophic phytoplankton is determined by their ability, which is dependent on light penetration, to accomplish air excess assimilation.

Because animals are dependent on plants for their nutrition the bulk of the zooplankton does not extend markedly below the water-air interface. However, the lowermost portions of very deep lakes exhibit a generally sparse population feeding on the organic remains floating down from above. In general at depths of 100 to 160 feet the numbers of individuals already have declined to very small values.

With the beginning of autumnal circulation, eddy diffusion becomes more pronounced and involves increasingly deeper strata and its influence on the distribution of plankton becomes continually stronger. During complete circulation the vertical distribution of plankton is virtually uniform, but under the winter ice cover stratification phenomena again occur. The amount of inflow-outflow in a lake affects the vertical distribution.

Temperature is one of the most effective regulators of vertical distribution. However, the reaction curve for temperature is overlaid by those of other factors, especially light. Among the plankton that prefer low temperatures are several diatoms, desmids, and blue-green algae. Temperature affects the activity of the organs of locomotion and the orientation of the direction of movement within a thermal gradient. Like temperature, light influences both the reproduction and the movements of plankton.

The diurnal vertical motion of plankton has been observed. There tends to be a downward movement at dawn and an upward movement at evening. The decrease in oxygen content has a pronounced effect on the composition of the plankton community. The majority of plankters in the metalimnion or hypolimnion can still respire at low concentrations of oxygen because of low temperatures. The vertical range of distribution of the zooplankton corresponds in general with that of the phytoplankton and affects the distribution of phytoplankton. A large number of zooplankters perform diurnal vertical migrations and graze in different layers at night than during the day (Ruttner, 1963).

Of the various factors important to life, temperature exhibits the greatest variations during a year in lakes. The succession of individual populations in the course of a year is determined by environmental conditions external to the lake and by changes that populations bring about in their environment. The volumes of plankton beneath a unit surface area present do not always bear the expected relationship to the trophic level of lakes as deduced from other properties. However, the content in a unit volume of zones are in good agreement. The decrease in population density can be compensated for by corresponding increase in thickness of one zone of production.

The hypolimnetic decrease in oxygen has led to the formulation of the concepts of oligotrophy (waters with a small amount of nutrients and hence a low organic production), and eutrophy (waters with a good supply of nutrients and hence a rich organic production). The nutrients which are set free by decomposition in the depths and which accumulate there are locked in the hypolimnion and prevented from re-entering the production cycle as long as a stable stratification exists. The amount of such materials in the hypolimnion is very great, especially in eutrophic lakes. During the summer stagnation the region of production (trophogenic zone) is essentially the epilimnion (often the metalimnion is included) while the breakdown region (tropholytic zone) coincides with the stagnant hypolimnion. These differences in the distribution of chemicals brought about by living organisms are termed biogenic chemical stratification (Ruttner, 1963).

The natural solutions of calcium bicarbonate, which comprise the majority of natural waters, are continually under the influence of plant and animal metabolism. Oxygen and carbondioxide are the two great complements in metabolism. Wherever a chemical gradient of biogenic origin occurs in nature, the distribution of these two substances is exactly opposite. When CO_2 content of the trophogenic layer decreases owing to photosynthesis, the oxygen content increases proportionately. As the oxidation processes of breakdown decrease the oxygen in the lower tropholytic region, it is enriched with carbon dioxide (or its salts).

A lake behaves like an assimilating plant: it gives off oxygen in the light, and at night or in cloudy weather the oxygen loss due to decomposition and respiration can be replaced again through the surface. The productivity of a lake can be estimated in many cases from the nature of the oxygen curve. In tropical lakes, temperature is the determination factor and the oxygen curve loses its importance as an indicator of the magnitude of organic productivity.

The optical properties of the water are affected by the different content of plankton organisms, some of which are pigments. A lake with very transparent and dark, blue-green or green water is always oligotrophic. On the other hand, eutrophic lakes always have a relatively low transparency and are yellow-green to yellow-brown in color; but the determination of these optical properties alone will not establish the productivity type, for the turbidity can have an inorganic origin and the color can come from humic substance.

Phosphorus is not taken up by the plankton algae solely in proportion to their demands for growth and reproduction. An excess over natural needs is stored if the supply allows this. While silicic acid is not a constituent of protoplasm it forms the basis of the skeletal structure of the most important group of algae in the water, the diatoms. Plants cannot utilize an abundant ion because they suffer from lack of another (Law of the Minimum). Thus, productivity is limited by the nutrient present in the least amount at any given time. Phosphorus and nitrogen often act as limiting actions.

The higher aquatic vegetation, the marsh and water plants, are fugitives from the land. Adaptations to life under water include: a reduced cuticle for curtailing transpiration; the vascular bundles and supporting elements are not arranged peripherally as in the stems of land plants, but rather centrally as in their roots; stomata are lacking on the submersed portions, and in floating leaves are shifted to the upper surface; aerial leaves tend to have a reduction in their outer surface; thin aquatic leaves consist of two to several layers of cells often finely dissected; a very large, gas-filled, intercellular system dominating the entire anatomy; and specialized organs for the performance of ventilation. Marsh plants occur where the substrate is continuously flooded. Their roots, growing in ooze free of oxygen, require an increased aeration. The intercellular system is well developed but the supporting elements are still arranged peripherally because of the requirements for bending. Reeds and rushes extend farthest into the lakes. Marsh plants seldom advance beyond a water depth of three feet. Farther out occur the floating-leaf plants represented at places by water lilies and floating pond weeds in which the stomata is shifted to the upper surface of the leaves. At a depth of ten feet a plant must either withdraw its roots from the bottom and become freely floating or submerge its organs of assimilation and assume a completely aquatic life habit. The aeration system of aquatic plants affords to a number of animals the opportunity for maintaining their original aerial life habit beneath water. Living as 'respiratory parasites' on water plants are for example the larvae and pupae of the reed beetle (Ruttner, 1963).

Aufwuchs are organisms that are firmly attached to a substrate but do not penetrate into it. The Aufwuchs have modifications for attachment. In addition to attached species there belong to the Aufwuchs family a large number of free living plant and animal forms which crawl upon the substrate, swim about in the dense confusion of the sessile species, or even undertake farther temporary excursions into the open water. On stones, crust-like growths predominate, whereas on living leaves and stems the coverings are light and flocculent. Living portions of plants serving as substrate for the Aufwuchs are usually transitory, very short-lived formations. The Aufwuchs begin to change considerably at depths coinciding with the thermocline, where life is influenced by decreasing light intensity and temperature.

Organic substances transform the lake bottom into an abode of life of very intense organic activity, the metabolism of which is able to affect significantly the processes on free water. Sedimentation of plankton plays a leading role in the formation of the organic components or ooze. Organic remains are washed in from the watershed. The organic and inorganic matter, after being worked over by bottom animals and bacteria in the lake bottom force a finely divided sediment called gyttja. The interior of the ooze is free of oxygen; there is a steep diffusion gradient of ogygen in the layers of water immediately overlying the surface of the ooze. Uppermost layers of ooze are at places aerated.

In oligotrophic lakes with an abundance of oxygen in the deep water and negligible quantities of reducing substance in the sediments, many species of animals live in and upon ooze. In eutrophic lakes new species occur. If the oxygen content of the hypolimnion disappears and if in addition the water layers adjacent to the bottom are loaded with quantities of reducing substances, then only anerobic protista are able to thrive. Life exists to depths of about eight inches in the loose sediments of the deeper layers of ooze. Numerous species construct long tubes to obtain dissolved oxygen for respiratory needs.

Bog waters are distinguished primarily by poverty of dissolved electrolytes, a strongly acid reaction, and a high content of humic materials. Bog pools continually have an excess of carbon dioxide. The microflora is dominated by the desmidiaceae and Mesotaeniaceae and by a few blue-green algae. A predominant role in the microflora of bogs is played by desmids. Besides the acid reaction and low salt content, the large quantity of humic colloids dissolved in the bog water is important in the composition of the community. Plants of the acid environment are: sedges, cotton grasses, marsh trefoil, and mosses.

EVOLUTION OF LAKES

A prime objective of paleolimnology is to illuminate the evolutionary stages through which a lake has passed. The sequence must be established by inference from the stratigraphic record and by further inference from the chemical, mineralogical, and organic composition of the sediments. A lake continuously undergoes change; the morphometry of a lake changes progressively as its sediments accumulate and as the earth's crust deforms. In the evolution of a lake there is a tendency to come to equilibrium with the controlling factors of climate and deformation of the earth's crust. These two dynamic factors are themselves influenced by the antecedent geologic history. Paleolimnologists reconstruct the history of a lake in terms of its stages and reconstruct the paleoclimata, hydrography, and physical geography of the surrounding terrain. A most important objective is to quantify dimensions and the rates at which events took place (Hutchinson, 1964).

In reconstructing the history of a lake, virtually all the evidence is fragmentary. All interpretations draw heavily on inference and analogy. Facts are obtained by observing and measuring stratigraphic sections of the layered rocks that were laid down as muds. There are four means by which scientists can interpret the more or less lithified representatives of muds deposited in lakes: analogy with known geologic processes, inference that the fossil organisms lived in the same kinds of environment as their living counterparts do now, analogy with limnology and sediments of existing lakes, and inferences drawn from the chemical composition and mineralogy of the sediments.

BOGS AND SWAMPS

A bog is the end stage in the life history of a lake (though not all lakes end as bogs). Its chief distinctive characteristic is a floating vegetal mat attached to the shore. True bogs occur most commonly on the areas where lake basins produced by glaciation are abundant. The regions dominated by a cold climate and constantly high relative humidity, such as the glaciated regions of northern Europe and North America, contain abundant bogs. In tropical regions, bogs occur only in the mountainous areas, where climatic conditions of the more temperate latitudes are duplicated.

A typical bog contains a floating mat of vegetation which may cover the entire water surface in late stages of development. The mat may be several feet thick. Peat in organic accumulation of fibrous or woody material, is the organic sediment resulting from the dead and partially decayed vegetation of the bog mat. A boring through a peat bed will penetrate woody peat near the surface, and will encounter the remains of rushes, sedge, and sphagnum moss plant at depth. The presence of a continuous bog mat on a lake prohibits the deposition of mineral sediments; the bottom of a bog lake consists wholly of organic material, which eventually becomes peat. The surface of the lake bottom is not sharply defined, but grades from a fine bottom upward to a colloidal sludge, or muck, commonly known as a false bottom. Chemically, bog lakes are generally strongly acid, with a low percentage of oxygen saturation, a condition which explains the scarcity of aquatic animal life in bogs (Hutchinson, 1957).

Aside from lake basin origins, swamps originate on floodplains of rivers, on deltas at mouths of rivers entering freshwater lakes, along lake margins, or in the vicinity of springs. Swamps lack the characteristic floating mat of vegetation which makes them different from bogs. Swamp sediments, although high in organic content, may also contain considerable amounts of inorganic material. Some floodplain swamps receive a heavy influx of mineral sediment each time the main stream overflows its banks. Swamps do not generally contain false bottoms, although, where finely disseminated organic sediment and ooze predominate, the swamp bottom may be very soft and possess very low bearing strength.

RESERVOIRS

A reservoir is formed by placing a dam across a stream. The simplest type of dam allows use of stored water only and excesses pass out over a spillway. Slightly more complicated dam structures have spillways through which the volume of discharge may be regulated by a system of gages to correspond to downstream water needs. Other dams allow flow only through tunnels near their bases. Reservoirs with hydroelectric power units discharge through penstocks to the generators and also have spillways to tunnels for irrigation or flood-control releases and water-level control. Large multiple purpose reservoirs usually have penstocks, against long-term floods. Maximum depth of such impoundments is normally measured at the level of the spillway crest. Multiple-purpose dams have intake structures, either incorporated in the dam or shortly upstream, that regulate flow through penstocks and flood control or irrigation release tunnels. Large capacity flood-control tunnels have air ducts to expedite flow, and stilling basins are usually constructed in the downstream areas that receive reservoir discharges. Penstocks and flood-control tunnels withdraw water from just above the dead storage level, but selective level releases are often practical for control of silting.

Inlets and outlets of natural lakes are near the surface, but water may leave a reservoir at one of several depths or from two or three levels simultaneously. The lower depression in a natural lake may occur anywhere in its basin, but the maximum depth of a reservoir is always near the dam, unless a natural lake is included in the impoundment area. A reservoir bottom has a regular slope from head to tail that was established by the river before damming. A similar slope is found in natural lakes that are formed by earthquakes, but basins of natural lakes were scooped out below river level, and non-uniformity of bottom slope is to be expected.

Natural lakes normally begin as oligotrophic bodies of water. Increases in productivity of their waters are gradually brought about by contributions of organic material originating in terrestrial life in their drainage basins, and development to the eutrophic condition usually requires a great number of years. Reservoirs, on the other hand, inundate rich bottom lands and fertile topsoils on river slopes and normally begin their lives with high productivity potential. Reservoirs tend to suffer productivity declines with passage of time and never seem to regain their initial productivity level. The life of a reservoir may be assumed to begin with closure. Erosion of readily soluble bed minerals, such as gypsum, often proceeds at a fast rate.

Reservoirs may have wave-cut terraces and reservoir-induced landslides that have markedly altered the physiography of their basins. Most sedimentation occurs in the upper ends of reservoirs where it usually forms deltas, but silt is subject to down-reservoir displacement by later currents or by bed and bank erosion of channels cut through the silt deposit following water-level declines. The degree of silting is generally dependent upon amounts carried into the reservoir, but where quantities are carried in density currents, withdrawals of water at proper levels can significantly decrease settled loads (Chow, 1964).

Reservoirs often develop typical thermal stratification with the formation of epilimnion, metalimnion, and hypolimnion. However, they are subject to periodic, intermittent, or even prolonged entrance of large quantities of water that differ markedly in density from any water stratum existing in them. These invading flows sink or rise to the proper density level and then move on down-reservoir as sharply defined layers that pass over the surface or wedge their way between or under existing water strata. They continue until they break on the dam and then come to rest and form additional water strata. Density of these currents is often affected by suspended materials which normally make them heavier than reservoir surfaces and frequently increase their density above that of any reservoir layer.

By stilling flow and precipitating suspended silt, reservoirs often greatly increase the plankton productivity of their watercourses. Dams usually make their impounded river reaches more attractive to migration waterfowl. Low temperatures maintained over warmer seasons by reservoir releases have permitted development of trout fisheries for varying distances below dams in rivers previously too warm for these species.

Chapter 7

Streams

Streams of the world provide commercial, industrial, irrigation, and municipal water supplies and are used for navigation, power development, and recreation. Waterways have always been important avenues of commerce in world history. The total capacity of the world's hydroelectric plants in 1959 was slightly over 160 million horsepower. Vast power resources still remain to be developed in Africa, Asia, and South America, if and when industry and commerce require more power. The importance of water-based recreation to man's well being continues to grow year by year.

Adverse effects are experienced when erratic streamflows occur, particularly those causing damaging floods. During floods, water spreads over the flood plain and generally comes into conflict with man. Since the flood plain is a desirable location for man and his activities, it is important that floods be controlled. In many areas, measures have been taken to eliminate or control floods. Such measures include construction of flood-control reservoirs, levees, and flood walls; channel improvements; etc. Engineers have been building dams and reservoirs and otherwise managing rivers for more than 3,000 years. The purpose of reservoirs is to smooth out the peaks and valleys of streamflow to obtain greater beneficial use of streamflow. Water is stored at times of excess flow either for the purpose of reducing downstream flood damage or to conserve water for later use at times of low flow. The release of stored water may be for a variety of uses: power generation; irrigation; industrial and public water supply; fish and wildlife preservation; condensing water for steam-electric power plants; maintenance of navigation depths; prevention of salt-water intrusion; dilution for sanitary purposes; and fishing, boating, and swimming. Some of these are the major uses for which a reservoir project is designed; others are of minor significance; and still others result incidental to the planning for major purposes.

In areas with a large concentration of population the liquid wastes (sewage) which must be disposed of in streams to maintain heathful living conditions include: domestic, or sanitary, sewage from toilets, sinks, and other plumbing fixtures; industrial wastes from manufacturing plants; and in many communities storm runoff from streets and other surfaces. Urbanization, industrial growth, and the improved standard of living have increased the strength and quantity of municipal sewage in recent years to the point where stream dilution alone can no longer be relied upon to prevent the undesirable effects of pollution. In many areas more advanced treatment of sewage is essential to prevent undue pollution.

Rivers are both the means and the routes by which the products of continental weathering are carried to the oceans of the world. Except in the most arid areas, more water falls as precipitation than is lost by evaporation and transpiration from the land surface to the atmosphere. Thus, there is an excess of water, which must flow to the ocean. Rivers, then, are the routes by which this excess water flows to the ultimate base level.

STREAMFLOW

Surface water in flowing rivers and creeks represents drainage from the land. Lakes and reservoirs may be viewed as streamflow in storage. Precipitation is the source of streamflow and sets an upper limit on surface runoff. Annual surface runoff ranges from more than 100 inches in rain forests to less than an inch in deserts. Rainfall is not the sole source of water for streamflow. Snow may remain on the ground for some time, but eventually it melts and contributes to surface runoff. Not all precipitation is discharged to streams. Some precipitation penetrates into the soil and is stored temporarily in the ground, from which it is discharged into the atmosphere by direct evaporation from soil pores and by the transpiration of vegetation. Surface runoff is the difference between precipitation and evapotranspiration. Temperature largely controls the amount of precipitation that is lost in evapotranspiration. In general, the higher the temperature, the greater the evapotranspiration loss and the less surface runoff. The excess of precipitation over evapotranspiration losses to the atmosphere is a surprisingly small percentage of the average precipitation. For the land area of the continental United States precipitation averages 30 inches while surface runoff averages 9 inches.

Streamflow fluctuates widely from year to year, season to season, and day to day. High flows occur during wet periods in many areas, but the time of seasonal high water in streams draining mountain areas is primarily associated with the melting of the accumulated snow, which reaches its climax with the onset of the warm season. Valley tributaries may reach their seasonal high stages some months earlier than high altitude, snow-fed tributaries. The flat area bordering most channels, the flood plain, must flood to some extent on the average every other year. To overflow the flood plain is an inherent characteristic of a river.

Streamflow consists of surface runoff, interflow, and groundwater runoff. Surface runoff is precipitation traveling over the land surface (overland flow) and through channels to reach the basin outlet. Interflow is precipitation which infiltrates the soil and moves laterally in the soil towards streams. Groundwater runoff is precipitation which infiltrates to the water table and moves laterally in deeper horizons towards streams. Channel precipitation is precipitation falling directly on the water surface of streams. Base flow is the sustained or fair-weather runoff and consists of groundwater runoff and delayed interflow.

Factors affecting streamflow include: precipitation—form (rain, snow, frost, etc.), type, intensity, duration, time distribution, areal distribution, frequency of occurrence, direction of storm movement, antecedent precipitation, and soil moisture; interception—vegetation species, composition, age, density of stands, season of the year, size of storm; evaporation—temperature, wind, atmospheric pressure, soluble solids, nature and shape of evaporative surfaces; transpiration—temperatures, solar radiation, wind, humidity, soil moisture, type of vegetation; and basin characteristics—size, shape, slope, orientation, elevation, stream density, land use and cover, surface infiltration conditions, soil type, geological conditions, presence of lakes and swamps, artificial drainage, and channel characteristics.

Prior to the beginning of rainfall and after an extended dry period, streamflow is maintained by groundwater seepage to streams. As the water table declines, streamflow continuously decreases. In some areas where the water table declines below the stream channel the channels are dry. As rain starts, the disposition of precipitation is divided among channel precipitation, interception by vegetation, infiltration into the soil, and temporary retention in surface depressions. There is little overland flow and evaporation and transpiration are slight. Groundwater runoff may continue. If snow is present, it will absorb part of the rain; if frost is present infiltration will be reduced, and runoff will be augmented only when thawing releases stored water in the snow, ice, and frost.

As rain continues interception and retention of surface depression capacities are reached, and excess precipitation becomes a source of runoff. Overland flow occurs when precipitation exceeds the infiltration into soil and detention storage on land surfaces and in channels. The infiltrated water will cause the water table to rise and groundwater runoff will increase. Interflow will contribute to streamflow as the soil is saturated. If the stage of the stream rises rapidly it may rise above the water table and streams will contribute water to the flood plain in the form of bank storage. When all natural storage has been satisfied, overland runoff becomes predominant.

Precipitation terminates and channel storage and surface retention becomes depleted. Evapotranspiration is active and infiltration continues. Some water temporarily stored in soils reaches the water table or the stream channel. Peak groundwater runoff and interflow rates are reached and streamflow begins to recede.

A river generally increases downstream in size owing to the increase of drainage area as tributaries enter. This increase in size is manifested not only in the amount of streamflow but also by an increase in channel width and depth. Variations in width, depth, and velocity are neither random nor unpredictable. Width increases downstream faster than depth, and depth faster than velocity, the latter being very nearly constant along the river length. In general the flow of the mountain streams, although perennial in their headwater and the middle courses, decreases downstream as it traverses the zones of increasing aridity. Upon debouncing from mountains, much of the flow is absorbed by the valley fill and the streams become intermittent. Farther out on the valley, streams may disappear entirely (Linsley and Franzini, 1964).

Relations between precipitation and runoff are developed for hydrologic analysis and design. The relation between rainfall and peak runoff has been represented by many empirical or semiempirical formulas. Usually the time of concentration, which is the time required for the surface runoff from the remotest part of the drainage basin to reach the point being considered, is involved in these formulas.

Studies of the world distribution of annual runoff show that South and North America have more runoff than any other continents and that the drainage area tributary to the Atlantic Ocean is roughly double that tributary to the Pacific Ocean, although the total runoff is only one and one half times as large. Areas of internal drainage total 24 percent of the earth's surface; they are dominantly arid and are located largely in Asia, Africa, and Australia. Total annual discharge of the rivers of the world represents about one third of the annual precipitation or about 8,200 cubic miles (Leopold and Davis, 1966).

Though the amount of water carried off the continent to the oceans each year is large, so also is the total length of river channels in the United States; including all the minor creeks and draws, it amounts to about 3,000,000 miles. The Mississippi River from its source in Montana to its mouth below New Orleans has a length of 3,892 miles. The Soviet Union has more major rivers than the United States, China, and Brazil combined. The ten great rivers in the world ranked in order of drainage area and average discharge are: 1) Amazon in Brazil, 2) Congo in Congo, 3) Mississippi in USA, 4) Nile in Egypt, 5) Yenisei in USSR, 6) Ob in USSR, 7) Lena in USSR, 8) Parana in Argentina, 9) Yangtze in China, and 10) Amur in USSR. The Amazon discharge is more than 5 times the discharge of the Congo (Leopold, 1962).

Streamflow measurement
Observations of streamflow are made regularly at gaging stations located on many principal rivers and a large number of their tributaries. Stream gaging consists of two parts: obtaining a

record of stage, called the gage-height record; and using a current meter to define the relation of stage to discharge, called the stage-discharge relation. The term stage refers to the water-surface elevation at a point along a stream. Principal stage indicators are the staff gage; chain, tape, and wire gages; pressure transmitters; and crest-stage indicators. Automatic instruments used in stage measurement are float or probe actuated water stage recorders or automatic printers, radio and land-line transmitters, a bubble gage, and a tensometric recorder. The oldest stage documents are the markings of flood stages of the Nile River carved in the cliffs between Semneh and Kumneh, 255 miles upstream from Aswan some 38 centuries ago (Linsley and Franzini, 1964).

Staff gages consist of a graduated scale attached to a bridge pier or along the river bank in such a position that the height of the water surface can be read directly on the scale. Water-stage recorders are generally enclosed in a shelter built over a stilling well. The stilling well, located along the river bank or attached to a bridge pier, is connected to the river by a pipe, called the intake. The water surface in the stilling well is the same as the water surface of the river. The water-stage recorder consists of two elements: the clockwork, designed in most instruments to move the recording paper at a constant predetermined rate, and the float and float cable, designed to move a pen across the chart, in a direction perpendicular to the paper travel produced by the clockwork and in an amount proportional to the raising or lowering of the float produced by the fluctuations of the water level in the stilling well.

A mechanical means for measuring stream velocity was proposed by Domenico Guglielmini in 1692. Current meters for measuring discharge were introduced in 1790 and are of two general designs: the propeller type and the cup type. The propeller type generally is used in continental Europe and the cup-type is in general use in the United States, Canada, and Great Britain. The cups or propellers rotate at a rate proportional to the velocity of the water due to the difference in pressure by the moving water on opposite sides of the cups or propellers (Isaac, 1967).

Various chemical and electrical methods have been proposed for stream velocity measurement. The chemical methods include salt velocity, salt dilution, and the detection of radioactive tracers. The electrical devices include oxygen polarography, the hot-wire anemometer, electromagnetic voltage generation, and supersonic waves.

The discharge of a stream is equal to the product of its cross-sectional area and its mean velocity. The cross-sectional area of the river is measured by sounding the depth of the stream at intervals across the stream from one bank to the opposite bank. During low stages discharge measurements usually can be made by wading across the stream. At flood stages, discharge measurements are made from a bridge or a cup run on a special cableway. Current-meter measurements of all floods cannot be obtained. Indirect methods are often used to compute the discharge of a stream at its peak. The foremost of the indirect determinations is known as the slope-area method. Mean velocity is a product of friction, depth and slope. Soon after a flood has passed, the engineer determines the width, transverse area, mean depth, and the slope of the water surface from water marks on stationery objects in the flood plain. Friction or roughness coefficients are selected according to the conditions of the channel (Linsley and Franzini, 1964).

The water-stage record is translated into one of discharge by means of the stage-discharge relation. At some point along the stream a given rate of flow is closely associated with a given stage, and a fixed stage-discharge relation exists. The river bed configuration at a point is called the control. The rate of flow at the control at a number of river stages is measured by using the current meter. The results of the measurements are plotted against the stage prevailing during the measurement to define the stage-discharge rating curve for the station. Sufficient measurements are made to include the lowest and highest stages experienced as well as intermediate stages. The rating curve rarely remains fixed because the action of flowing water and other factors changes the river channel and produces corresponding changes in the stage-discharge relation. Frequent measures are made at each gaging station to detect changes in the rating curve.

Streamflow graphs
A graph showing stage, discharge, velocity or other properties

The World of Water

of stream flow with respect to time is known as a hydrograph. The hydrograph can be regarded as an integral expression of the basin characteristics that govern the relations between rainfall and runoff of a particular drainage basin. The hydrograph represents the distribution of total runoff in a stream at a given gaging station. Numerous methods of hydrograph analysis have been developed including watershed models which utilize daily, hourly, or smaller time increments of rainfall as an input to generate continuous mean daily or hourly hydrographs for a drainage basin. The development of the model parameters consists principally of adjusting the infiltration capacities, groundwater recession rates, and evapotranspiration losses in a general digital-computer model to match those characteristics of the particular basin. The general model is constructed so that the model parameters are closely related to the corresponding physical parameters (Linsley and Franzini, 1964).

Variations in flow with time can be conveniently shown graphically by flow-duration curves, flood-frequency graphs, and low-flow frequency curves. The flow duration curve shows the cumulative frequency distribution of flows greater than specified amounts. Comparison of flow-duration curves from two or more basins which have the same climate yields information about the characteristics of each basin. A flow-duration curve with a small slope indicates a large contribution from groundwater. Flood-frequency graphs show the approximate frequency of recurrence of floods of given magnitudes. Flood-frequency graphs furnish design data for planning culverts, bridges, and reservoir spillways. Low-flow frequency graphs show streamflows that cities and industries can depend upon with construction of storage reservoirs. A power-duration curve is a useful tool in the analysis for the development of water power. A flow-mass curve has many useful applications in the design of a storage reservoir, such as the determinition of reservoir capacity, operations procedure, and flood routing.

Electronic digital computers and streamflow data have been used to solve streamflow problems. Applications include computations of backwater curves; unsteady flow for analysis of floods; surges in hydropower-plant tunnels; river tides; streamflow routing; total sediment load; grain-sorting in rivers; reservoir yield; water quality; and analysis, design, and planning of water-resources projects. Electronic analog computers also have been used to study flood flows in rivers, flood routing, unsteady flow in open channels, runoff simulation, and storage routing.

GEOMETRY OF DRAINAGE BASIN AND STREAM-CHANNEL SYSTEM

Systematic description of the geometry of a stream drainage basin and its stream-channel system requires measurement of linear aspects of the drainage network, areal aspects of the drainage basin, and relief aspects of channel network and contributing ground slopes. Quantitative descriptions of drainage basins and channel networks require consideration of the following factors: stream segments (stream order); stream lengths; length of overland flow; arrangement of areal elements; frequency distribution of basin areas; relation of area to length; relation of area to discharge; basin shape; drainage density; watershed surface required to sustain channel stream frequency; channel cross-section geometry; ground surface gradients; and relief measures (Leopold, 1962).

A river is both the product and the architect of its environment. A river has evolved through geologic time and the processes of change that may be observed at present are the same processes by which this evolution took place. The changes during the river history in geologic time were brought about by changes in the external conditions, such as a change in climate, a change in elevation of the continental mass and the concomitant changes in vegetation, in rates and types of weathering, and in the amounts and kinds of materials flowing under the influence of gravity toward base level.

The base level of a stream is defined as the lowest point to which a stream can erode its channel. The base level of a stream may be controlled by lakes, layers of resistant rock, the level of the main stream into which a tributary drains, and ultimately by the ocean. Base level is subject to change and can be either raised or lowered; the stream adjusts itself to a rise in base level by building up its channel through sedimentation, and it adjusts to a fall in base level by eroding its channel downward. Water transports debris, erodes the river channel deeper into the land, and deposits sediments in valley flats, lakes, and the ocean (Leet and Judson, 1965).

The World of Water

The fundamental mechanism in the evolution of a landscape by water erosion is the recession of the valley slope into the upland. As a stream cuts downward and lowers its channel into the land surface, weathering, slope wash, and mass movement come into play, constantly wearing away the valley walls, pushing them farther back. In addition, a stream cuts from side to side, or laterally into its banks. Rapids, like waterfalls, occur at sudden drops in the channel.

The over-all pattern developed by a system of streams and tributaries depends partly on the nature of the underlying rocks and partly on the history of the stream. A dendritic pattern, resembling the branches of a deciduous tree, develops when the underlying bedrock is uniform in its resistance to erosion and exercises no control over the direction of the valley growth. A radial stream pattern is likely to develop on the flanks of a newly formed volcano, where the streams and their valleys radiate outward and downward from various points around the cone. A rectangular pattern occurs when the underlying bedrock is crisis-crossed by fractures that form zones of weakness particularly vulnerable to erosion. The master stream and its tributaries follow courses marked by nearly right-angle bends. The trellis pattern, like the rectangular pattern, is caused by zones in the bedrock that differ in their resistance to erosion. The tributaries in the trellis pattern are examples of streams flowing in zones of less resistant rock. Continued erosion leaves the more resistant rocks standing as ridges or hills above narrowed segments of the valleys and antecedent streams. These stretches of valley are called water gaps. If one of two streams in an adjacent valley is able to deepen its valley more rapidly than the other, it may also extend its valley headward until it breaches the divide between them. When this happens, the more rapidly eroding streams capture the upper portion of the neighboring stream.

All river systems appear to have basically the same type of organization. The river system is dynamic in that it has portions that move and can cause events and create changes. There is not only unity displayed by important similarities between rivers in different settings, but also an amazing organization of river systems. This in part results from a delicate balance between the forces of erosion and the forces of resistance. The manner in which a channel moves across the valley floor, eroding one bank and building a nearly flat flood plain on the other, all the while maintaining a cross section similar in shape and size, is another aspect of the dynamic equilibrium that appears to characterize many channel systems (Leet and Judson, 1965).

All bends of a river are called meanders and the zone along a valley floor that encloses a meandering river is called a meander belt. Both erosion and deposition are involved in the formation of a meander. A meander grows and migrates down-valley by erosion on the outside of the bend and by deposition on the inside. Under certain conditions, the downstream sweep of a series of meanders is distorted into cutoffs, meander scars, and oxbow lakes. The length of a meander is proportional to the width of the river. A similar relationship holds between the length of the meander and the radius of curvature of the meander.

On some flood plains a stream may build up a complex tangle of converging and diverging channels separated by sand bars or islands. This braided pattern is commonly found in alluvial fans, glacial outwash deposits, and along certain rapidly depositing rivers. In many flood plains, the stream is held above the level of the valley floor by banks of sand and silt known as natural levees (Linsley and Franzini, 1964). Measurement data show that there is a constant relationship between channel width and the radius of the curves which the channel exhibits. Also, the meander length or wave length is generally proportional to channel width. There is essentially a linear relationship between the wave length of the channel curves, channel width, and the radius of curvature. The relation of radius of curvature to channel width is consistent. The tendency for a constant ratio of radius to width makes all rivers look quite similar on planimetric maps.

CHEMICAL AND BIOLOGICAL COMPOSITION

The chemical composition of river water is highly variable, in part due to the relative contribution of groundwater and surface runoff. During low flows, rivers are largely sustained by highly mineralized groundwater. When rainfall is heavy and river stages are high, the flow is almost entirely surface runoff. Moderate to heavy loads of suspended sediment (clays, silts, and sand) are commonly transported by storm runoff, whereas, groundwater discharge to streams is normally sediment free.

Streams as they flow from their headwaters to their mouths in general tend to become more mineralized. Geologic influences control composition of river waters. The mean concentration for the river waters of the world in milligrams per liter (mg/1) of the major constituents has been computed to be: silica 13·1; iron 0·67; calcium 15·0; magnesium 4·1; sodium 6·3; potassium 2·3; bicarbonate 58·4; sulfate 11·2; chloride 7·8; and nitrate 1·0. The minerals in rivers are not present in equal amounts or in equal proportions, but are dissolved in accordance with geologic and climatological influences in the earth's environment.

The plankton entering rivers from the lakes or flood plain waters decreases quantitatively downstream. Potamo-plankton is the true stream plankton in large rivers, which forms its own community independent of tributaries and flood plain waters. With respect to the biotas of the shores and bottom of streams, the slower the current is the more the composition and configuration of these communities approach those of standing water. In the rushing water of the rapids of streams the stones are often thickly overgrown with mosses and algae, and in addition there is a richly developed animal life. Stones acquire much smaller Aufwuchs and usually fewer animals as well. Rubble that can be rolled by the current forms an unfavorable substrate for colonization by algal Aufwuchs and an unsuitable dwelling place for animal life.

The adaptations that animals have developed to life in flowing water are greatly varied. The stronger the current is, the less prominent are the free swimming forms. Only fishes, (for example, the salmonids with their muscular, almost round, stream-lined bodies) are able to swim upstream in rushing water and to overcome rapids. In weaker currents, swimmers also occur among the insects, such as the nymphs of mayflies.

A biotape similarly protected from the current is that represented by the cracks and small fissures in rocks as well as the spaces between the individual stones of the substrate. The under surfaces of stones, which are often densely populated, also offer excellent protection. Free-living protozoa, algae, and small animals of the most diverse groups can live here under these conditions (Ruttner, 1963). Aerial respiration is more difficult for insects of flowing water than in standing water; they are forced to extract oxygen from the water. Flowing water is physiologically richer in oxygen than standing water and a reduction of respiratory surface is commonly observed in stream animals. Currents of water are also commonly utilized in the feeding of animals.

The decrease in light intensity by turbidity can be so extensive under certain conditions that an assimilating plant life cannot develop on the bottom of a stream. A factor that brings about a regular change in the composition of the biocoenoses of a river course from its source to its lower course and also brings about zonation along the shore bottom is temperature. The influence of increasing temperature on the composition of the community manifests itself in two different ways; in the progressive exclusion of species, genera, and entire families, and in the occurrence of specific thermal forms.

SEDIMENT TRANSPORT AND EROSION

Year after year, the streams of the earth move staggering amounts of debris and dissolved materials through their valleys to the oceans. The transport of sediment debris by rivers to the oceans is a phenomenon known to everyone. It is far less well known that the quantity of dissolved materials carried by rivers to the ocean is also very large. Because the transport process is not visually evident, nor are deposits of dissolved materials obvious, it is hard to visualize that slightly more than half of all the materials carried by river water from continent to ocean is carried as a dissolved load.

A stream is an effective agent of erosion and removes material from its channel or banks. The solid particles carried by a stream may themselves act as erosion agents, wearing down larger fragments in the bed of the stream. Runoff, flowing as a sheet of water or in closely spaced shallow channels transports a great amount of material downslope toward stream channels. Under natural conditions in the more humid areas, dense vegetation affords protection against erosion. Disturbance of this cover by man's activity, such as overgrazing of grasslands, removal of timber by logging or burns, and breaking of sod cover by plowing, disturbs the natural conditions, and the rate of erosion becomes greatly accelerated.

Water erosion may be classified into two general types: sheet erosion and channel erosion. Sheet erosion is the detachment of the material from the land surface by raindrop impact and its subsequent removal by prechannel or overland flow. Channel erosion is the removal and transport of material by concentrated flow. The total amount of sheet and channel erosion in a watershed is known as the gross erosion. All eroded materials in a watershed do not get into the stream system. Particles detached on comparatively level areas, with little or no surface runoff, for example, move only short distances and consequently are not transported downstream. Some material may be carried to the stream system, only to be deposited on flood plains, and some may be deposited in the form of bar materials in the channels themselves. The total amount of eroded material which does complete the journey from source to a downstream control point, such as a reservoir, is known as the sediment yield. The ratio between the amount of sediment yield and the gross erosion in a watershed is called the sediment delivery ratio (Water, 1955).

Size of drainage area is a most important consideration in respect to the total yield of sediment from a watershed. The important topographic features which appear to influence the delivery ratios and sediment-production rates are the degree and length of watershed slopes and the channel density of the watershed. The delivery ratio of sediment is much higher for steep watersheds with well-defined channels than it is for watersheds of low relief and poorly defined channels. Precipitation, in respect to amount, location, and seasonal distribution, influences both the sediment yield and the sediment-delivery ratio. Where high-intensity storms occur on watersheds at a time when cover conditions offer minimum protection against erosion, rates of gross erosion are high. Where maximum rainfall energy occurs during periods when the ground surface is frozen, lower rates of erosion prevail.

In most streams the finer part of the load (wash load) is limited by its availability in the watershed. The coarser part of the load (bed load material), the part which is more difficult to move by flowing water, is limited in its rate by the transporting ability of the flow between the source and a particular cross section of the stream. In any channel with a given sediment bed the bed material load is a function of the flow called the bed-load function. Values of the bed-load function can be determined by direct measurement of the load. Such load measurements show large variations with time and the location on the bed. In constrast to the bed material load, the wash load is represented in the streambed only in very small amounts. In most rivers wash load constitutes the predominant bulk of the sediment load. As a rough estimate, it is between 80 to 90 percent of the total load.

The sediment supply from a watershed is usually not a function of the stream discharge. At the beginning of a storm the water may find much more loose material ready to move than at the end of the storm. A winter storm may find entirely different watershed conditions from those of a summer storm. One tributary may contribute a much higher sediment concentration than another, making the sediment supply dependent on the exact location of the storm center.

Where a river discharges into a lake or ocean, it deposits its sediment in the form of a delta, continually extending the length of the river channel. With the lake or ocean at a constant level, the slope in the channel is constantly reduced, causing deposition. In many rivers tectonic elevation changes cause changes of the river slopes, which the river counteracts by deposition of scour. Change of land use in the watershed or change of climate may gradually change the sediment supply. Similar effects stem from forest fires in mountainous areas. All such changes of supply call for the adjustment of the channel slope or section. The construction of reservoirs in the watershed may change both the sediment supply and the hydrology of the stream, calling for readjustment of the bed-load function to new conditions. Improvements of the river channel upstream may prevent local flooding and deposit of sediment, but often cause the sediment load and the flood heights to increase in the downstream (Leet and Judson, 1965).

Sediments in general are classified according to size, specific weight, shape, mineralogical composition, color, and other aspects. With respect to its movement by the water, the grain size is the most important factor since it causes the widest range of mobility. The gravel and boulders may be expected to move predominantly as bed load, while silt and clays move predominantly in suspension. The sand will undergo both types of motion. Only few sediments have sufficiently different specific gravities to cause a significant change of their property of being moved. The movement of flocculated particles is governed by the size and bulk density of the flocks, but not of the minerals. The various shapes of sediment grain have little influence on the ability to move. Only for some very flat materials such as mica is their property to be moved by water significantly dependent on their particle shape. Sediment grains in the bed layer are not vertically supported by the flow, but rest on the bed almost continuously while sliding, rolling, and jumping along.

As a part of the hydrologic investigation of a watershed, it is often necessary to determine the sediment load passing a given stream section. This information is required for the prediction of the useful life span of proposed reservoirs, and may also be required for the design of other flood-control structures such as the height of levees, the depth of footings of levees, bridge and other foundations, and the proper width of regulated river sections. For the bed material load it is required to measure the rate at which grains of various sizes of the bed move along the channel. This movement is either as bed load only or partially as bed load and partially as suspended load. The bed material load is a function of the discharge and channel characteristics and is generally calculated.

Sediment measurement
Samplers in general use for bed material load are of several types: box, or basket type; pan type; pressure-difference type; and structure type. The box-type, or basket-type sampler consists essentially of a perforated container as a catcher. The pan-type sampler is a wedge-shaped box, with the downstream half of the top surface open to catch the sample. The pressure-difference type is a sampler of improved design which provides a larger exit than entrance in order to reduce the flow disturbance at the upstream side and approximate and intake velocity to that of the stream. The structure-type sampler is designed for measurements of long intervals of time. It is a permanent struc-

ture built in a small stream or canal for taking intermittent or continuous records of the total rate of transport. The usual design consists of open or grated depressions on the bottom of the channel at the end of an essentially uniform reach. The materials settled and collected in the depressions are withdrawn for measurement by pumping or sluicing.

The calculation of the bed material load in a given channel requires knowledge of the bed composition. Bed sampling under flowing water is very difficult because of the danger of losing the fine particles. Clamshell and similar grabbing devices are often used. Also, bucket-type samplers have been used, which will sample the bed as they are dragged over it. Empirical formulas are used to determine the sediment load as a function of the bed composition and the flow (Linsley and Franzini, 1964).

Modern samplers for measuring wash load are depth-integrating and point-integrating samplers. A series of depth-integrating samplers have been developed. A typical sampler of the series consists of a streamlined case carrying a standard milk bottle as a sample collector. At a uniform speed, the sampler is lowered to the bottom of the stream and then raised to the surface. The sample thus collected is an intergrated quantity, with the relative portion collected at any depth in proportion to the velocity at that depth. The point-integrating sampler is designed to collect continuously at a given point over an interval of time. It is generally used in deep swift streams, where the depth-integrating sampler is unsuitable.

It is still impossible to make consistent and accurate measurements of the amounts of debris being transported as bed load in natural rivers. Instruments have long been in use that measured adequately the sediment being transported in suspension, but bed load, being concentrated in a thin zone near the stream bottom, is interrupted by the insertion of an obstacle, no matter how streamlined. The insertion of a sampling device at the stream bed changes the conditions of transport locally in such a manner that a representative sample of the bed load in transport is impossible. Though rates of bed load transport can be successfully measured in experimental flumes, the conditions represented in the laboratory are much more limited than those in the field.

FLOOD CONTROL

Floods for design purposes may be measured hydraulically or determined hydrologically. Floods are measured as to height, area inundated, peak discharge, and volume of flow. The height of the flood is of interest to those planning to build structures along or across streams; the area inundated is of interest to those planning to occupy the flood plains; the peak discharge is of interest to those designing spillways, bridges, culverts, and flood channels; and the volume of flow is of interest to those designing storage works for irrigation, water supply, and flood control. The height of a flood may be measured at a point, as at a gage in a fixed location, or in a reach, as is defined by a profile along one or both banks. The area inundated is measured by outlining the edge of water on a map (Linsley and Franzini, 1964).

The time that a stream remains at flood stage is important in many instances. A high peak of short duration usually has a relatively small volume of flow and may be completely controlled by a reservoir, while a lower peak of long duration and large volume will not be controlled by a reservoir of the same size. Many roads are built across flood plains on low embankments that will be overtopped by the higher floods. It is important to know how long the road will be flooded. The design of flood walls and embankments must consider only the height of the flood peak. The design of storage reservoirs must also consider the volume of flood flow. The duration of flood peaks varies widely; some rise and recede within hours, while others remain at a high stage for days. The peak discharge is computed from empirical formulas, from a frequency concept, or from flood records. Knowledge of the magnitude and probable frequency of recurrence of floods is necessary to the proper design and location of many flood structures. Either overdesign or underdesign of the structure involves excessive costs on a long-time basis.

The maximum probable flood has been defined as the largest flood for which there is any reasonable expectancy in this climatic era. This is a very large flood and seldom would be used in design except for reservoir spillways, where failure could lead to great damage and loss of life. The determination of the maximum probable flood involves a detailed study of storm patterns, transposition of storms to a position that will give maximum runoff, and computation of the maximum flood by the unit-hydrograph method. A design flood is the flood adopted for the design of a structure after consideration of economic and hydrologic factors. It is seldom economically practicable to design for the maximum probable flood and not for the maximum of record. The design flood is usually selected by exercise of engineering judgement after consideration of the pertinent facts.

Flood routing has been defined as the procedure whereby the time and magnitude of a flood wave at a point on a stream is determined from the known or assumed data at one or more points upstream. Flood routing may be considered under two broad but somewhat related types, namely, reservoir routing and open-channel routing. The former type provides methods for evaluating the modifying effects on a flood wave passing through a reservoir. In design and planning it applies to the determination of the location and capacity of reservoirs, of the size of outlet structures and spillways, etc. Open-channel routings are used to determine the time and magnitude of flood waves in rivers, to develop design elevations for flood walls and levees, to estimate benefits from completed or proposed reservoirs, etc.

All flood routing-methods are based on some knowledge of the river reach under consideration. The knowledge may be as meager as maps defining topographic features, with no record of floods, or it may include a rather complete history of floods, profiles, cross sections, etc. Generally, routing procedures are based on the relationship between stage and storage or discharge and storage. Two methods are available for developing this relationship. The first involves the determination of volumes of storage at different levels from valley cross sections or detailed topographic maps. The second method, more commonly used, determines the storage volumes by the analysis of floods of record, assuming that the relationships established by the record will be valid for future floods. Data required for this analysis are the flow records at the upstream, downstream, and tributary stations, as well as the precipitation records for the ungaged areas.

The World of Water

Dams

The first dam for which there are reliable records was built on the Nile River sometime before 4000 B.C. It was used to divert the Nile and provide a site for the ancient city of Memphis. This dam is no longer in existence. The oldest dam still in use is the Almanza Dam in Spain, which was constructed in the sixteenth century. Dams are constructed to create retention or detention water storage or to maintain a static water-surface level. Examples of retention reservoirs are those designed to store water for such purposes as irrigation; municipal, industrial, and domestic water supply; and hydropower. These reservoirs accumulate water during periods of plentiful supply and store it for relatively long periods of time, to be used when the demand exceeds supply. Detention reservoirs are those designed for flood-prevention purposes, groundwater recharge, and other purposes where storage is of temporary nature, and release rates are regulated to provide downstream discharge rates in accordance with the objectives of the project. Dams which do not depend on carryover storage for proper functioning include run-of-the-river dams to create head for power purposes; water-diversion structures; debris dams; and dams to control water levels for other purposes, such as navigation and erosion control (Linsley and Franzini, 1964). A dam on a stream channel changes the hydraulic characteristics of flow and the sediment-transport capacity. In the process of adjusting to the equilibrium for the new conditions, additional problems may be created, both upstream and downstream from the structure.

Dams are classified on the basis of the type and materials of construction as gravity, arch, buttress, and earth-fill. The first three types are usually constructed of concrete. A gravity dam depends on its own weight for stability and is usually straight in plan although sometimes slightly curved. Arch dams transmit most of the horizontal thrust of the water behind them to the abutments by arch action, and may have thinner cross sections than comparable gravity dams. Arch dams can be used only in narrow canyons where the walls are capable of withstanding the thrust produced by the arch action. The simplest of the many types of buttress dams is the slab type, which consists of sloping flat slabs supported at intervals by buttresses. Earthfill dams are embankments of rock or earth with some provision for controlling seepage by means of an impermeable core or upstream blanket. More than one type of dam may be included in a single structure. Curved dams may combine both gravity and arch action to achieve stability. Long dams often have a concrete river section containing spillway and sluice gates and earth or rock-fill wing dams for the remainder of their length. The selection of the best type of dam for a given site is a problem in both engineering feasibility and cost.

A spillway is the safety valve for a dam. It must have the capacity to discharge major floods without damage to the dam or any appurtenant structures, at the same time keeping the reservoir level below some predetermined maximum level. An overflow spillway is a section of dam designed to permit water to pass over its crest. Overflow spillways are widely used on gravity, arch, and buttress dams.

River forecasting

Water-control structures such as dams, levees, etc., offer a positive method of reducing or eliminating the damages caused by flooding. In numerous situations, however, topographic and/or economic factors make the control of floods impracticable or unjustifiable. In these situations river forecasting provides an alternative means of reducing flood damage and loss of life. Advance warning of an approaching flood permits evacuation of people, livestock, and equipment. The warning time available determines how much evacuation is possible. River forecasts are required for estimating inflow to reservoirs in order to permit the most efficient operation for flood control or other purposes. In addition, there is an increasing demand for day to day forecasts of river stages and discharges by those interested in navigation, water supply, stream pollution, and many other related fields (Linsley and Franzini, 1964).

The tools of the river forecaster include rainfall-runoff relations, unit hydrographs, routing methods, recession curves, and stage-discharge relations. Because of the importance of the time factor, great stress must be placed on the development of forecast procedures that will enable flood warnings to be issued at the earliest possible time. Methods for collection and handling of basic data, preparation of forecasts, and dissemination of these forecasts must be carefully organized in order to speed the operation and minimize human and mechanical errors. A warning received too late to permit evacuation of people and removal of property from the threatened area is of no value.

A forecasting service is dependent on adequate data. The primary data required operationally are precipitation, snow on the ground, air temperature, and river stage or discharge. The number of reporting stations depends upon hydrologic need and availability of observers and communications. Where adequate data are available and forecasts of the complete hydrograph are required, a reasonably standardized approach to river forecasting has been developed. Rainfall-runoff relations are used to estimate the amount of water expected to appear in the streams, while unit hydrographs and streamflow-routing procedures, in one form or another, are utilized to determine the time distribution of water at a forecast point. Stage-discharge relations are utilized to convert these flows to stages.

HYDROELECTRIC PLANTS

Hydroelectric plants may be classified as run-of-river storage, or pumped-storage. A storage-type plant is one with a reservoir of sufficient size to permit carry-over storage from the wet season to the dry season and to develop a firm flow substantially more than the minimum natural flow. A run-of-river plant generally has very limited storage capacity and can use steamflow with little or no direct storage. Some run-of-river plants have enough storage (called pondage) to permit storing water during off-peak hours for use during peak hours of the same day. Run-of-river plants are suitable only for streams which have a sustained flow during the dry season or where other reservoirs upstream provide the necessary storage (Linsley and Franzini, 1964).

A pumped-storage plant generates power for peak load, but, at off peak, water is pumped from the tailwater pool to the headwater pool for future use. The pumps are powered with secondary power from some other plant in the system, often a run-of-river plant where water would otherwise be wasted over the spillway. Under certain conditions a pumped-storage plant will be an economic addition to a power system. It serves to increase the load factor of other plants in the system and provides added capacity to meet peak loads. A unique feature of some pumped-storage plants is that very little water is required for their operation. Once the headwater and tailwater pools are filled, only enough water is needed to take care of evaporation and seepage. Pumped-storage plants have been widely used in Europe, especially in Germany.

A hydroelectric development ordinarily includes a diversion structure, a conduit (penstock) to carry water to the turbines and governing mechanism, generators, control and switching apparatus, housing for the equipment, transformers and transmission lines to the distribution centers. In addition, trash racks at entrance to the conduit, canal and penstock gates, a forebay, or surge tank, and other appurtenances may be required. A tailrace, or waterway, from the powerhouse back to the river must be provided if the powerhouse is situated so that the draft tubes cannot discharge directly into the river. No two power developments are exactly alike, and each has its own unique problems of design and construction. The type of plant best suited to a given site depends on many factors, including head, available flow, and general topography of the area.

WATER SUPPLY AND SEWAGE

The first step in the design of a waterworks system is a determination of the quantity of water that will be required, with provision for the estimated requirements of the future. Next a reliable source of water must be located, and finally a distribution system must be provided. Usually water in a stream is not fit for drinking, and water purification facilities are ordinarily included as an integral part of the system (Linsley and Franzini, 1964).

To be safe for drinking, water must be free of disease-producing bacteria (pathogens). In addition, the water should not possess undesirable tastes, odors, color, turbidity, or chemicals. The principal waterborne diseases are typhoid fever, dysentery, and gastroenteritis. Between 1900 and 1950, deaths from typhoid fever in the United States dropped from 36 to 0·2 per hundred thousand of population. A substantial portion of this decrease resulted from improvement in purity of water supplies. Typhoid fever death rates in small communities are generally higher than in large cities because of the poorer supervision and control over the water supply of small towns.

Sewage consists almost entirely of water with a small amount of solids in solution or suspension. It usually contains disease bacteria and other harmful and obnoxious products. In the modern community, sewage is removed in underground conduits called sewers. The process of collecting sewage and delivering it to a disposal point is called sewerage, and the system of conduit and appurtenances for accomplishing this is known as a sewerage system. An adequate sewerage system and, when necessary, a sewage-treatment plant are of the greatest importance to the health and welfare of a community. Storm drains are designed to collect only storm runoff. A combined sewer conveys domestic and industrial sewage as well as storm water and must be designed to handle their peak flow. A sanitary sewer carries only domestic sewage and industrial waste (Linsley and Franzini, 1964).

When raw sewage is discharged into a body of water, sewage solids may be washed up on shore near the point of disposal, where they decompose and create unpleasant odors. In addition, the sewage will contaminate the water with pathogenic bacteria. Thus, even though sanitary sewage is about 99.9 percent water, it often requires treatment if nuisance is to be avoided. The required degree of treatment depends on the character and strength of the sewage and the disposal facilities. A small community at the seaside might discharge untreated sewage directly into the ocean without any ill effect, but if this city were located inland on a small stream, the sewage might require a high degree of treatment, particularly during the season of low flow.

The organic matter in sewage is unstable and decomposes readily through chemical and bacterial action. Fresh sewage generally contains two to four millegrams per liter of free oxygen. In the process of aerobic decomposition this free oxygen is rapidly consumed by the action of aerobic and facultative bacteria on the organic matter in the sewage. Within 20 or 30 minutes the free oxygen is used up, and anaerobic bacteria begin to act on the organic matter. During the process of anaerobic decomposition (putrefaction) the complex organic compounds are broken down into simpler forms, and gases such as hydrogen sulfide (H_2S), ammonia (NH_3), carbon dioxide

(CO_2), and methane (CH_4) are produced. The final step in the decomposition of sewage is oxidation, in which oxygen absorbed from the air combines to form sulfates, nitrates, and other stable and unobjectionable compounds. Several types of bacteria found in sewage are dangerous because they produce disease. Most bacteria found in sewage, however, are important aids in the process of sewage decomposition. Biochemical sewage-treatment processes rely on an accelerated natural cycle of decay, and the objective of treatment-plant design is generally to provide an environment favorable to the action of the aerobic and anaerobic bacteria that stabilize the organic matter in the sewage.

Ordinary sanitary sewage contains between 500 and 1000 mg/l of solid matter. Sewage-treatment processes utilize biological, chemical, and physical means to remove a portion of these solids and to transform them to forms which will be safe for disposal. The solids in a sewage sample consist of insoluble or suspended solids and soluble compounds dissolved in the water. The suspended-solids content is found by filtering the sewage sample. About 60 percent of the solids in an average sewage are dissolved. Some of the suspended solids settle quite rapidly, but those of colloidal size settle rather slowly or not at all.

The most important chemical test of sewage is the test for biochemical oxygen demand (BOD). If adequate oxygen is available, aerobic decomposition of sewage will continue until no oxidizable matter is left. The amount of oxygen consumed in this process is the BOD. Polluted water will continue to absorb oxygen for many months, and it is impracticable to determine the ultimate oxygen demand of sewage. The standard test for BOD consists in diluting a sewage sample with water containing a known amount of dissolved oxygen and noting the loss in oxygen after the sample has stood for 5 days at 20°C. The rate at which BOD is satisfied (deoxygenation) depends on the temperature and the residual oxygen demand. It is generally assumed that the average BOD of domestic sewage is 0·17 lb/day per capita, excluding industrial wastes. This figure of 0·17 lb/day is often used to compute the population equivalent of industrial waste. Many cities base their charges for treatment of industrial waste at least partly on the computed population equivalent. The dissolved oxygen is the effluent from a sewage-treatment. If there is no dissolved oxygen, the BOD has not been satisfied and decomposition is still proceeding. After sewage has passed through a treatment plant, it is often chlorinated. Other tests of sewage include tests for pH, free ammonia, organic nitrogen, nitrates, nitrites, and chlorides (Linsley and Franzini, 1964).

If a large supply of diluting water with adequate dissolved oxygen is available, the BOD of the sewage can be satisfied without odorous conditions developing. The solubility of oxygen in water depends on the temperature. At high temperatures, when the bacterial action is most rapid, the solubility of oxygen is reduced. Hence conditions in a polluted stream will be worse in warm weather, particularly if it coincides with the low-flow stream. Oxygen deficit is the difference between the actual oxygen content of the water and the saturation content at the water temperature. When polluted water is exposed to air, oxygen is absorbed to replace the dissolved oxygen that is consumed in supplying the BOD of the sewage. The processes of reoxygenation and deoxygenation go on simultaneously. If deoxygenation is more rapid than reoxygenation, an oxygen deficit results. If the dissolved oxygen content becomes zero, aerobic conditions will no longer be maintained and putrefaction will set in. The amount of dissolved oxygen at any time can be determined if the rates of reoxygenation and deoxygenation are known. Knowledge of the rates of deoxygenation and reoxygenation is of practical value in predicting the oxygen content at any point along a polluted stream. It permits an estimate of the degree of sewage treatment required, or of the amount of dilution necessary, in order to maintain a certain dissolved oxygen content in the stream.

If sewage is discharged into a stream with inadequate dissolved oxygen, the water downstream of the outfall will be turbid and dark. Sludge will be deposited on the stream bed, and anaerobic decomposition will occur. The dissolved oxygen content will decrease downstream, and a zone of putrefaction may occur from which hydrogen sulfide and ammonia and other odorous gases will arise. Since fish require a minimum of 4 mg/l of dissolved oxygen, there will be no fish life in this portion of the stream. Farther downstream the water will become clearer and the dissolved oxygen content will increase until visual observation indicates no pollution.

Several processes transform sewage discharges into water into a stable and unobjectionable form. An ample quantity of diluting water helps to assure the presence of free oxygen. This permits aerobic bacteria to play an active role in the decomposition of the sewage. Aerobic conditions will be enhanced if the stream is turbulent and reoxygenation is rapid. In some instances mechanical agitators have been used to put oxygen into streams, rivers, and ponds. Sedimentation of sewage solids on the stream bed permits anaerobic bacterial action. Finally sunlight kills bacteria and stimulates growth of algae which produce oxygen and hence aid in the oxidation process.

There are two general methods of disposing of sewage, dilution, or disposal in water, and irrigation, or disposal on land. Disposal by dilution is the more common of the two methods. Disposal by dilution in a lake or estuary or in the ocean depends very much on the currents near the outfall. If these currents are not sufficient to mix the sewage with an adequate volume of diluted water, undesirable conditions will develop. Dilution in salt water is less effective than dilution in fresh water because at the same temperature salt water can contain only about 80 percent as much dissolved oxygen as fresh water. The higher specific gravity of the salt water also retards sedimentation slightly.

There are many different ways to treat sewage. Treatment processes are classified as primary, secondary, or tertiary processes. Primary treatment consists solely in separating a portion of the suspended solids from the sewage. This is usually accomplished by screening and sedimentation in settling basins. The separated solids are conveyed to a tank where they are decomposed by bacterial action and the liquid effluent is disposed of by irrigation or dilution. The liquid effluent from primary treatment will ordinarily contain considerable organic material and will have a relatively high BOD. Secondary treatment involves further treatment (or oxidation) of the effluent from a primary treatment process. This is generally accomplished through biological processes using filters, aeration, oxidation ponds, and other means. The effluent from secondary treatment will usually have little oxygen demand and may even contain several milligrams per liter of dissolved oxygen. Tertiary treatment is often accomplished by passing the effluent from secondary treatment through a fine sand filter. The choice of treatment methods depends on several factors, including the disposal facilities available. Actually the distinction between primary and secondary treatment is rather arbitrary since many modern treatment methods incorporate both sedimentation and oxidation in the same operation (Linsley and Franzini, 1964).

The treatment of industrial wastes often presents special problems because toxic metals and other chemicals may hinder or destroy the bacterial activity depended upon in most treatment processes. Certain organic wastes impart undesirable tastes and odors. Often it is advantageous to require preliminary treatment of the wastes at the industrial plant before discharge into the public sewer. Such treatment usually includes screening and chemical sedimentation. Occasionally a large or remotely located industry must provide complete treatment of its wastes. In most instances, however, industrial wastes are combined with domestic wastes.

Chapter 8

Water-based Recreation and Wildlife

In the past in many parts of the world, few people have had any real leisure. All their efforts were or are required to produce food, clothing, shelter, and the other necessities of life. Only the very rich or the privileged classes have had much leisure. Rising productivity has enabled many to increase their material standard of living while at the same time making it possible to have leisure time for play, relaxation, enjoyment, and personal self-fulfillment. Some leisure is used for outdoor recreation. People of all ages, both sexes, all income levels, all occupations, and of a variety of other characteristics, now take part in outdoor recreation. The kinds of outdoor recreation most people take part in today are relatively simple: walking and driving for pleasure, playing outdoor games and sports, swimming, sightseeing, picnicking, fishing, bicycling, boating and hunting.

Water is a prime factor in most outdoor recreation activities; water also enhances recreation on land. Choice camping sites and picnic areas are usually those adjacent to or within sight of a lake or stream, and a pond or marsh enriches the pleasures of hiking or nature study. The demand for water-based recreation is increasing more rapidly than the demand for outdoor recreation in general. Swimming, for example, appears likely to be the most popular outdoor activity by the end of the century. Some of the most difficult problems of water management and development that nations will face in the next generation involve the use of water for recreation. In the pursuit of recreation there is a large economic turnover of money and goods. An important segment of the economy is stimulated by and derives gains from the financial resources of the recreationist (Clawson, 1963).

Until recently very little was known of the private lives of fishes, the animals that dominate the underwater realm. But modern scientific developments have opened new underwater vistas. Diving vehicles capable of exploring the ocean bottom, electronic devices to measure the movements and habits of fishes, improved underwater techniques, and specially equipped vessels for studying the science of the sea and the science of fresh waters are now available. Fishes are almost ubiquitous and virtually numberless. In the ocean they live at all levels from shallow depths down to the cold, sunless deep waters. In fresh waters, they range from the tropical well-lit hill-streams to the dark and cool recesses of the deepest lakes.

A good many species, whether by breathing close to the surface, or through the acquisition of air-breathing organs, exist in stagnant, tropical swamps. Whatever move they make, whether in exploring their surroundings, taking food, evading enemies, migrating, courting, mating, and so forth, fishes cleave through a medium that is eight hundred times denser than air. The more streamlined they are the less energy is lost in overcoming the resistance of water. Fishes have adopted many different, though essentially similar, ways of using their fins and bodies (Hylander, 1964).

Everything that swims or lives in the water is not a fish even though it may be called so. Jellyfish, for instance, are not fishes but softbodied animals known as coelenterates, a group that includes the corals and sea anemones. Starfish likewise are not fishes but members of another group known as echinoderms to which sea urchins and sand dollars also belong. Shellfish are not fishes, either. Some, like crabs, are crustaceans; others are mollusks, such as clams. There also are water-dwellers that look like fishes but are really sea-going mammals—the porpoises and whales.

Fishes are significant in many ways. Of all the forms of wildlife they are by far the greatest single source of food. Fisheries provide much of the human diet in many parts of the world. Fishes also play a key role in recreation. Millions of men and women of all ages spend countless hours pursuing elusive game fishes. Some fishes, because of their appearance or interesting habits, are popular as aquarium animals, bringing a new kind of nature into the home.

Fishes are aquatic, gill-breathing, cold-blooded vertebrates, which bear fins that are stayed by an inner skeleton of rod-like fin-rays. A fish has an internal skeleton of cartilage or bone which places a fish in the same category as the other back-boned animals: the amphibians, reptiles, birds, and mammals. Jellyfish, starfish, and shellfish lack such an internal skeleton. A fish belongs to the vertebrate group of animals, a large and important assemblage in which is man himself. A fish is equipped with special respiratory organs known as gills by which it can breathe under water. Oxygen is essential for every living organism, and the chief source of oxygen available to a fish is the air dissolved in the water. Water, taken in through the mouth, passes over the gills in the back of the throat. In the gills, dissolved air passes from the water into the blood. An aquatic organism with gills is perfectly adapted for staying under water continuously. On the other hand, an animal with lungs, be it an alligator, a loon, or a whale, must come to the surface periodically to breathe. Gill-breathing is a handicap to living on land; yet some fishes can survive for long periods breathing air if the gills are kept moist.

A fish has paired appendages in the form of fins. With only a few exceptions, such as lampreys, two sets of paired appendages are typical of fishes, as they are of most vertebrates. The fins of a fish are such paired appendages. A fin lacks the framework of jointed bones that attaches a limb to the body. Fins also lack terminal digits, such as fingers in humans, and the muscles that enable the limb to be used in locomotion. All fishes have a head and a definite brain, which is protected and connected by nerves to elaborate sense organs—the eyes, ears, nasal organs, taste buds, tactile endings, and lateral line system. The axial framework of the trunk and tail is the vertebral column, which forms the inner attachment of nested series of muscles segments. Most fishes move by the activity of these muscles. The fins are used as propellors, rudders, stabilizers, brakes, hydroplanes, or even as limbs. The tail fin is the most versatile, for it may serve all of the first four functions. The body of a fish is covered with scales. Scales are an ideal body covering that provides protection, at the same time permitting the flexibility essential in a swimming animal. Only a few kinds of fishes, notably the moray eel and cat-fish, lack scales (Marshall, 1966).

The migration of birds has been observed with awe or curiosity over the centuries. Only in this century, however, when it became painfully clear that nature's bounty was in serious danger of depletion, did man begin to take inventory of this resource, to give thought to preserving its habitat, and to study the many aspects of the requirements and values of waterfowl.

The many species of swans, geese, and ducks that frequent continental areas share certain broad similarities: all have webbed feet; more or less wide, flat bills; short legs and tails; and rather long necks. All can live in a watery environment of one sort or another. Each species of ducks, geese, and swans has different requirements for food and cover plants. The requirements change with the season and with daily changes in weather. The best waterfowl marsh must meet the varied food and cover requirements of many species during the time the birds are present. The species utilize nearly every available aquatic habitat, from ocean surf to inland pothole; from arctic sea to semitropical lagoon. Each species has its own unique set of habits and adaptations, of food preferences, nest sites, migration pattern, general distribution, and local habitat. The amount of open water needed varies with the season and species of ducks and geese. Natural wetlands are the backbone of waterfowl production. Several management devices permit the maximum recreational use of waterfowl consistent with its perpetuation. One is the establishment of wildlife refuges, on which proper conditions can be maintained. They permit man to control part of the distribution of the birds and the rate of their movement southward from their nesting places to their wintering grounds (Linduska, 1964).

There are many species of wild creatures that often are seen at watering places, the frogs and other amphibians that must spend a part of their life cycle in water, and those, like the beaver, that are in and out of the water. The need of wild animals for water varies. Some apparently obtain all they need from the succulent vegetation or soft-bodied insects they eat. Many terrestrial animals like deer, elk, and moose require clear, open water for drinking. Others like quail and pheasant are able to meet their water needs from dew and by eating available succulent plants and fruits. Resident animals which inhabit swamps, marshes, sloughs, lakes, ponds, streams, and ditches include some of the most important fur-bearing animals. To this group belong the muskrat, beaver, mink, otter, and racoon. These wildlife do much of their feeding either along the margins of water areas or in the adjacent agricultural land. Skunks, foxes, and weasels invade waterfowl breeding, feeding, and hunting grounds. Coyotes and bobcats work around the wetlands. Blackbirds and crows sieve through grain crops, or compete with ducks for water bugs, crawdads, and fairy shrimps. Simultaneous occupation of wetlands by furred and feathered faunas lends both aid and attrition to the birds. The water needs of aquatic or semiaquatic animals like fish, frogs, ducks, geese, and swans are readily apparent.

As a class, the reptiles are represented in marine and fresh waters and the intermediate estuary. The Galapagos iguana is the only marine lizard. Snakes are common in estuaries. A few snakes are fully marine, being found in the open seas. Crocodiles inhabit fresh waters and estuaries. Turtles occur in both marine and freshwater environments, but there is apparently little mixing of the two faunas in the estuary. The aquatic reptiles are primarily carnivorous, although some freshwater turtles feed upon plants to a certain extent.

The number of insects known to spend part, or all, of their lives in fresh waters exceed 5,000 species. Included in this figure is a great array of forms exhibiting a remarkable variety of adaptations to all types of fresh waters. Waterbased insects include: the stoneflies, dragonflies, mayflies, alderflies, dobsonflies, and spongeflies. Stonefly nymphs are common inhabitants of swift, cool streams and the shores of temperate lakes. The beetle order is represented in fresh waters by a variety of forms which have aquatic larvae, terrestrial pupae, and aquatic adult stages. Another order includes a vast number of insects such as the midges, houseflies, mosquitoes, blackflies, and craneflies. The nymphs of mayflies are common inhabitants of most streams and standing water containing sufficient oxygen. Lakes contain burrowing types and bottom dwellers. The larvae of alderflies, dobsonflies, and spongeflies are found widely, though usually not abundantly, in lakes, ponds, and streams (Reid, 1961).

WATER FOR OUTDOOR RECREATION

A great deal of outdoor recreation requires or uses water.

However, this use does not consume water in the same sense that irrigation consumes water. Recreation is often dependent upon a body of water or upon a flowing stream of water. A substantial proportion of all water bodies is used for recreation to some degree.

As with land, the usefulness of water for outdoor recreation hinges on three factors: proximity to population, physical and legal accessibility and suitability for recreation purposes. For certain kinds of uses (sailboating), the principal requirement is one of distribution in space of the water resource; for another type of use it may be distribution in a time which is most important (white water canoeing). In still a third type of use, (swimming), the principal requirement may be one of water quality.

Data suggest that the intensity of recreational use is governed to a large degree by the general character of the region itself, relative to availability of recreational waters, the concentration of population, and the distance from urban centers. If water bodies are few in a given area, use may be very intensive despite obvious disadvantages of a widely fluctuating water level, local competition, crowding of access points, and other adverse factors (Outdoor Recreation, 1962).

Each year as Social Security and retirement systems affect more people, more of the older population group have funds to finance recreation. Trends in industry and business are toward shorter workdays, shorter workweeks, and longer vacation periods, frequently with full pay benefits. The recent rise in family incomes in many parts of the world since 1939 has been phenomenal and has made it possible for a steadily increasing number of families to finance annual vacations. The increasing importance of recreation is revealed by statistics: the mileage of automobiles driven to recreational areas, the sales of sporting goods, the number of boats sold, and the number of people visiting national parks. As mobility continues to increase, more people travel farther to enjoy outstanding scenic, wildlife, and wilderness areas. Continuing transportation improvements, higher incomes, and longer vacations will result in increased pressures on high quality recreation resources that now seem remote from population centers. With the probable rise in total recreation activity in the future, intensity of use will almost certainly rise much further (Clawson, 1963).

Only about three or four percent of all leisure time is used for the outdoor recreation activity. This superficially very low figure results in part because about 40 percent of all leisure is daily leisure, after work or after school, during which it is often difficult for many people to get to an outdoor recreation area; and much leisure is at seasons when outdoor recreation is not attractive to the average person.

Excluding daily leisure, outdoor recreation occupies only about seven percent of the remaining leisure. An average person in the United States has about eleven days outdoor recreation on public areas or in hunting and fishing annually, six or more visits in local parks, about two days in intermediate areas, about one day on a more resource-based area, and about two days of fishing and hunting.

Recreational benefits connected with water-resource development have been difficult to evaluate, because they are not entirely comparable with the project benefits for which evaluation procedures are already available. It is obvious that the monetary value of recreation depends on the intensity of use. Mass recreation provides the greatest financial returns; specifically, the number of users or visitors per unit of time determines the financial gain. However, the intensity of recreational use of any area tends to reduce the quality of the recreation provided, in that the esthetic attributes are diminished in value in proportion to the intensity of use.

Of the many outdoor recreation environments, mountains, seacoasts, deserts, and woodlands, the shoreline appears to have an unusually strong appeal. Coastal areas provide opportunity for a wide variety of active or passive pleasures such as: surf-riding, skindiving (spearfishing, underwater exploration), beachcombing, coastal hunting and fishing, swimming, boating (motorboating, sailing, canoeing), water skiing, fishing, hiking, and walking, sunning, bird watching, horseback riding, picnicking, camping, photographing, sketching, painting, sightseeing (scenic, scientific, historical), and nature study (biological, geologic, botanical). While all of the shoreline has some recreation value, and the entire shoreline constitutes a recreation resource, not all of the shoreline is equally sought out for outdoor recreation. Of the three categories of shoreline, marsh, bluff, and beach, the latter is by far the most popular in present patterns of outdoor recreation activities (Outdoor Recreation, 1962).

An important difference between rivers and most other land resources for outdoor recreation depends on factors associated with the linear characteristic of rivers. Recreation in a wilderness area depends on the whole area, its flora, fauna, and topography, and its network of lakes and streams as a setting. Trails in a wilderness area are lines of access to that setting. A river, on the other hand, is both a primary part of the environment and the line of access. Often a fine sense of detachment from civilization is obtainable on rivers that are quite close to highways, farms, and even towns. By its very nature, a river can be a slim thread of undisturbed nature winding through well-developed countryside. Often the banks are high and overgrown with screening vegetation, or the river may run deep in a canyon, far removed from activity on the canyon's rim. Besides the physical screening effect of a river's topographic setting and flora, there seems to be a psychological screening effect induced by the river itself. In a wilderness area, a trail is usually unobtrusive, and the traveler's eye is drawn to the mountains, forests, lakes, and wildlife around him. By contrast, on a river, the traveler's attention is caught and focused by the river itself.

A large amount of water is now available for angling. Inland fresh waters within the 48 conterminous United States cover some 95,000 square miles. This water is in almost a million miles of streams and rivers and more than 100,000 natural lakes; 10 million surface acres of it are in artificial impoundments; and over half of the total area is in the Great Lakes.

Almost no large reservoirs have been created primarily or solely for recreation, but most of the reservoirs built for other purposes have significant recreation potentials. Even in the most arid regions, reservoirs have made water-based recreation available to large numbers of people.

Swimming is one of the most popular single outdoor recreation activities. Boating is normally done in combination with other activities, such as fishing, picnicking, and sightseeing. Swimming, sunbathing, picnicking, sightseeing, and camping also are often done in combination with boating. Racing both sailboats and motorboats is a popular sport. Paralleling closely the recent tremendous boom in boating is the increase in water skiing. A few short years ago, water skiing was seen only at exhibitions, in the movies, and on television. Now few lakes are without their water ski groups unless it is zoned against them (Outdoor Recreation, 1962).

The most intensively used portion of a lake is the area around an access point with boats going in and out of the water at all times of the day. Next might be picnic areas where families enjoy their picnicking between boating, skiing, or fishing expeditions out into the lake. More remote sections of shorelines also offer picnic sites, swimming, water skiing, and general enjoyment of the water away from the crowds. The least intensively used portion of the larger lakes is that area in the center, a mile or more from shore.

Summer, winter, and health resorts are among the most valued recreational land uses. In the majority of the larger parks accommodations of four kinds are provided to take care of the visitors: hotels, cabin camps, tourist cabins or motels, and tourist camping grounds.

Some people own land and water areas for their own use and enjoyment; these may be either solely for recreation, as a cottage at the seashore or in the mountains, or they may nominally be for other purposes, as a ranch or forest where the recreation value to the owner is a major consideration. Some land and water is owned by one individual but is used by others for recreation, on payment of a fee. Camping areas are thus provided in some circumstances. Permission to hunt upon private land may be sold by the owner of the land to other persons; in the U.S., game belongs to the state and cannot be sold, but permission to enter private land for hunting can be sold. Some large landowning companies, forest industry corporation and public utility companies, in particular, allow the general public to engage in outdoor recreation on their land often free of charge, and sometimes provide facilities for the comfort of the users. In these latter cases, recreation is usually not the only, or even primary, kind of land use, but is subordinate to other major land uses, such as forestry.

In recent years the growing interest of the public and public agencies in recreation and conservation has resulted in conflicts over the use of land and water resources. In projects built by governments, the demands of recreation have conflicted with the primary project purpose, whether the latter was power, flood control, or water supply. Some recreational uses, power boating, water skiing, swimming and fishing, conflict with each other.

The use of lakes, rivers, and reservoirs for recreational purposes is limited by certain factors. Among these limitations are impairment of water quality, lack of accessibility to the body of water, variation on water level, and conflicts of both use and economic interest. Water quality requirements for recreation consist of three classes: water used for swimming and bathing, water used for aquatic life, and water used for camping and boating. Adequate water quality for recreation can be maintained by administrative devices such as pollution control laws and governmental agencies and industry regulation.

There are three major outdoor recreation areas. At one end of the scale are the user-oriented areas. These are characterized by their close proximity to the residences of their users. City parks of all kinds are major examples of this type. Such areas have only modest requirements for natural resources; a relatively few acres, some of which are moderately well drained and reasonable level, will suffice for a playground or city park, for instance. Location of such areas is highly important; they must be near enough to where people live to be used in the time available, usually after school or after work. Playgrounds must ordinarily be within a half mile of where children live in order to be useful. Areas of this type are intensively used, with hundreds or thousands of visits per acre annually (Clawson, 1963).

Intermediate outdoor recreation areas are located farther from the users' homes, but usually within a distance (less than 100 miles) where they can be used readily for all-day outings. Some of these areas may be for general outdoor recreation activities, with emphasis upon activities. In the last two decades or so, particular interest has focused upon water-based recreation, and the most popular outdoor areas of the intermediate type usually include some water. In some instances, the water may be dominant and the surrounding area more or less incidental.

A third major type of outdoor recreation area is the resource-based. Here, primary emphasis is upon the natural or human qualities of the site, much less emphasis upon the activities of the site, and almost none on the location factor. One common type of such areas is the national park; here the emphasis is upon the unique natural characteristics of the area, which give it national significance. Such areas mostly lie at some distance from where most people live, hence fairly long travel is necessary to reach them; they are visited primarily during vacations. Other examples of resource-based areas are the outstanding historic sites, where early or present day man has carried on some activity which gives the spot special significance. Such sites are often small, only a few acres or less in extent. Among the natural areas, the degree of access may vary greatly, from many favorite spots in the most popular national parks which are accessible by auto, to the more remote wilderness areas which are accessible by pack-train, on foot, or by canoe (Clawson, 1963).

An outdoor recreation experience consists of five more or less separate phases: anticipation, travel to, on site, travel back, and recollection. Each of these is present in every outdoor recreation experience although their relative importance may vary greatly. Anticipation is the planning stage of an outdoor recreation experience. It takes place in the recreationist's home town, usually in his own home. This is when he decides where to go, when, with what equipment, for what specific activities, which members of the family will go, how long they will stay, and how much they can afford to spend. The planning may be careful and methodical, based upon ample accurate data; or it may be impressionistic, uninformed, mere wishful thinking; or it may be something intermediate. This is perhaps the most important stage of the whole experience, for what takes place later all has its origins here.

Travel to the actual recreation site is usually necessary. Travel may be short, as to a neighborhood playground or a city park; or it may be long, as when one visits a national park across the country; or it may be intermediate in length. For most outdoor recreation activities, travel to the site requires an appreciable proportion of the total time spent on the whole experience; often as much time is spent in travel as later is actually spent on the site. Considerable costs are also involved in this travel. Many people report sightseeing and travel as the chief attraction in their outdoor recreation experiences (Clawson, 1963).

On site experiences are those commonly thought of in connection with outdoor recreation. They run a gamut of specific activities: organized sports of all kinds, hunting and fishing, camping and picnicking, the variety of water sports, all sorts of specialized activities such as rock climbing and cave exploration, and much just plain resting and loafing. For the general outdoor recreation experience, participation is often on a family basis, and a variety of activities to appeal to different age and sex groups is essential.

Travel back is in some ways the counterpart of the travel to the area, but it may have important differences. The routes need not be the same, nor even the money spent. Perhaps most important of all, the recreationist and his family may approach this travel in a different spirit than they did travel to the site.

Recollection is the last of the major phases. Like the first, it takes place primarily in the recreationist's home town, in his home or office or in the homes of his friends. It may be supplemented by pictures taken on the trip, or by souvenirs brought back. No small part of the payoff of the whole experience takes place here; it is the memories that people carry with them that determines whether they will go back. Recollection of one experience gradually merges with planning for the next.

FISHES

All fish species are segregated in three categories or classes on the basis of their skeleton and type of mouth. All fishes with a skeleton of cartilage, or gristle, and with a mouth that lacks movable jaws are known as the jawless fishes. The fishes that have a cartilage-type of skeleton but possess a mouth with movable jaws are known as the cartilaginous fishes. Fishes with a skeleton of bone are known as bony fishes; bony fishes possess a mouth with movable jaws (Hylander, 1964; Marshall, 1966).

The jawless fishes are the most primitive of living vertebrates.

They are eel-like fishes with a circular suckerlike mouth. The slimy body lacks a covering of scales, which is typical of the other two classes of fishes. The gill chamber opens to the exterior by means of a series of pores, like small portholes along the side of the head. The most common representative of this class is the lamprey, a fish of both salt and fresh waters.

The cartilaginous fishes, a larger and more important class, are more advanced than the jawless fishes in structure and habits but in other ways are more primitive than the bony fishes. Cartilaginous fishes have a body covering of placoid scales; the gill chamber opens to the exterior by a series of slits on the side of the head or on its under surface; the mouth in most species has jaws well armed with sharp teeth. In addition, these fishes possess paired fins. All members of the class live in salt water only and reveal two trends in body design. In one group, which includes the sharks, the body is elongated and streamlined. The other body design, typical of the skates and rays, is that of a flattened body, triangular or circular when viewed from above.

The bony fishes form the largest and most varied group of living fishes. They make up the most familiar and common of the native fishes: the game fishes, food fishes, and aquarium fishes. Like the cartilaginous fishes, bony fishes have paired fins and mouths usually provided with teeth. They differ, however, in being covered with ganoid, cycloid, or ctenoid scales instead of placoid ones, and in having a single large opening on the side of the head, which leads into the gill chamber, protected by a gill flap. The most primitive group is that of the sturgeons with ganoid scales and a skeleton that consists mainly of cartilage with some bone. A second group includes the gars and their relatives, also with ganoid scales but with a skeleton made up of more bone and less cartilage. The third group includes all the remaining fishes with skeleton made up more completely of bone; they are known as the teleosts.

Fishes exhibit a greater range in size than any other group of vertebrates. A whale, the largest mammal, is only 500 times greater in length than the shrew, the smallest mammal. But the largest fish, a whale shark, is 2,000 times the size of the smallest fish, a Philippine goby. The undisputed giant among fishes is the tropical whale shark, reaching a length of over 40 feet and a weight of at least 13 tons. Sport fishermen consider that they have hooked a huge fish when they have landed a California sea bass measuring 7 feet and weighing 1,600 pounds. Heavyweights among saltwater fishes are: white sturgeon, black marlin, swordfish, bluefish tuna, ocean sunfish, manta, white shark, basking shark, and whale shark (Hylander, 1964; Marshall, 1966).

Freshwater fishes do not reach huge proportions. An angler considers he is battling a giant when he hooks a muskellunge 5 feet long and weighing 70 pounds. Even the mighty alligator gar grows to a length of only 9 feet, and a weight of 300 pounds. A large freshwater fish is the white sturgeon of the Pacific Coast waters. This champion attains a length of 12 feet and a weight of 1,300 pounds.

A tiny fish must have the same complex internal organization of bones, muscle, nerves, glands, and digestive organs as larger fish. The smallest fishes are found among the minnows, blennies, bogies, and killifishes. Blennies are common little fishes of tidal pools and floating masses of seaweed; they range in size from two to four inches. Midgets among fishes are: minnow, stickleback, dwarf herring, dwarf sea horse, seaweed blenny, naked goby, mosquitofish, least killifish, and pygmy Philippine goby (Hylander, 1964; Marshall, 1966).

Among the varying factors which affect the distribution of fishes are the chemical composition of the water (whether it is fresh, brackish, or salty), its temperature, and the amount of dissolved gases. The last two conditions are associated closely with the depth of the water and its rate of movement.

Marine fishes are four times more diverse than those of fresh waters, but the latter easily outnumber the species of deep-sea fishes, which have the largest living space on earth. Most fishes that live on an average from five to ten years, such as goldfish, salmon, trout, freshwater bream, pike, haddock, cod, herring, pilchards, and mackerel, keep growing after maturity.

Water forms about four-fifths of the weight of most fishes: extreme values range from about 50 to 90 percent. Most of the water is within or around the cells, but a small proportion, usually from two to ten percent of the body weight, is the fluid basis of blood and lymph.

Adequate amounts of dissolved oxygen and fish food, reasonable water temperatures, and the absence of toxic chemicals are prerequisites for sustenance of aquatic life. Fishes obtain oxygen by moving water over their gills. The oxygen diffuses from the water into the blood that flows in the gills where it is chemically caught by the haemoglobin of millions of red cells and then circulated as oxyhaemoglobin to all parts of the body. In most jawed fishes the respiratory current enters the mouth, and after flowing over the gills, is expelled backward through appropriate external openings. A fish breathes and feeds to acquire the energy needed for its daily activities. Much of this energy goes to the muscles used in swimming. Through the evolution of a gas-filled swimbladder, which keeps them weightless in water, most of the boney fishes have acquired a means of saving their breath. They can hover or swim at one level without using energy to stay at this level. Two living pumps are at work when a cartilaginous or a bony fish is breathing. Contraction of the mouth cavity, together with that of the gill pouches in sharks and rays, acts as a pressure pump to force water through the gills. The other kind of pump generates suction to draw water from the mouth cavity into compartments of the far side of the gills (Hylander, 1964; Marshall, 1966).

The scavengers feed on detritus, particles of broken-down organic matter that fall to ocean, stream, or lake beds. Many freshwater fishes feed on plants. Compared to the carnivorous species, they usually have a long intestine, suited to the slower digestion of plant material. In fresh waters, the small carnivorous fishes depend for much of their food on the aquatic larvae of insects, particularly on those of midges and mosquitoes. Catfishes are among the larger predators. The sizeable species take frogs, fish, and shrimps. Besides consuming flowering plants, many fishes feed on the algae that grow attached to such plants or to other suitable sites. Plankton-feeding fishes are more prominent in the ocean than in rivers and lakes. Certain freshwater fishes also depend on planktonic plants. In tropical coastal waters, garfishes, trumpet-fishes, groupers, barracuda, snappers, bluefish, and amber-jacks, and certain drum-fishes prey on small fishes and crustaceans.

As in other vertebrates, preliminary digestion of proteins takes place in an acid medium produced by the stomach. But a number of fishes have no stomachs; examples include lungfishes, sea-horses, and skippers. The food passes straight from the gullet into the intestine, where all the digestion occurs.

The diverse forms of fishes reflect both their ways of motion and their means of living. A deep-sea angler fish, who lures her prey to a trap-like mouth, has no need for the fine shape of a herring, much of whose life is spent in a search for its food, the plankton. The mouth of a fish may be located on the upper side of the head, at the top of a pointed snout, or on the under side. The teeth of fishes are not used for chewing, as a fish gulps its food whole. The chief function of teeth is to get a firm hold on slippery prey.

A fish is weightless in water if the capacity of its swimbladder is about five or seven percent of its body volume, depending on whether it is a marine or freshwater species. Ideally, the swimbladder must be kept inflated at this proper volume and a pressure equal to that of the surrounding water, which increase by one atmosphere, or 14.7 pounds per square inch, for a descent of 33 feet. A fish swimming very close to the surface will be subject to the pressure of the atmosphere, but if it dives to a depth of 33 feet, the pressure will increase to two atmospheres. At this depth the swimbladder will be compressed to half the volume it had at the surface.

Locomotion in fishes, as in all vertebrate animals, is brought about by contraction of muscles. These muscles are concentrated in the posterior part of a fish, chiefly in the tail region. Only a few muscles are found elsewhere, such as those that open and close the gill covers and move the jaws. Because the muscles make up most of the posterior portion of the body, the vital organs (liver, heart, digestive tract) are crowded into a small space behind the head. Muscle tissue or meat, of a fish is white or grayish in color due to the complete oxidation of food during muscular contraction. The muscle in deep-seated tissues is a darker brown in color. The pink color of salmon muscle is caused by a pigment derived from the small invertebrates on which salmon feed (Hylander, 1964; Marshall, 1966).

A fish swims by alternate contractions of the muscles segments, first on one side and then on the other. This brings about an undulation of the body, which is transmitted to the main propulsive organ, the tail. Wavelike undulation of the entire body is typical of slow-swimming fishes with cylindrical bodies, such as eels; this is the least effective way of utilizing the muscle contractions. Far more efficient is the side-to-side movement of the tail.

In many fishes propulsion is centered largely in the tail and tail fin, but in numerous species the tail and its fin are not the usual means of locomotion. Surgeon-fishes cruise by rowing with their pectoral fins, but use the tail if necessary. Trigger-fishes swim by a side-to-side flapping of their dorsal and anal fins, while in puffer-fishes, these two fins and the pectorals are used as propellors. Sea-horses, which have prehensile tails and and very small tail fin, swim by means of undulating along their pectoral and dorsal fins. The maximum observed speeds of fishes range from about half to forty-four miles an hour. A blue-fin tunny has been observed to travel at rates exceeding 40 miles per hour.

The unpaired fin along the back of a fish is the dorsal fin. Such a vertical fin gives stability to the elongated and often compressed body of a fish, which otherwise might roll from side to side. It also functions as a keel in keeping the fish on a steady course. A single dorsal fin characterizes many common fishes. This may be tall and situated far forward as in the swordfish; it may be located midway along the back as in trout; or it may be set far back near the tail as in muskellunge. Some fishes have several dorsal fins: in cod there are three; in barracuda, two. Many fishes have a dorsal fin consisting of two sections, a forward region stiffened with spines and a posterior soft-rayed portion. Fishes with this type of dorsal fin are known as spiny-rayed fishes.

The anal fin is an unpaired fin on the ventral side of the fish, between the anus and the tip of the tail. Most fishes have a small and single anal fin, in others it may be larger and more conspicuous. The cod has two anal fins, but in some fishes this fin is lacking entirely. A peculiar type of unpaired fin known as an adipose fin can be seen on the back of trout and catfish. This is a fleshy fin of small size located between the dorsal and tail fins.

Variations in the shape of the tail fin are useful in identifying fishes. In the majority the backbone does not extend into the tail fin, which is symmetrically lobed. In sharks and sturgeons, however, the tail fin consists of two lobes of unequal size, and the backbone extends into the enlarged upper lobe.

The paired fins of a fish correspond to the limbs of a land animal. The pectoral fins are the two fins that develop, one on either side of the forward end of the fish, near the head. The ventral fins, or pelvic fins, are also paired, but they are less constant in their position. In sturgeon and gar the ventral fins are set far back near the tail. In salmon and trout they are near the middle of the body. In members of the perch and sunfish families they are located far forward near the pectoral fins and below them. Paired fins are useful in balancing and leisurely swimming; during more rapid swimming the paired fins are folded back against the body. Slow movement of the paired fins enables the fish to remain motionless in spite of the tendency of the stream of water ejected from the gill openings to propel the fish forward. Perhaps the greatest value of the paired fins is their use of maneuvering, making precision movements, and acting as brakes in making quick stops (Hylander, 1964; Marshall, 1966).

Scales are nonliving structures produced by the skin of a fish. A fish's skin, unlike that of man, is made entirely of living cells. They can remain alive because the skin, being bathed by water, is rarely exposed to drying out. The fish's skin secretes a slime, or mucus, that produces the slippery surface so typical of most fishes. This acts as a lubricant, enabling the fish to slip through the water. It also protects the body against invasion by bacteria, fungi, and other disease-causing organisms present in water. Only in a few fishes are the scales eliminated entirely as in the catfish family. The number of scales on the body of a fish remains the same throughout its life. Thus, as the fish grows and its body increases in size, the individual scales also must increase in size. Scales reveal other details of life. In salmon they show how many years were spent at sea and how many times the individual has spawned. Even the length of the fish can be estimated from the size of a single scale.

Though water is much less transparent than air, fishes are long-sighted. Many deep-sea species have eyes that are superbly designed to see in dim surroundings, but some abyssal forms and cave-fishes are able to live without eyes. But no fish ever loses its ears. Fishes also have gained a distant water touch sense through the evolution of lateral line organs. The main use of these is in prompt, short-range detection and location of disturbances in the water, such as those stirred by moving prey, predators, associates and so forth. Many teleosts, including some that live near the deep-sea floor, are sound producers. Sound signals are a good means of communication on the dim and sunless waters. Fishes have also risen above visual restrictions through the evolution of light organs and electric organs. The former are most highly developed in teleosts that live in the twilight zones of the deep ocean. But light organs may be adapted to lure prey or confuse enemies as well as to flash signals. Through the discharges of their electric organs, fishes may not only keep in touch with each other, but also have a means for navigation and the location of prey or predators in turbid, tropical fresh waters (Hylander, 1964; Marshall, 1966).

Besides striving to maintain their health and vigour, fishes have ways of concealing and protecting their lives. One of the remarkable aspects of protective coloration is the ability of many fishes to change their color and pattern to match that of the surroundings.

Most fishes reproduce by eggs that are made fertile after they are laid. This is true despite the fact that fertilization is internal in sharks and rays. In no more than one kind of fish out of twenty-five are the eggs made fertile within the female. Fishes are not invariable male and female. Individuals of some kinds of sea-perch, maenids, and sea-bream are functional hermaphrodites; one fish can produce both ripe sperm and eggs. In the open ocean most kinds of fishes lay floating eggs. In coastal seas, especially in near-shore waters, many species have taken to nonbuoyant eggs. Such eggs are produced by nearly all of the fishes that live in estuaries, where sea and land waters meet. In fresh waters non-buoyant eggs are almost the invariable rule. Most kinds of marine fishes start life as eggs that float in the sea. A good many, principally species that live near the shore, lay their eggs on the bottom, or in nests, or fasten them to rocks, shells, sea weeds, sponges and so forth. Some of these fishes guard their eggs, but parental care is more advanced in those other kinds that carry their eggs or use part of the body as a brood chamber. In still more advanced species, represented by many sharks and rays and some teleosts, the eggs develop within the female, who nourishes the embryos after they hatch (Hylander, 1964; Marshall, 1966).

Except when courting and mating, many fishes lead separate lives. Yet the schooling habit, whereby the same-sized members of a species swim together in orderly and peaceable ways, is widespread among marine and freshwater teleosts. Individuals of one out of every four species school during some part of their life. By living in associations, fishes improve their chances of survival. During their evolutionary history, some kinds of fishes have taken to associating with other kinds, and in one order, the shark-suckers, their way of life is imprinted on their design. Other fishes have discovered means of living together with various kinds of invertebrate animals. A school is not just a group of fishes belonging to one species. One special feature is that the members of a school are of much the same size. When startled, a school of fishes will quickly come together and move almost as though it were a single organism. Schooling fishes can swim with some precision along more or less parallel paths, and in doing so, they may be formed in close array. When a school is feeding it may be more closely knit than at some other times.

The diversity of fishes sharply reflects their mastery of water. There are some twenty thousand living species, which are arranged in many families and larger groups. One of the most obvious differences in the environment of fishes is that of the salinity, or saltiness, of the water; as a result of this, most fishes are adapted for life in either fresh or salt water. Among the strictly freshwater species are such familiar fishes as minnows, suckers, and sunfishes. Among the common marine fishes are the sharks, mackerels, and flounders. Some families of fishes include species living in fresh water and species living in the sea; this is the case in the salmon, sturgeon, and sculpin families. A small number of species (salmon, trout, eels, and shad) live part of their life in the sea, part in freshwater habitats. Saltwater game fishes include: amberjack, barracuda, bass, bluefish, bonito, cod, dolphin, drum, marlin, permit, pollock, sailfish, swordfish, tarpon, tuna, and weakfish. Herring and menhaden, cod and haddock, flounder and halibut make up the few families that constitute the majority of the commercial harvest from the sea. The common freshwater game and food fishes belong to six families: the salmon, catfish, pike, sunfish, perch, and sea bass families. The salmon family includes trout, white fish, and cisco. The pike family includes pickerels and muskellunge. Sturgeons are the largest of our freshwater fishes (Hylander, 1964; Marshall, 1966).

Marine fishes often are classified into three groups on the basis of where they live. Some species are pelagic, wandering over the open sea; such are the swift-swimming tuna and swordfish. Other species are littoral, staying close to shore in the sheltered waters of inlets and bays or in the surf zone along beaches. Many of these are popular game fishes: striped bass, tarpon, bonefish, and bluefish. Still another group spend their lives on the ocean bottom, grubbing for the mollusks and crustaceans, which are abundant in such places. These are the benthic fishes, the bottom dwellers. Some, such as sculpin and flounder, favor the shallow water of bays and harbors. Others, such as cod and halibut, prefer deeper offshore waters.

Many fishes live in coral reefs and atolls: these include moray-eels, squirrel fishes, cardinal-fishes, parrot-fishes, trigger-fishes, file-fishes, and puffer-fishes. Fishes that find much of their food over bottoms covered with coral sand are red-mullet, flounders, silver-perches, and flat-heads. Coral reefs are also full of predatory fishes, notably carcharhinid sharks, lizard-fishes, garfishes, barracuda, kingfishes, little tunny, amberjacks, groupers, snappers, and scorpion-fishes. Many reef fishes have deep bodies, much compressed from side to side, for instance file-fishes, butterfly-fishes and angel-fishes; others are elongated and slim in form, for example trumpet-fishes, cornet-fishes, and pop-fishes; and there are many serpentine species in the eel order, such as moray-eels and snake-eels. Away from the corals, on sandy bottoms, live certain kinds of flounders. The body is deep and compressed, but they rest, as do all flatfishes, on one side, the blind one of the body.

Updwelling makes these equatorial regions the most productive in the tropical and subtropical ocean. The phytoplankton flourishes, providing food for swarms of herbivorous planktonic animals such as copeheads, which directly or indirectly support the life of fishes. Copeheads, for instance, are taken by flying fishes, which are the prey of dolphin-fish, snake-mackerel and other predatory fishes.

The World of Water

Centered about the equatorial divergence, particularly in the easterly half of the ocean, there are large populations of yellow-fin tunny and skip-jacks, together with abounding wahoo, dolphin-fish, marlin, and lying fishes. Oceanic sharks, such as the white-tip shark are also common in the easterly equatorial belt. The same is true of the blue-shark, which is not confined to tropical waters. There are corresponding aggregations of tunny in the equatorial regions of the Atlantic and Indian Oceans (Hylander, 1964; Marshall, 1966).

North and south of the equatorial current systems, extending to latitudes of about $40°$, are the great central water masses which circulate in immense, slowly-moving eddies. Mixing between the layers above and below the thermocline is so limited that these central waters are the least productive of life in the warm ocean.

The coastal fish fauna in the temperate North Pacific, which consists of more than a thousand species, is several times richer than that of the temperate North Atlantic. Rock-fishes, sculpin, sea-poachers, sea-snails, kelp-fishes, eel-blennies, and flat-fishes are represented by different species in both areas, but they are more diverse in the North Pacific, which also contains certain families, such as the greenlings and the surf-perches. There are more cod-fishes in the North Atlantic. The two faunas are not closely related, though closely allied species of cod, herring, and halibut live in both regions. Different populations of cod, herring, and halibut occur on the American and European sides of the North Atlantic. Other species common to both sides include the spiny dog-fish, pollack, haddock, mackerel, lump-sucker, and short-horn sculpin.

Arctic fresh waters are dominated by salmonid fishes, notably by species of char and white-fish. The salmonids range over most of the north temperate zone but are absent in the tropics. There are over a hundred kinds of fishes in the waters fringing the Antarctic Continent islands. Nearly three-quarters of these belong to a division of perch-like fishes. Other kinds of skates, eel-pouts, and sea-snails are found in arctic coastal waters. The eel-pouts and sea-snails, together with species of cod-fishes, bullheads, armed bullheads and flat-fishes, are the dominant fishes of arctic shores. Like the antarctic fishes, most of these species are bottom-dwellers.

The living space of the most highly evolved flying-fishes is in the clear blue surface waters of the tropical and subtropical ocean. When disturbed by a ship or harassed by their enemies, they leave the sea for the air, to glide rapidly and briefly over their element. Glides lasting from four to seventeen seconds and consisting of two take-offs are not uncommon. The distance covered may be from twenty to several hundred yards, the flight being along a straight line or a curve.

A number of freshwater and marine teleost fishes are able to move over land. A fish in water has little or no weight to carry, but once it walks on land the out-of-water weight must be supported as soon as its body is raised off the ground. Only one group of fishes, the mud-skippers are really adept fin walkers.

Most kinds of freshwater fishes live in land-waters that are out of reach of the sea. Few tolerate brackish waters; most of these must seek fresh waters when ready to spawn. Still fewer kinds, such as carp, bream, roach, and barbel are more adaptable. Some freshwater fishes have established themselves in ice cold, fast-flowing mountain streams and deep cool lakes, others in warm stagnant ponds and sluggish rivers. Brook trout make their home in cold swift brooks and streams; smallmouth black bass live in equally cool clear lakes. Other slower streams and warmer waters are the home of rainbow trout and white sucker as well as largemouth black bass. Sunfish and perch abound in the smaller warmer ponds, and even somewhat stagnant shallow ponds support great numbers of carp. The oxygen-poor waters of sluggish southern bayous provide a home for the alligator gar (Hylander, 1964; Marshall, 1966).

A well-rounded freshwater fish population does not occur where the dissolved-oxygen content is less than 3·0 ppm. Even a coarse fish population cannot occur where the dissolved oxygen content is less than 3·0 ppm. Fish can survive in water outside these limits. Although fish can tolerate less than optimum amounts of dissolved oxygen for short periods of time, decreased levels of oxygen can destroy the fishing potential of streams. The effect of toxic materials upon aquatic life varies with the species, its size, and the composition of the water. Tolerance limits of many chemicals of many species have been determined; however, little is known about the toxicity of mixtures. A mixture of several chemicals in water may cause more damage to aquatic life than the sum of the damages by the individual chemicals; a mixture of several chemicals in water may cancel each other and cause less damage than the sum of the damages by the individual chemicals. Thus, the toxicity of chemicals cannot always be predicted. Sometimes streams may become intermittent and lose all fish. The reduction of the flow of springs and the loss of streamside shade may raise the temperature of streams above that required by trout. Increased erosion of the watershed may accelerate sedimentation in lakes and reservoirs and produce a habitat in which only rough fish can live. Winterkill of fish may result from the lack of oxygen, which often develops in such shallow, weedy waters. Pollution by the discharge of industrial and domestic wastes into streams and lakes has also been a major destroyer of fish habitat (Hylander, 1964; Marshall, 1966).

WATERFOWL

Waterfowl come in many sizes (30 tiny green-winged teal would barely balance a good-sized trumpeter swan) and many colors, from the frosty snow goose through the multihued drake wood duck to the drab and sooty scoters. They have a complete chorus of voices: honking, trumpeting, quacking, whistling, purring, and croaking. Most swan species are large and white and have extremely long necks. The geese are intermediate in shape and size between swans and ducks. Their bodies are less flattened and their necks are longer than those of the ducks. Both sexes are alike in coloration, as is true of the swans. Geese, however, have a wider range of colors and sizes. The species of ducks are grouped by certain structures and habits. The surface-feeding ducks, the 'dabblers' or 'puddle ducks', favor, as their name implies, the smaller shallower inland lakes, ponds, and marshes. To make a fast getaway from such restricted waters, they bound vertically into flight. Legs are set farther forward than most ducks giving the dabblers good locomotion on land (Linduska, 1964).

Their ability to forage ashore, to feed efficiently in the shallows, and to dive moderately well makes the dabbling ducks the most versatile feeders of all waterfowl. As a group they make use of dozens of submerged and emergent aquatic plants; scores of aquatic and terrestrial animals; and many kinds of farm crops, grasses, and weeds. Food preferences range from the 40 percent animal material of the mottled duck to 90 percent vegetation of the wood duck. The canvasback is a member of a major group of ducks, the divers; they usually feed underwater. Specialized for the underwater pursuit of aquatic animals are members of the mergansers. Their streamlined bodies are tipped by a narrow bill, whose edges are serrated with backward-pointing teeth that are ideal for grasping the fish that make up most of their food. The little hooded merganser nests in treeholes and prefers wood-bordered streams and ponds. The two larger species seek more open waters, but the redbreasted merganser always nests on the ground, generally farther north than the common merganser, which may nest in tree cavities, cliffs or on the ground.

The mallard is prized by gunners. The pintail has a wide breeding range. The blue-winged teal spends the summer in the north and may winter in the south. The American widgeon always nests on dry land; the black nests anywhere from the ground to a duck-blind roof or a treetop crow's nest; wood ducks seek out tree holes and nest like woodpeckers. The ruddy and his close relative, the redhead, prefer prairie potholes and sloughs, the redhead often preferring the larger, more open marshes. Both nest over water, in clumps of reeds or cattails. The ruddy is specialized for diving, with stubby legs set far astern, and is helpless on land. A better submariner than any diving duck or merganser, it feeds largely on plants, not fish. Though it dives well and nests among overwater reeds like a redhead, it prefers muddy creeks and little ponds (Linduska, 1964).

Waterfowl habitat is in direct competition with other uses. The human population is steadily expanding; it requires more land and water to sustain itself; and at the same time it demands more birds for recreational hunting. Man is trying to make maximum recreational use of waterfowl while staying within the abilities of waterfowl to keep their numbers up. In practice, this has resulted in an increased take of under-harvested species and in a reduction of bag limits or complete closure of species in danger of overharvest.

The World of Water

Over the years many birds have been banded, and information from this source is useful in developing regulations. Recoveries of the bands, mostly by hunters, have provided data concerning the relationships between breeding, harvest, and wintering areas. Data from bands also provide a basis for determining mortality rates, the importance of hunting as a mortality factor, and rates of harvest in relation to changes in hunting regulations. The recovered bands show that each species has its own routes and its own destinations. Different species raised in the same slough may winter in entirely different parts of the continent. At the same time all members of the same species utilizing the same nesting slough will not have the same wintering grounds. Birds that share one wintering ground may have been hatched thousands of miles apart from each other (Linduska, 1964).

From inspection of wings, a bird's identity, age, and sex can be ascertained. Information provided by hunters provides additional facts about distribution of kill by location, time of day, and day of the season. All these bits of information help to determine the relationship between hunting regulations and harvest.

Waterfowl prepare for migration by donning a new or partly new suit of clothing. If the trip is to be a long one, they acquire a supply of fuel in the form of fat under the skin. In spring, a chain of physiological changes takes place, stimulated partly by increasing day length. The reproductive organs enlarge, and the urge to migrate becomes strong. The birds are finally ready, physically and psychologically. But the releasing mechanism for their journey is not their condition. Rather, it is the condition of the atmosphere through which they must ply their way. In migration, waterfowl neither loaf nor hurry. They move along at a speed normal for the species, pausing as they go to feed and rest. The cruising speeds vary for different species, but for ducks and geese they are about 40 to 60 miles an hour. The intervals reported between banding in the north and recovery in southern regions indicate that a month or more may be taken to cover an airline distance of a thousand miles (Linduska, 1964).

Most ducks and geese flee southward each fall ahead of cold polar and arctic airmasses. As winter wanes, the cold air tides lose their force and begin to recede northward. When winter wanes, the numbers of ducks and geese reach low ebb. Birds lost during the past must be replaced if species are to endure. The losses can be compensated for during nesting seasons to come. Each spring waterfowl undertake the journey north to nesting grounds. En route they must have enough food, sunlight, warmth, and other things that make them physiologically ready to mate and nest. At their destination, early-nesting species, such as pintails and mallards, must find nesting territories ready for immediate occupancy. Environmental conditions must remain favorable during the weeks they need to incubate eggs and rear the young.

Large numbers of birds use certain routes regularly. Some of their travel lanes are like a narrow path close to some definite geographical feature, such as a river valley or a coastline. Other lanes may resemble a broad boulevard alongside a land mass or body of water. A migration route usually is a generalized pattern, rather than an exact course followed by individual birds, and may vary because of local storms, water conditions, and many other factors.

Two kinds of flyways are recognized by waterfowl specialists: biological flyways, those established by the birds themselves, and administrative flyways, those delineated by people for efficient management of the resource.

Of the zones of aquatic vegetation, emergents are the vital ones for waterfowl. Their patterns largely determine the degree to which waterfowl will use fertile breeding ponds and marshes. Clumps of emergents well interspersed with open water offer excellent nesting cover for overwater nesters, such as redheads, ruddy ducks, canvasbacks, and coots. Such habitat also serves as fine escape cover for many species of waterfowl. In contrast, shorelines supporting dense stands of emergents, such as cattail, exclude open edges preferred by ducks for loafing and shallow-water feeding. An edge, or line of change in habitat, exists in places where open water borders emergent vegetation or the shoreline. It offers the basic requirements of food, cover, and protection within a shore distance. The marsh with the largest amount of edge generally supports the most waterfowl. Crooked shorelines or scattered patches of emergent vegetation increase the amount of edge (Linduska, 1964; Water, 1955).

The World of Water

A good waterfowl marsh contains an abundance of different food plants intermixed with enough emergent vegetation to protect the birds against rough weather and natural enemies. The birds will use water that is choked with sago pondweed and other submergent food plants, but the density and total area of the emergents are critical factors.

Wetlands furnish breeding sites for most of the North American ducks and geese and contribute an important part of the habitat used during migration and wintering. The prairie pothole region makes up only ten percent of the total waterfowl breeding area of the North American continent, yet it produces 50 percent of the duck crop in an average year. This region covers about 300 thousand square miles in south-central Canada and north-central United States. It extends in a great arc from Edmonton in Alberta, eastward to Prince Albert in Saskatchewan, south and east to Winnipeg in Manitoba, and across the border to include the western parts of Minnesota and South Dakota. There the Missouri River marks the western and southern border as it crosses western North Dakota and northern Montana to Great Falls. At that point, it extends northward along the foothills of the Rockies to Calgary and Edmonton. Averaging 300 miles in width, this great expanse of prairie is about a thousand miles in length from northwest to southeast.

Drought is the greatest single diaster that can overtake a waterfowl population on prairies. Vast areas of grasslands may lose all potholes and lakes except the ones fed by irrigation or springs. Land clearing and farming, which normally follow drainage, have further eliminated much of the habitat. Logging has reduced the value of other areas by removing trees needed for nesting and mass production. Forestry practices, such as culling deformed trees and girdling or poisoning species of no economic value, have further reduced the environment of wood ducks. Northern deltas are important in the year-to-year production of waterfowl. They are especially important when drought hits the prairies and parklands. Waterfowl densities of the woodlands and tundra are comparatively low, but the expanse of land and the myriad lakes and streams make possible a substantial contribution to the total waterfowl population. Although the climate is severe and the summers are short, waterfowl breed even in the most northern parts (Linduska, 1964; Water, 1955).

Many kinds of algae grow in waters that ducks use; most of them are harmless. A few are poisonous to wildfowl if they occur in large numbers. When a toxic strain becomes predominant in a water bloom, hundreds of birds may die in a few hours. Extensive algae blooms are potentially dangerous to waterfowl, especially where the principal component is Anabaena flos-aquae or Anabaena lemmermanni, which may be the same algae. Not all blooms are poisonous, and not all species that produce a bloom are toxic. Waterfowl get lead poisoning by swallowing lead shot that they pick up on the bottoms of lakes and marshes. The average hunter fires five shots for every duck he bags. A 12-gauge shell contains about 280 pellets of number-6 shot. Accordingly, as many as 1,400 pellets may be deposited on waterfowl hunting grounds for every duck killed.

Botulism, a disease of both birds and mammals, is a bacterial poisoning. The causative agent, Clostridium botulinum, does not invade the living tissues of its victims. Each of its cells can form a spore highly resistant to physical and chemical agents, and in this form it may lie dormant for many years. When conditions are favorable (suitable temperature, an organic medium to satisfy food requirements, and an absence of atmospheric oxygen) the spores germinate and multiply. In so doing, they produce a potent nerve toxin which birds absorb through the lining of the digestive tract. By way of the blood stream, it reaches the peripheral nervous system. In some manner not yet clearly understood, it attacks the nerves and causes paralysis. If the dose of toxin is large enough, death of the bird results from paralysis of the respiratory system. There appears to be no such thing as a typical botulism area. Most marshes and lakes on which outbreaks occur are shallow, brackish, and on the alkaline side of neutrality; but depth, salt concentration, and alkalinity may vary widely from one marsh to another and within the same marsh from year to year. The kinds and abundance of vegetation and invertebrate life also vary within wide limits on such marshes. The mode of spread within a waterfowl population is in doubt. The disease agent is present in both the nasal excretions and the feces of infected birds, and the environment, particularly on a densely populated lake, will quickly become contaminated. Domestic fowl appear to be more susceptible to experimental infection by the intranasal than the oral route. This supports the belief that the natural disease is primarily a respiratory infection (Linduska, 1964; Water, 1955).

Fowl cholera, unlike botulism, is an infection. A tiny bacterium, Pasteurella multocide, must invade the tissues of its host to bring about its ill effects. Different strains of the organism vary with respect to the severity of the disease they induce. Some cause an acute, rapidly fatal infection; others, a more chronic form of the disease. Among the many causes of disease in waterfowl are the blood parasites. The black flies that transmit Leucocytozoon to ducks show a strong preference for them and consequently are essential in spreading the parasite from duck to duck.

Present-day waterfowl refuges differ in many respects from those of the past, although they have points in common. Their object may be to preserve from extinction a notable piece of habitat, a distinct ecological unit of plants and animals, or a single species. Some refuges are as small as an acre in size; others may exceed a million acres. Two thoughts lie behind the modern concept of wildlife refuges; the first is the idea of sanctuary. Any creature much sought after by hunters must have areas where it is safe and undisturbed. The purpose of sanctuaries is to limit the harvest of the species concerned and thus promote their long-term welfare, and to serve as reservoirs from which surplus stocks may emerge. The second idea is that of the preserve. The environment of the species is necessary for its survival; the essential elements of the environment must therefore be preserved.

Chapter 9

Conservation

The universal need of water, its worldwide distribution, and apparent inexhaustibility have led to various human attitudes towards its utilization, one of which is not the conservation of this important natural resource. It is indeed an anomaly that a resource that not infrequently creates a deluge of extremely destructive proportions needs on occasion to be conserved. Both too little and too much water are, in part, the result of the unwise use of water resources. The universal importance of water as a basic necessity of all forms of life makes its utilization a most complicated problem of conservation. The two major conservation problems affecting water for uses are the quantity of water available and its quality for the purpose for which it is to be used. To the average individual of our modern civilization water is too often taken for granted; it is always available at the tap.

The problem of water conservation is not one that can be solved independently of the conservation of the other natural resources. Man is but one species living in a world with numerous others; he depends on many of these others not only for his comfort and enjoyment but for his life. Plants provide the principal mechanism whereby energy from the sun can serve the earth's inhabitants. In doing so, they maintain the oxygen content of the air and furnish the basic habitat and food of animals and men. Animals serve man as great converters, changing plant-stored energy into forms of food he prefers, and supplying him with a wide variety of materials: leather and furs, oils and pharmaceuticals, ivory and pearls, bristles, and wool. Many insects are beneficial, some as pollinators; others as predators on harmful forms; some as makers of silk and honey. As contributors to happiness and the quality of life, plants and animals provide opportunities for enjoyment of natural beauty, for hunting, fishing, gardening, scientific study, entertainment, and the satisfaction of our human curiosity.

In the control of pollution, plants, animals and microorganisms are directly useful in two ways: first, living things, especially micro-organisms, have a capacity for absorption and decomposition of pollutants, with resulting purification of water. Second, many species of organisms, each with its own particular range of sensitivity to each pollutant, stand as systems for environmental bioassay and monitoring, and for warnings of danger to man and his environment.

Because living things are interdependent and interacting, they form a complex, dynamic system. Tampering with this system may be desirable and necessary, as in agriculture, which involves artificial manipulation of the balances of nature on a huge scale. But such tampering often produces unexpected results, or side effects, and these are sometimes very damaging. The delicate interrelationships between living creatures on and beneath the land and in the rivers, lakes and oceans, are dimly appreciated and little understood (Restoring Our Environment, 1965).

An immediate joy in living and learning that is experienced in wild and natural areas has given man a consciousness of the values of returning to the primitive for recreation, for inspiration, and for knowledge. Areas of the wilderness itself have come to be valued as wilderness: areas that, in contrast with those parts of the earth's landscape that are dominated by man and his works, are untrammeled by man; areas where man is himself a member of the natural community, a transient whose travels leave only trails.

The world's seashores, lakeshores, and riverbanks are a priceless possession. They have provided the harbors that serve our commerce and sites for basic industries. Great cities have been built on their shores. They have grown in importance as a prime resource for recreation. However, the coastlines, shorelines of lakes, and the banks of many rivers have been neglected, underdeveloped, and polluted. The rights to the shorelines have been left for acquisition by whoever wanted them. The magnificent stretches of beach and surf that remain in their original and beautiful state, where oceanwide overlooks invite campers, picnickers, and naturalists, are dwindling rapidly as other uses encroach. Public access to river, sea, and lake shores often is severely limited. The cost of acquiring such access, high now, rises constantly, especially near cities. The limitations of public access to shoreline recreation areas exclude many persons from waters legally open for common use. Sometimes land surrounding such waters is privately owned or controlled. Sometimes there are no roads or paths by which people can reach the water (Place to Live, 1965).

Water that once remained in low spots and provided habitat for waterfowl now collects in ditches and tile lines and is rushed to the nearest stream. Millions of acres that once grew cattails, wildrice, and pondweeds now support wheat, corn, houses, factories, airports, and roads. Waterfowl is a renewable resource which is subject to management by man. The basic needs of waterfowl are adequate food, water, and cover to meet their specific requirements and protection from decimating factors which reduce their numbers. These needs can be met only by proper management of the land upon which they live and by control of such factors as drainage. Although many species formerly common or abundant are now rare, the esthetic value of those remaining is great. Public demand for recreational use of waterfowl exerts enormous pressure on the supply and in some species necessitates complete protection and drastic restrictions on the use of others to ensure their welfare (Place to Live, 1963).

The control and useful development of water in our streams constitutes an important segment of the larger problem of water conservation. In the operation of the hydrologic cycle the return of the water to the sea from which it was originally derived provides an opportunity to use the water beneficially and as far as possible to prevent destructive floods.

CONCERN OVER POLLUTION

Pollution touches all mankind as pollutors and sufferers from pollution. Pollution adversely affects the quality of our lives. In the future, it may affect their duration. Present levels of pollution of water in many parts of the world are for the most part below the levels that cause disease or death in people. At the same time water pollution is causing deaths at many places.

The World of Water

The documented cases of pollution-caused injuries to plants, fish, birds and mammals are extensive and the economic loss from these injuries has been considerable. Some waters no longer support any useful fish or invertebrates. Some areas have been rendered unsuitable for useful plants. Many natural waters throughout the world are becoming continually less beautiful and less usable. Prudence and self interest dictate that men exert themselves not only to prevent further buildup of pollutants but to reduce present burdens of pollution in our waters (Restoring Our Environment, 1965).

The full effects of environmental changes produced by pollution cannot be foreseen before judgements must be made. The responsible judgement, therefore, must be the conservative one. Trends and indication, as soundly based as possible, must provide the guidelines; demonstration of disaster is not required. Abnormal changes in animal populations, however small, at whatever stage in the life history of the individual, or in whatever niche of the species complex, must be considered warnings of potential hazard. Many kinds of pollution problems could be prevented by the exercise of ecological foresight. Given a reasonable knowledge of persistence, biological effect and expected initial distribution and amount at least part of the impact on living things can be predicted. In the future, such advance evaluations will be essential.

Disposal of wastes is a requisite for domestic life, for agriculture, and for industry. Traditionally, waste disposal was accomplished in the cheapest possible way, usually by dumping in the nearest stream. This tradition is no longer acceptable; industrial and agricultural waste disposal must now be accomplished in such a way that pollution is avoided. The pressure to pollute in the past has been an economic one; the pressure to abate must in the future also be economic.

Although flowing water exposed to the sunlight and air tends to purify itself, the problem of pollution has become more complex as domestic and industrial uses have placed an ever-increasing drain on the volume of water. Sewage and industrial wastes have increased enormously; aquatic life has been partially destroyed; and silting due to increased erosion has been accelerated. Likewise groundwater is polluted, especially in shal-

Conservation

low and open wells. Seepage from barnyards and from cesspools in more thickly populated areas is a source of contamination.

Purification of water and the processing of sewage and industrial waste are two of the important steps in the program of conservation of surface water, since sewage and industrial waste in the rivers and lakes are among the major causes of pollution. Beginnings have been made by both cities and private industry to process sewage and industrial waste, returning only harmless residues to the streams and lakes. If these processes are carried to their logical ends, reclaiming usable materials from industrial waste and producing fertilizers from sewage, only pure water would be returned to the streams and lakes, and one of the conservation problems would be solved.

From a conservation viewpoint, the fisheries are perhaps the most poorly managed of all our world resources. In most commercial operations, where fish are regarded as free goods provided by nature and the only law is the law of capture, the following well-defined pattern is recognized (Guy, 1965):

1. A period of abundance, with large catches per man, per boat, or other unit of effort. The apparently inexhaustible supply at this stage is frequently a temptation to indulge in reckless overfishing.

2. A period of declining catches, with the return per unit of effort falling off to a marked degree.

3. Intensification of fishing efforts. This understandable attempt of the fisherman to keep up the poundage generally means more and larger boats, more efficient gear, and a wider cruising radius. Intensification helps to keep up the amount marketed but makes still deeper inroads into the remaining parent stock.

4. Depletion and abandonment of the grounds. Depletion often occurs with scant warning, since, by the more intensive combing of the sea or by taking constantly larger percentages of schooling fish such as mackeral or salmon, the impending exhaustion may be concealed for some time. When operations become unprofitable the fished-out area is usually abandoned.

The remedial measure for all fisheries, however, tend to have certain similarites, which may include (Guy, 1965):

1. A program of scientific research until the complete life history is known.
2. Flexible regulations which may include one or more of the following measures: (a) provision for adult escapement; (b) a quantity limit on the catch; (c) restrictions on the size or age of the catch; (d) a closed season for part of the year, or possibly for a term of years if the stock is badly depleted; and (e) refuge zones or nursery areas where fishing is prohibited.
3. Restrictions on type of fishing gear.
4. Removal of obstacles to migration or the construction of fishways.
5. Artificial propagation by means of hatcheries, if practicable.
6. Abatement of stream and coastal pollution.
7. Licensing of vessels or other fishing media to insure more effective control.
8. Securing the cooperation of the fishing industry and the public by a program of education.

It is always easier to preserve an original stock than to rebuild an exhausted one; fishery experts try to act before exhaustion is reached. Preservation of fisheries depends largely upon public willingness to recognize the danger, grant adequate appropriations for research, and submit to reasonable regulation. The ultimate goal of all such measures is a sustained yield and a permanent abundance.

Scientific fish farming is on the increase, including the construction of artificial ponds that are stocked with suitable varieties of game or pond fish, such as bass, crappie, bluegill, and catfish. Hatcheries supply millions of fry to stock ponds of this type. By adding chemical fertilizers to the water microscopic plants and insects multiply, serving as the base for a highly productive pyramid of fish food.

Oyster farming is already far more profitable than the unrestricted exploitation of public oyster grounds. There has been no comprehensive survey of the food-producing possibilities of the great ocean margins. Mollusks and crustaceans seem especially adapted to aquiculture. Pelagic and anadromous fish present more obvious difficulties in management, and it may be impossible to apply this method to demersal types. In the not too distant future, however, man may find it profitable to cultivate the sea as carefully as he is now cultivating the land.

POLLUTION AND ITS CONTROL

Man's concern with the quality of water differs from place to place and in time. His earliest preoccupation was to have water for drinking free of bacterial contamination; most present treatment of wastes and water is to assure this level of purity. A second concern has been to correct nuisances resulting from odors, soils, trash, and visible pollutants; here again some success has been achieved. Man is now beginning to be more concerned about the esthetic quality of natural waters, about the suitability of these waters for municipal, agricultural, industrial, and recreational uses, about harmful substances present in small amounts, and immediate and long-term changes in lakes, streams, and estuaries (Restoring Our Environment, 1965).

The relative importance of the various water quality problems depends on the uses to which the water is put and upon the priorities assigned these uses. It is not desirable to attempt to maintain a busy industrial harbor in the same degree of cleanliness as a municipal water supply reservoir. All streams cannot be trout streams. Some deterioration or changes must accompany the growth of municipalities, the development of industry, and the exploitation of agricultural and mineral resources.

During and following World War II apprehension has become widespread about the threats to health from chemical pollution of the environment. Some of the important factors are the rapid growth of population, urbanization, the rise of nuclear power and greatly expanded chemical technology, the use of pesticides, and the redefinition of health to include mental and social well-being. The tremendous growth in the production of synthetic chemicals for all kinds of uses is producing an entirely new type of pollution problem. Wastes from the manufacture and use of these chemicals are reaching natural waters in significant amounts. Their effects on plants and animals are poorly understood, and many do not undergo decomposition as readily as do most biologically produced materials. Synthetic chemical pollutants are known to create taste and odor problems that are difficult and expensive to solve. Some of these chemicals, particularly the pesticides, are toxic to various forms of aquatic life. Others are suspected of interfering with aquatic food chains. With the trend toward larger electricity generating stations, disposal of this heat in our rivers is becoming increasingly burdensome (Restoring Our Environment, 1965).

The most intense water pollution is in or near great metropolitan areas and the industrial complexes associated with them. Sewerage systems and waste disposal practices were developed in early years as means for reducing the severe health and nuisance problems resulting from individual responsibility for waste disposal. Sanitary sewerage systems are undoubtedly the most significant of all the sanitation measures of modern society. Unfortunately sewers impose the burden of disposal on nearby waterways. For a variety of reasons, waste treatment has not completely solved the problems associated with municipal, sewage disposal. Even if treatment could remove all undesirable constituents from sanitary and industrial sewage, a great deal of pollution would reach streams in metropolitan areas.

Pollutants can be carried long distances down rivers, and those that remain in solution or suspension and are not broken down by chemical or biological processes reach the estuarine zone. A large part of the pollution load originates near our sea coasts. Evidence points to the lowlands bordering the sea coasts as an area where pollution problems merge and concentrate.

The drains of a city carry two types of liquids; storm water or surface runoff from streets, roofs, lawns, and paved areas; and used or spent water from houses, industries and all other kinds of establishments that are supplied water from either a public or private source. In the separate system of sewage, storm water is collected, transported and disposed of through a storm drainage system, while the spent water supply or sanitary sewage is carried by a sanitary sewerage system. When both types of waste water are collected in a single set of underground drains the system is a combined one.

Ancient cities had elaborate drainage systems to remove runoff from rainfall. In those times domestic wastes were cast into the streets and flushed intentionally or otherwise into these drains. Combined systems of sewerage have thus been in use for some thousands of years. The problems associated with them remain still to be solved. In modern times, as in ancient, drainage systems grew piecemeal. Water courses were first walled to save space, then covered, then used for the disposal of every kind of liquid and water-carried waste. Nearby discharge points were foul smelling, so larger drains were built to collect the effluent from smaller ones and the nuisance points were moved elsewhere. These systems had dozens if not hundreds of outlets along the major water or river fronts of older cities. The idea of building separate sytems to collect sanitary sewage was tried about the beginning of the twentieth century but first efforts failed and the combined system of sewerage continued to be favored. The problem of combined sewage overflow can be attacked by: separation of sewage systems, increasing interceptor sizes, construction of express sewers, reducing input of storm runoff, reducing solids load in storm runoff, reducing input of sanitary sewage, reducing solids load in sanitary sewage, storage of flow in the system, removal or alteration of solids in the system, terminal treatment of overflows, installation of measuring and monitoring, and improved operation and maintenance.

Suspended solids usually accompany organic materials from domestic and industrial sources, but may also arise from mining and quarrying operations, poor control of erosion on agricultural lands, or through milling processes and construction. Non-toxic salts are waste products from some kinds of mining and industry, from oil drilling, or from irrigated agriculture, and may increase the salt content to quite high levels. Pesticides used in the control of plants or animals in orchards and other agricultural enterprises may be washed into waterways following heavy rains, where they may be highly toxic and frequently are cumulative. Some pesticides used for weed control in waterways are toxic to animals as well as to the plants.

Radionuclides from industrial reactors are a potential source of pollution, especially in the event of accidents, and will become more so as more power reactors are placed in operation. The amounts of heavy metals and the levels of dissolved gases toxic to aquatic organisms are well known and can easily be measured by simple chemical procedures, and simple detection devices can reveal the amounts of radioactivity known to be harmful to man. However, in many instances, the effects of pollution may be so subtle that they cannot be detected until some parts of the biota have been eliminated.

In fresh as well as in marine waters, inert pulp wastes from paper processing plants have been shown to cover the stream or ocean bottom to such an extent that the entire area was rendered unfit for the survival of bottom fauna. Much of the same sort of condition is traceable to the accumulation of coal dust, and tailings from plants. In oil-producing areas, there is abundant evidence that waste materials from oil wells render entire stream systems devoid of most aquatic life. Many such streams have high salt contents, in addition to phenols, sulfides, etc. Seepage from coal mines has resulted in almost complete acidification of some streams and brought about a virtual elimination of aquatic life.

Agriculture has done an excellent job in increasing farm production and in providing the nation with the food it requires for high health and economic standards. Clearly, it is now necessary to be concerned as well with the various wastes of the production operations. Disposal of farm animal wastes has created a major and evergrowing production problem for farmers. The problems of farm waste disposal, and pollution arising from agricultural sources, are aggravated by the large animal population, the sheer volume of material to be disposed of, and the unavailability of suitable disposal procedures or facilities (Restoring Our Environment, 1965).

The excreta of farm animals may be a major source of water pollution; animal wastes enter the streams, rivers or lakes either in the form of surface runoff or through seepage. In some watersheds, farm animals contribute considerably more wastes than humans and the drainage from certain land areas supporting large animal populations probably leads to significant water contamination. Pollution from animal manure is known to have reached such proportions in some areas that downstream fish kills and groundwater contamination have been observed. As the human population increases, the animal population continues to rise; however, the usable land area becomes no greater.

The problem of agricultural waste disposal has grown to such dimensions that the major unsolved issue in the confinement housing of livestock and poultry is the handling and disposal of manure. The magnitude of the problem may be visualized by comparing the wastes voided by man and by the animals he raises. For example, a cow generates as much manure as 16.4 humans, one hog produces as much waste as 1.9 people, and seven chickens provide a disposal problem equivalent to that created by one person. As a result, farm animals produce ten times as much waste as the human population.

Groundwater pollution arising from the disposal of livestock and poultry wastes may be evidenced in undesirable changes in taste, odor and color of the water. When manure treatment or storage areas are improperly located, the nitrate levels in immediately adjacent groundwater supplies may become disturbingly high. The organic nitrogen in the barnyard manure is converted to nitrate, which in turn may pollute rural wells despite the absence of indications of bacterial pollution.

Treatment processes do not remove much of the inorganic phosphorus and nitrogen that enter the sewage plant, and the treatment operations permit the release of nitrates and phosphates in large amounts into natural waters, leading to unwanted chemical and biological enrichment of the waters of ponds, lakes, rivers, and estuaries. Certain agricultural operations may also contribute substantially to these effects. Problems associated with the increasing enrichment of waters merit immediate study not only to minimize present but also to avoid future degradation of the world's water resources. Research aimed at ascertaining the causes of problems resulting from the overenrichment of water resources is urgently needed, and corrective measures must be established for specific bodies of water which continuously or seasonally no longer meet present and potential use requirements because of overfertilization (Restoring Our Environment, 1965).

Nutrients attributable to man's activities come from several possible sources; the most important of which are domestic sewage, garbage, industrial wastes, remnants of manufactured chemical products, drainage from fertilized lands, wastes from domestic animals and sewage from ships and boats. The amounts and proportions any water receives from these several sources differ in different situations and from time to time. Drainage waters vary considerable in the concentrations of nutrients they carry. Urban street drainage and return flows from both surface and subsurface irrigation contain concentrations of nitrogen and phosphorus several times greater than that observed in streams of forested areas with little habitation and land use. Sewage and sewage effluents, however, are a much more concentrated source of nutrients. Investigations of the chemical composition of the effluents of sewage plants indicate that the phosphorus concentrations are considerably higher than was common in sewage effluents 20 years ago.

A proportion of the nutrients in sewage is removed by common methods of sewage treatment and is accumulated in sludge. Such sludge, when dried, is usually too poor in nutrients to be of commercial value as a fertilizer. Sludge produced by activated sludge plants is higher in nutrients, and some have a commercial use, but this is usually a marginal or non-profit making operation. Lime can be employed for removal of phosphate from sewage effluents; the resulting material could be put to use. Sewage nutrients could also be used for the commercial production of algae, which might possibly serve as a poultry feed or as a source of biochemicals of economic value.

Fertilization speeds up the ecological aging or eutrophication of waters. Such change is usually most rapid and most noticeable in impounded waters of lakes and reservoirs which, if they remain undisturbed, eventually become filled with organic debris along with silt and material settling from the water as a result of chemical precipitation. Europhication will be an increasingly important problem in the future with increased use and re-use of potable and industrial waters and as more reservoirs are built to impound and store water.

Prime consideration has been given to the importance and effects of the addition of phosphorus and nitrogen, particularly as orthophosphate and nitrate, to waters. These two essential elements for plant growth are singled out because often, but probably not always, the supply of other nutrients needed for aquatic plant growth is present in excess of the biological demand, and phosphorus or nitrogen are the elements limiting the extent or severity of the aquatic algal blooms or excessive growth of other plants. It should be emphasized, however, that many other nutrients are essential for the growth of algae and rooted aquatic plants, and in specific situations, one or more of these nutrients may be more important in promoting unwanted blooms than inorganic forms of either nitrogen or phosphorus.

There are very few municipal plants which are being operated to minimize the nitrogen and phosphorus content in the effluent stream. In conventional biological treatment plants, organic nitrogen, urea, and ammonia nitrogen are converted to protein (in bacterial cells), ammonia and nitrates in the effluents. Further nitrogen removal from the effluent may be accomplished by algal ponds which convert more of the soluble nitrogen to algal cells. At some laboratory and pilot installations, the nitrified sewage is subjected to anaerobic conditions and the nitrogen converted to gaseous nitrogen with subsequent release to the atmosphere. Passing of sewage plant effluent through selected soils has resulted in nitrogen removal, possible through dentrification. Chemical means for removal of nitrogen have not progressed beyond the laboratory research phase. Suggestions have been made regarding the removal of nitrogen through ion exchange, but no quantitative data are available. The application of current treatment technology can result in the removal of approximately 50 percent of nitrogen to domestic wastes. The nitrogen removed in the form of bacterial or algal protein can be used as soil additive and potentially as animal feed supplements. The conversion of the nitrogen to a valuable product could make it more attractive to remove nitrogen from wastes (Restoring Our Environment, 1965).

Phosphorus removal is only accomplished to a very limited extent currently in biological treatment plants. Any removal that does occur is from the precipitation of phosphates and the removal of phosphorus in the excess biological mass developed. In conventional municipal waste treatment facilities, the inorganic nitrogen and phosphorus levels in the effluent generally exceed the level of the inflow. Removal of phosphate can be accomplished by chemical coagulation. Chemical coagulation can reduce the concentration of all forms of phosphorus compounds, ortho, complex, and organic. Lime, alum, ferric salts, and polyelectrolytes are being used, and reduction of greater than 90 percent has been accomplished. Work on the effectiveness of biological removal of phosphates by bacteria has not yet been substantiated by field or full scale plant operation. Removal of phosphates by algae in ponds can be accomplished, but there is limited information on the percentage reduction that is achieved.

Techniques of waste treatment now being developed are aimed at complete removal of nitrogen and phosphorus from waste streams. Those processes, including absorption, foaming, electrodialysis, ion exchange, precipitation, evaporation, and reverse osmosis show promise of complete removal of all contaminants from waste streams. Wastes from boats or ships can either be treated aboard the vessel or else stored and discharged to an acceptable system. Nitrogen and phosphorus currently entering streams in the form of land drainage from farm animal wastes can be treated by the installation of suitable facilities. Improved agricultural practices could reduce the amount of nutrients lost into receiving waters. In critical situations, land drainage can be intercepted and treated for removal of undesirable elements, or diverted to a disposal point where objectionable conditions would not be created, or stored for controlled release. If nitrogen and phosphorus enter receiving bodies of water, eutrophication of the nutrients is a major consideration, efforts can be made to reduce the concentration of nitrogen and phosphorus in the stream by providing proper means for dispersion of wastes, or possibly by regulation through dilution by flow augmentation.

Problems arising from eutrophication can be controlled by preventing the excessive development of undesirable plant growths. Chemical control, which has not proven particularly effective, or biological controls, such as through algal viruses and the biochemical or biological modification of a receiving body of water, are considered as possibilities of preventing eutrophication.

Once critical nutrient levels are reached and eutrophication takes place, the natural sequence is self-perpetuating through the death and decay of the algae with the subsequent release of nutrients. To solve adequately the problem of eutrophication in certain locations, not only must the addition of nutrients be curtailed, but the nutrients already present in the lake must be removed, reduced in concentration, or made unavailable. A number of solutions for removing nitrogen and phosphorus by the harvesting of algae, rooted plants, and the fish population have been suggested. The role played by the sludge deposits in lakes, their composition and what effect they have on the release of nutrients is still to be determined. Large scale engneering projects aimed at modifying oxygen gradients, temperature gradients, sludge dredging, and construction of physical barriers in lakes may be effective in solving the problem of eutrophication (Restoring Our Environment, 1965).

FISHERIES

The easy-going assumption that man can never exhaust the sea placed upon nature the entire responsibility for replenishment. Public reliance upon this theory, which demanded neither care nor restraint on the part of the fishermen, was based on general ignorance concerning most types of underwater life. The old-fashioned biologist, in considering fisheries inexhaustible, also under-estimated the ingenuity of modern fishing methods. It was impossible to foresee the effect of otter trawlers, large-scale operations, and numerous improvements in fishing gear, all of which added to the efficiency of production but also intensified the pressure upon the basic resource. The theory of inexhaustibility has now been abandoned or, at least modified. The modern biologist prefers to think of fisheries as a replaceable resource, needing scientific study and responding readily to good management. Knowledge concerning marine life was extremely meager until early in the twentieth century, and even today little is known concerning the abundance, habits, growth, reproduction, and migration of many valuable food fish. Fortunately, biologists and oceanographers have now developed various techniques of marine investigation, and their research on problems of fish life is providing exact data of great value (Guy, 1965).

Every spring and summer the rivers of the Pacific, from California to the Bering Sea, are the scene of one of the world's most spectacular fish runs. Millions of salmon appear at the river mouths, swarm across the bars, and move steadily upstream. Packing plants are located from northern California to western Alaska, usually near river mouths. By means of traps purse seines, and gill nets, the fish are caught by thousands and taken to canneries.

Salmon running began on the Sacramento River in 1864.

The runs at that time were excellent, and the pack increased to 200,000 cases in 1882, then dropped steadily until it disappeared. The decline was caused, first, by overfishing to the point where the adult escapement was insufficient to replenish the stock and, second, by the obstruction of rivers by power and irrigation dams. The Sacramento and the San Joaquin are now insignificant as salmon streams.

During the period of abundance in the early 1900's most of the fishing off the coast of British Columbia and southeastern Alaska was within a radius of about 500 miles from Seattle and Vancouver, B.C. Gradually, as the numbers declined within this area vessels pushed farther to the north and west, returning with even larger cargoes of fish. Peak production was reached in 1915 when the total catch was 63,254,000 pounds. Any catch between 50,000,000 and 60,000,000 was considered normal, and in order to maintain this figure both Americans and Canadians went to more distant grounds (Guy, 1965).

One of the most popular food fishes in America is the halibut, found in both the North Atlantic and the North Pacific. This great deep-sea flounder early became one of the staples of the Atlantic coast fish trade. It was not until some sixty years ago, however, after the inauguration of fast transcontinental rail service between Puget Sound and eastern United States, that Pacific halibut began to reach the market in quantity. Once landed to the extent of 14,000,000 pounds per year, Atlantic halibut has been heavily overfished and has decreased to about 1,000,000 pounds annually.

For many years the decline of halibut in the North Pacific was partially concealed by the fact that as an area was depleted the fisherman widened their radius of operations and still managed to bring in the usual poundage. Little was known about actual sea-bottom conditions, many fishermen contending that there was still an abundance, but that halibut migrated from one bank to another and that it was necessary to shift fishing operations to follow them. Finally the limits of lateral expansion were reached.

The International Fisheries Commission was appointed in 1924 with a membership of two Americans and two Canadians and was given authority to investigate and recommend halibut conservation measures. Biologic data collected by the Commis-

Conservation

sion concerning habitat, spawning, and rate of growth were correlated with other data, particularly those of ocean currents, and by 1930 it was possible to present a fairly comprehensive life history of the Pacific halibut. It was ascertained that there were distinct populations of halibut each living, spawning, and dying within its own area with little migration between areas. Hence, it is difficult for a depleted area to be restocked from an adjoining one. Artificial propagation of deep sea fish such as halibut is impracticable; it is also impossible to control the food supply or enemies of the fish. Each stock must be managed so that the catch from it will be fully balanced by natural propagation and growth.

The practicability of the Commission's regulations involving division of the convention waters into areas, limiting the catch from each area, licensing of vessels for the halibut fishery, collection of statistics of abundance and locality of capture, modification of the closed season, and closing of nursery grounds has been satisfactorily proved. Regulation by the Commission has brought about remarkable changes in the halibut fishery. The abundance is twice as great as it was in 1931, the year before regulations began; annual catches are 12,000,000 to 15,000,000 pounds greater; and these larger catches are taken with one-third less fishing effort. Rehabilitation is well under way (Guy, 1965).

The shift of whaling centers, from Norway and Iceland to the shores of New England, thence to the North Pacific with headquarters in the Hawiian Islands, and finally south to New Zealand, the Falkland Islands, and the Antarctic, provides a case history of the progressive exhaustion of a world resource. Active whaling long ago disappeared from the North Atlantic and is now only a minor activity in the North Pacific. The great deep-sea mammal has been pursued so ruthlessly for more than a century that a reliable estimate of the whale population is less than 350,000, a mere remnant of the hordes which once frequented the seas.

The most active center of present-day whaling is in the Antarctic waters, particularly around Ross Sea. Most of the world's whaling is where the cold waters are especially rich in the tiny crustacea and other minute sea organisms which make up the food supply of whales. During the short Antarctic summer, November to February, the great mammals feed along the edges of the southern ice floes and have attracted the modern whaling fleets of several fishing nations. Large steel vessels, powerful enough to plow their way through pack ice, have been turned into floating factories, completely outfitted for modern whaling. Each of these mother ships employs a number of small but high-powered chaser boats. Equipped with a Norse invention, the Foyn harpoon gun, which shoots a harpoon carrying a bomb in its tip, the chaser hunts down a whale and then tows it back to the mother ship. The carcass is dragged up a runway to the cutting floor inside the vessel where it can be completely processed in a few hours. Present-day whalers are required to utilize every part of the carcass. Not only is oil reduction greatly improved, but the Antarctic factory ship is equipped with canneries for whale meat which has long found a ready market in the Orient; whale meat is also frozen or dehydrated for the European market. Bone and scrap are made into poultry feed or fertilizer. At the end of the season the mother ship returns to the home port to dispose of its cargo. Much of the oil goes into the manufacture of margarine, soap, cosmetics, or lubricants.

A high degree of mechanized efficiency is making heavy inroads into the remaining whale supply. Japanese scientists report that the gray whale is seldom seen in the North Pacific; several other varieties are now quite rare. Sperm, white, and humpback whales are diminishing all over the world, finback and blue whales accounting for the bulk of today's catch. Too many immature whales are being taken, and it is generally admitted that all varieties are being killed faster than they can reproduce. Unfortunately there is no sign of decreasing pressure upon the supply (Guy, 1965).

Since whales range the oceans freely from arctic to tropical waters and are not under the direct jurisdiction of any country, the preservation problem is difficult. Nationally speaking, whale conservation is nobody's business. The need is for an international whaling agreement to be signed by all nations concerned which will protect all species for a term of years. With a longer closed season, the killing of immature whales prohibited, and a production quota set for whale oil, this unique mammal might have a chance to survive.

FLOODS

With its carrying capacity and its competency greatly increased, a river in a flood becomes a powerful agent of destruction. Recurrent floods are characteristic of small streams as well as of the large, and locally the resulting damage may be great. It is difficult to determine exactly the extent of flood damage and to compare in a satisfactory manner one great flood with another. This is due in part to the tendency to overestimate flood damage, particularly at the time of the flood. Another complicating factor is the changing value of the dollar in which the damage is expressed. However, it appears that the floods are becoming more destructive.

Floods are the result of many conditions working singly or in combination. Usually no single cause can be assigned the whole responsibility. Although most floods are related directly to heavy precipitation and the immediate surface runoff, floods are also caused by dam failures, ice obstructions, high tides, and gales.

To escape the danger of floods various control measures either singly or in combination have been utilized to provide the necessary protection. Probably one of the earliest methods was to evacuate the area at the first warnings of impending danger. Flight to safe areas could hardly be interpreted as flood control, but it did mean the protection of life and a limited amount of property. This method is still used when there is a failure of other protective measures. Throughout the history of civilized man the fertile alluvial lowlands have been preferred areas of habitation; and, as high water menaced periodically the homes of the people, the protecting dike or levee became one of the first methods of defense against floods.

Local improvements in the channel planned to protect only the adjacent property may actually increase the flood hazard downstream. Improvements designed to facilitate the rapid downstream movement of water along the tributaries may heighten the flood crests along the main stream. It is because of the conflicts of interests within a drainage basin that all flood-control works should be co-ordinated, so that preventive measures applied in one area may not nullify the works in another.

The World of Water

Many of our principal cities are located upon the larger rivers, and wherever there is likely to be extensive damage to valuable urban property by inundation protecting levees have been constructed. Though rather expensive, the levees, if properly constructed and maintained, may give adequate protection against all floods except those classed as the great unprecedented floods. The confinement of a river between closely spaced levees creates a dangerous situation because the floodwaters, no longer having access to the floodplain, rise above former levels and increase the danger of breaks or crevasses. Along streams that have been gaged over a long period of time the flood crests may be so well known that protective dikes may be constructed to contain all but the great flood between them. Here the levees or dikes should not be placed to close to the river's edge, but set back somewhat, leaving room for other preventive works along the stream and providing a safety margin in anticipation of unprecedented floods. Such a system of protecting dikes will require a correlated system along the tributaries and a series of gates to provide for the drainage of the lowlands outside of the dikes in time of low water. In times of flood the gates will have to be closed, preventing drainage of the lowlands. To avoid local inundation it may be necessary to install pumping machinery to lift the water over the levee to the main stream.

The natural history of a river confined to a levee-protected course includes not only an overtopping of the levees in time of flood but also the breaking of wide gaps in the levees permitting the floodwaters to escape to the back swamp areas. Because a large river may at times need more of the floodplain than is available between the levees, an additional floodway may be provided in the lower back swamp areas. Such floodways are protected by dikes and coordinated with the levee system of the master stream and its major tributaries. Well-protected floodways are an effective means of lessening the danger of breaks in the levees where too much water is confined to a narrow watercourse. Along the larger rivers that have broad natural levees and expansive back swamp areas, retarding basins may be developed as a means of reducing the flood crests.

One of the best ways to prevent trouble is to avoid it, and one of the best ways to avoid flood damage is to stay out of the floodplains of streams. Zoning ordinances can prescribe areas within which structures which would suffer from floods could not be built. Parks could be created along streams where frequent flooding makes other uses impractical. Another form of zoning is to designate flood areas as zones where the owner builds at his own risk. In instances where only isolated units of high value are threatened by flooding, they may sometimes be individually flood proofed.

DRAINAGE

Accumulation of excess water can arise from heavy local precipitation, runoff from upstream areas, low-lying land in depressions, tidal action in coastal areas, impervious subsoil, buildup of a high water table as a result of irrigation or seepage, or from artesian or other underground movement of water. Drainage refers to the removal by artificial means, of excess water to improve the condition of the land. Excess water either in or on the soil, whether a permanent or a temporary condition, influences farm production, farm income, and farm values. Too much water in the soil adversely affects crop growth and the timely performance of operations such as tillage, seeding, cultivation, and harvesting.

Many individual farmers and some communities could profit by the drainage and improvement of agricultural lands in local areas. Wetlands, subject to drainage, constitute the greatest reserve of new land available for use at some future time when our growing population and expanding industry require additional materials. The question arises as to the desirability of draining additional land in order to have it ready for immediate use, when needed, to provide food and fibers for our growing population and industrial raw materials for our rapidly expanding industry. There is abundant evidence that marshland deteriorates more rapidly after it is drained than it does in its natural state. Several causes contribute to this deterioration, but the most serious one seems to be general subsidence of the land due to settling and accelerated oxidation of the organic matter in the drained soil. Also, fires may completely destroy peat and muck soil, thus lowering the level of the land surface. So long as the water table is maintained at the surface of the ground, little or no deterioration occurs, and the land is more likely to be available for full production use than it would be if it were drained and thus exposed to the hazards of subsidence and fire (Place to Live, 1963).

Many millions of acres of good waterfowl habitat have been destroyed by drainage and the loss continues. Dredges and ditches have had a profound effect on our waterfowl. They were not used deliberately to destroy waterfowl domain, but were used to convert waterways and wetlands to more profitable channels and lands. In many places throughout the world waterfowl are important economic assets and nearly everywhere they are desirable esthetic assets. The public, if it wants waterfowl, must be militant in seeing that vital habitat is not destroyed and that wetlands not now productive and not economically feasible of being drained are flooded and managed.

Chapter 10

Water Resources Planning, Development, and Management

The story of the development of water resources planning, development, and management ideas and techniques resembles the history of modern man's discovery, adaptation, and use of knowledge in many fields. The translation of intellectual endeavor into plans and thence into reality is a time-consuming process. Too often, the residents of a given river city do not understand that what happens to them, with respect to such factors as floods and polluted water, is determined not by the relatively short reach of the stream familiar to them but by occurrences elsewhere in the basin, sometimes hundreds of miles away. In any river basin at a given time numerous local or special foci of support for regional action may be found to exist; but they are so diffuse and so fragmented that it is next to impossible to marshal them effectively in a united movement.

Not only does the river basin generally fail to impress the people residing there as an entity with important public problems; there are also contrary forces exerting strong influences against the emergence of a regional spirit. Among them may be mentioned a series of persistent and widely prevalent intraregional conflicts. These are manifest in the urban-rural rivalries, the industrial-agricultural differences, the upstream-downstream controversies. It follows that a strong regional consensus on any particular issue is very difficult to achieve. The problem is further complicated by the fact that, in a given river basin, there are likely to be found hundreds of governmental units and agencies, and additional hundreds of private enterprises, each pursuing its own course without effective reference to regional issues or regional needs (Martin, 1960).

The most basic concept of planning requires a look at the future. This anticipates a basin's requirements, catalogs present and anticipated resources, and then advises a plan that will utilize resources to meet the requirements efficiently. In water resources planning, the resource base is assessed and its adequacy appraised both for present and future needs. Thereafter, a means must be devised by which the resource is brought into juxtaposition with the need.

There is probably no such thing as one and only one river basin plan. A plan is a compromise among a shifting set of alternatives. At any one point in time, based on facts that are available, there may be a hypothesis that certain engineering works are required, and the plan may include a schedule of the order in which work should be undertaken; however, by the time the first step in any such plan has been achieved, other developments, social, political, or economic have also taken place, and the assumptions, under which the first statement of plan was put forth, may no longer be valid. Thus, it becomes necessary to update the original plan. So it goes with each succeeding addition to the system of works that is devised to solve water problems. At each step new decisions must be made, and basic to the decision process is the examination of alternatives.

There are many types of criteria that must be used in the decision making process as it relates to river basin planning. First and most commonly recognized, there are economic criteria of feasibility. The most common device for judging economic feasibility is the traditional benefit-cost ratio. Benefit-cost ratios, under the best of conditions, represent inexact criteria. In this era, the benefit-cost ratio formula has been very greatly complicated by the necessity to attempt to evaluate recreation as well as other intangible costs and benefits. There are social criteria that must be considered in water resources planning. What is cheapest or what seemingly offers the greatest long-range economic benefit may not in fact be what the people want. Increasingly, people seem disposed to choose what they would like to have for esthetic or other social reasons, rather than for what is represented to them as being the most feasible engineering plan with the highest benefit-cost ratio. Social values and viewpoints are being upgraded. Each new proposal for water development presents a new set of political problems. Thus, there are political criteria to which water development plans must be adjusted. Finally, water occurs in a physical environment and hydrologic criteria of feasibility must be met.

Water Resources Planning, Development, and Management

There are five principal ideas that seem to encompass the current conceptualization of river basin development and management. First among these is the multiple-purpose storage project. The worth of the multiple-purpose project has been proven many times, and the limited experience with basinwide programs seems to show that concept to be valid. Basinwide development and management is the second major concept. This is the idea that a system of works can be geared together to maximize use of all the water in a basin. Comprehensive regional development and management, the third concept, represents an even more general attempt to formulate the connections between water development and management and the maximization of all other factors that go to make up general economic growth. Articulated land and water programs and unified administration, the fourth and fifth concepts, are logical accompaniments of the first three ideas. They represent attempts to theorize about the administration of the first three concepts. To varying degrees, the theories of comprehensive regional development, articulated land and water programs, and unified administration remain to be worked out and applied. The fifth concept, that of unified administration, represents an attempt to circumvent the imperfect nature of water as an organizing principle and to blend land and water problems by consigning both to a single agency for administration. Application of the concepts has gone slowly, awaiting first of all the evolution of basic scientific and engineering tools sufficient to the task (Martin, 1960).

RIVER BASIN COMPREHENSIVE PLANNING

United States

The concept of coordinated planning has been practiced in the United States since 1784 when a Commission was appointed by the Commonwealth of Virginia and the State of Maryland to study navigation improvement of the Potomac River. In 1879, the Mississippi River Commission was appointed and has been an active organization throughout the intervening years in the development of the lower Mississippi River and tributaries. There have been numerous other coordinating efforts, such as the Inland Waterways Commission of 1907, the National Resources Planning Board in the 1930's, the Federal Inter-Agency

The World of Water

River Basin Committees in the 1940's, and the Water Resources Policy Commission in the 1950's.

In the last two decades, the water and related land resource planning programs of Federal agencies have expanded greatly and new Federal agencies have been brought into the planning field. The need for close coordination of these programs became increasingly apparent, not only to the Federal establishment, but also to the State and local groups. Also, great concern was voiced by some States over the fact that planning for the water resources development within the sovereign States was being done largely by the Federal Government. In 1959 and 1960, a United States Senate Select Committee on National Water Resources held hearings throughout the country and prepared a report which has become historically of great significance in the planning program for water resources of the nation. Two of the recommendations pertaining to comprehensive planning that this Committee developed were that the Federal Government, in cooperation with the States, should prepare and keep up-to-date plans for comprehensive development for all major river basins, and stimulate more active participation by the States in water planning.

A further recommendation by the Committee was that Congress request the Executive branch to submit for congressional consideration, in January 1962, a program for preparing comprehensive plans for each major river basin or water resource region, toward the end of providing for development of plans for all basins by 1970, in cooperation with the States. The comprehensive plans, thus developed, should be kept up to date and each authorization of a project should show the relation of the project to the comprehensive plan.

In a special message to Congress, President Kennedy in February 1961 accepted the recommendation of the Senate Select Committee and committed his Administration to the goal of developing comprehensive plans for all major river basins by 1970. President Johnson renewed the commitment, although budgetary requirements have resulted in advancing the scheduled date of completion to 1972. As an initial step in carrying out this commitment, coordinated budgets were prepared for 18 studies whose geographic areas would blanket the nation, except for the two areas of Alaska and the Tennessee Valley

Authority. This action assured the working together of these agencies in a cooperative planning effort. The Bureau of the Budget and the Congress have recognized this as a forward step in agency coordination and respected the budgets as developed. In 1967, eight of these studies are being funded, and two are included in the budget for fiscal year 1968. The first of the studies scheduled for completion is the Ohio River Basin which is in its final stages. In fiscal year 1969, the Missouri and Upper Mississippi studies are scheduled for completion.

Largely as a result of the Committee's recommendations, the Water Resources Planning Act of 1965, Public Law 89-80, 89th Congress was signed into law July 22, 1965, by President Johnson. The act provides for the optimum development of the nation's natural resources, through the coordinated planning of water and related land resources, through the establishment of a Water Resources Council and River Basin Commissions, and through financial assistance to the States in order to increase State participation in such planning.

Title II of the Water Resources Planning Act provided for the establishment of a river basin commission which has as one of its responsibilities the preparation of a comprehensive coordinated joint plan for Federal, State, interstate, and nongovernmental development of water and related land resources. The framework plan has been viewed as a first step in preparation of this comprehensive plan. The basic objective of a framework study (also referred to as type I study) is to provide a broad guide for the best use of water and related land resources in the area under consideration.

The Water Resources Council has prepared guidelines for framework studies which go into detail as to what should be included. The six major elements of the study as indicated in these guidelines are as follows:

The projections and study of economic development. Economic base studies start with information from a nationwide study by the Office of Business Economics of the Department of Commerce and the Economic Research Service of the Department of Agriculture, to prepare economic projections, including population and growth in major economic sectors, to the years 1980, 2000, and 2020. A data bank has been prepared which will make it possible to assemble data and projections for subbasins or subregions. These projections are reviewed and revised in the field study.

Translation of economic projections into needs for water and related land resources uses. The economic projections are made for employment, income, and output for major economic sectors. In addition, information is needed on efficiency of water use in different economic sectors, on costs of substitutes and other factors that affect rates of water use in relation to economic activity. Relating projected economic activity to water use and pollution loadings is a responsibility of field planners in the respective studies. The Council is interested in improved methods for projecting water use in various economic sectors.

Appraisals of the availability of water supplies, including quantity and quality. The use of mathematical models and computers has provided substantial improvement in this technique in recent years and should be utilized to the extent practicable in the framework study.

Appraisals of the availability and characteristics of related land resources. This involves the classification of soils and relating them to potential agricultural use, including irrigation capabilities. Also included are urban land changes, outdoor recreation and wildlife needs, greenbelts, and other potential uses.

Outline of the characteristics of projected water and related land resources problems. Based on the collection of the foregoing data, the critical problem areas should surface, and the characteristics of the problems can be brought into focus.

Alternative approaches that appear appropriate for solution for the foregoing problems. This analysis will be based on the general knowledge of development opportunities and costs, reasoned approximations, available data, and judgement of experienced planners. Those basins or parts of basins that have problems will be described, including the possible solutions. Areas where no problems are expected in the immediate future will also be indicated.

The four types of studies that are being used in comprehensive planning in the United States are:

Type 1 (Framework Study). Framework studies will reach

conclusions as to the urgency of water and related land problems in the subregions and recommend priorities for more detailed studies in the near future (10 to 15 years) leading to the authorization of an action program.

Type 2 (River Basin Study). Studies by river basin Commission or other Federal Inter-Agency State coordinating organization of an area that extends the scope and intensity beyond the type 1 studies to define and evaluate projects in sufficient detail, including project formulation, to comprise a basis for authorization of those Federal and federally assisted projects to be initiated in the next 10 to 15 years. These type 2 reports will be in sufficient detail to provide for authorization of projects by the Congress.

Type 3 (Project or Single-Purpose Studies). These studies are made by a single agency and usually relate to one project or purpose involving a geographic area limited to the project. The study should indicate the relationship of the proposed programs and projects to the comprehensive plan where such a comprehensive plan has been prepared.

Type 4 (Cooperative State Studies). These are special studies that are being made by a State water resource agency in which one or more Federal agencies are cooperating. They generally are on subbasins and are more intensive than type 1 studies and are used primarily for guidance in developing State programs and policies and for establishing priorities for project development.

From the national view, logical order of comprehensive planning would be, first, the preparation of the framework plan which delineates the areas that need more detailed studies, followed by type 2 or type 4 studies that identify projects that should be constructed in the next 15 years. Type 3 studies which lead to project authorization should be made concurrently or follow.

Germany

The Parliament of the Federal Republic of Germany in 1957 enacted the Water Household Law to provide for the general planning of the subwatersheds of main rivers, such as the Rhine. The law provides for the development of plans to assure needed improvements in management of water and land for immediate purposes and for the next 30 years. The Federal Government establishes the standards and undertakes the coordination of water planning, but the actual planning is carried out by the German Lander (States) under the direction of the State ministeries of agriculture and forestry. One State, Hesse, has underway or has completed 10 watersheds management plans, comprising 76 percent of its total area of 8,147 square miles. The watersheds covered by the plans range from 52 to 2,682 square miles. All but four are within the 250 thousand acre size limit (Place to Live, 1963).

The plans are truly comprehensive. They include the present and future needs (up to 30 years) for flood control, use of surface and groundwaters for domestic and industrial supply, irrigation, improvement and maintenance of water quality, recreation, and other purposes. The planning takes into account the potential of planned economic development of the region. It also evaluates the potential downstream effects of whatever measures may be proposed in the watershed on navigation, hydro-power, and control of water quality. The planning process is aimed at establishing a balance between demand and supply of water. The plans include suggestions for administrative procedures and data on admissible maximum water extraction from groundwater and for granting of water rights to the use of surface water. Benefit-cost analysis as it is practiced in the United States does not provide the framework for German water resource developments. Decisions are based on whether a project is needed to maintain or develop the resource. Projects decided upon are designed to last forever, insofar as technical knowledge permits. The rate of undertaking projects is dependent on national and state budgetary considerations.

The watershed plans of Hesse are worked out by planning groups comprised mainly of experts of the Water Management Department of the Ministry of Agriculture and Forestry. A special working group or committee of consultants is established also for each plan as a body to look after the interests of the respective municipalities, the chambers of agriculture and forestry, the chambers of industry and commerce, various economic associations, and navigation authorities. The Water Management Department works closely with the Federal authorities who have responsibility for seeing that the uniform national procedures are followed and also assists in coordination where the watersheds extend into other States, as is often the case.

DEVELOPMENT AND
MANAGEMENT ORGANIZATIONS

England and Wales
While it is true that over England and Wales as a whole rainfall provides ample water to meet all foreseeable needs, it is no simple matter to ensure that water is available where and when it is needed in the right quantity and of the right quality. An ever-increasing volume of effluents from industrial and domestic use of water flows back into the rivers which are the chief natural sources of supply of water. There is a rapid growth of pressures on rivers and lakes for recreation from a growing population, mainly urban, with far greater opportunities for leisure than previous generations. Thus, water resources, which were in the past ample to meet all needs, are now hard-pressed, particularly in certain parts of the country. This situation calls for better management of the country's water resources. The Water Resources Act, 1963, sought to provide the machinery for the comprehensive management of the water resources of England and Wales (Goode, 1968). The Act set up a new organization of 29 river authorities each responsible for its own area, and a national Water Resources Board responsible for overall planning and for national policy.

Under the new system of river authorities all the water resources of a river basin, whether on the surface or underground, are brought under one authority. The river authority is given full control over all aspects of water in its area. The same authority is responsible for land drainage and flood protection, for controlling withdrawals and for prevention of pollution. The river authority is responsible for meeting the needs of those who withdraw water whether for public water supply, for agriculture or for industry. It is also responsible for meeting the needs of all who use or enjoy the waters in the rivers or lakes, such as the fisherman, the yachtsman or water skier, and for the preservation of amenity for its own sake. With

The World of Water

the exception of certain special arrangements dealing with navigation on a few rivers, the river authority has now been given all functions relating to management of its rivers. The administration of water resources is based on catchment areas. The boundary of each river authority follows the watershed separating one catchment from another. There is no division of authority within a river basin. A single authority is in charge throughout the whole area of the catchment giving integrated management of the river throughout its course to the sea, regardless of boundaries between counties or even the boundary between England and Wales. Each river authority area is a river basin or a group of river basins. The boundaries are determined solely by reference to hydrological considerations.

All withdrawals of water having any significant effect upon resources have been made subject to licensing. The river authorities have similar powers to control all discharges of polluting matter into non-tidal surface waters or into underground strata. They also have powers to control fishing and to look after freshwater fisheries, and to regulate other recreational uses of their rivers. Licensing provides the river authorities with comprehensive statistics of withdrawals from rivers and discharges back into them. Each authority is required by the 1963 Act to prepare a hydrometric scheme to provide the information needed to assess the resources of each catchment. The river authorities have a statutory duty not only to survey their resources, but from time to time to assess present and future demands on those resources and how best those demands can be met and to see that all necessary action is taken to that end. Thus, the river authorities are made responsible not only for preparing development plans to meet future water needs in their areas, but also for seeing that these plans are carried out. A river authority will not necessarily itself undertake every development scheme. Given sound planning, the execution of a plan can be organized as best suits the particular circumstances. Some schemes may best be carried out by public water supply undertakings, others by some special body constituted for the purpose, and others by the river authority itself.

One important provision of the 1963 Act assigns to the river authorities the duty of fixing a minimum acceptable flow for any river for which this may be desirable. This is the minimum flow in the river which the river authority considers is needed for safeguarding public health, for meeting all authorized withdrawals, and for satisfying the requirements of land drainage, natural beauty, navigation, and fisheries. Minimum acceptable flows are an integral part of the licensing system, and must not be impinged upon.

To provide coordination between river authorities and where necessary to provide regional or national planning, a central authority, the Water Resources Board, was established by the 1963 Act. The Board's functions cover the whole of England and Wales. Its first duty is to advise and assist the river authorities in the discharge of their water resources functions, in particular to give guidance over hydrometric schemes, over periodic surveys of resources and demands and on planning to meet demands. The Board is also responsible for advising Ministers on national policy. A majority of the membership of the river authorities is drawn from the major local authorities of the area. Other members are appointed by Ministers to bring experience of land drainage, agriculture, industry, public water supply, fishing and, where appropriate, navigation of the river. Thus, the membership of the authority should ensure that not only are all interests in the river fully taken into account in managing the river, but that other local interests and aspirations are understood and considered. The Water Resources Board and the river authorities are responsible ultimately to the appropriate Ministers of the central government with whom are the final powers of decision on appeals from planning decisions and control of finance.

The basic principle of finance adopted in the 1963 Act is that the management and development of water resources should be self-supporting. Just as the cost of providing water for public water supply has been paid by the consumers, so the river authorities will recover their expenditure on managing and developing water resources from those who benefit by a system of charges levied on the holders of withdrawal licences at rates to bring in amounts sufficient, but no more than sufficient, to meet expenditure, taking one year with another. The rates of charge must be specified in schemes requiring the Minister's approval and must be such as to remain in force for five years.

The World of Water

To facilitate capital works river authorities are empowered, with the Minister's approval, to borrow money on mortgage.

The Water Resources Act does not apply to Scotland where it was not considered that there were water conservation problems warranting major reorganization such as the ones in England and Wales required. Nevertheless, new legislation for Scotland is being considered which would establish both regional supply boards and a Central Board with powers to develop new sources of supply for use by certain of the regional water boards.

One of the principal tasks of the Water Resources Board is to establish an overall picture of the future pattern of demand for water, both geographically and to a time scale. Such a look into the future can be more readily produced in respect of public water supplies, as the period of record on which projections is based covers many years and so provides a more reliable trend than records for shorter periods. Industrial and agricultural demands are more difficult to estimate and it will be evident, that to be of any real use in planning new developments, regular reviews of demands must be made. This is provided for in section 14 of the Water Resources Act 1963, which requires the river authorities to review both the potential demands, and the developable resources of their areas at intervals of not more than seven years. This information then becomes available for coordination into a regional development plan aimed at the transfer of water from areas with a surplus of resources to areas no longer capable of meeting their own rising demands. In addition to these overall estimates, related to broad categories of water use, investigation is being made of the detailed ways in which water is used, both in the home and in industry. Investigations of this kind are likely to reveal the components of demand most likely to increase with rising standards of living and those which, by the application of technology (and possibly of economic pressures) are susceptible to reduction. In addition a greater understanding is being obtained of real needs (as distinct from those handed down by tradition over the years) as regards the quality of water required for different purposes of use. In the past much good quality water has been used for purposes quite capable of being met by water of lower chemical quality standards.

In practice, however, the pressures for new resource development have interposed an urgent need (for planning purposes) to complete assessments of demands and resources, covering regions which embrace the areas of several river authorities, prior to these authorities being able to commence their own individual surveys. As a result the Water Resources Board has already published a study covering the ten river authorities in the southeast of England and is engaged on a similar exercise covering six river authorities areas in northern England. These investigations, which are also subject to the need for regular revision, set the pattern for the planned development of resources. In very general terms water resource legislation seeks to ensure that water is made available whenever a would-be user requires it, providing that he is prepared to meet that part of the overall cost which is attributable to the quantity which he reserves. In practice this could mean that a river authority area with a surplus of resources capable of development at a low cost could either become a 'factory' manufacturing water for use outside its own boundaries, or a 'magnet' drawing water-using industry to it. This potential for the application of powerful stimuli to the geographical location of growth emphasizes the need for the regional co-ordination of the studies carried out by the river authorities.

A further advantage arising from the regular review of these studies is that regard can be paid to the results of research into alternative methods of water resource development and water treatment. The Water Resources Board is currently sponsoring research into specific aspects of desalination as a supplementary water resource. As was indicated earlier the proximity of the sea to all parts of Britain opens up the possibility of an alternative to the transport overland of water derived from surface flows, provided removal of the salt can be effected at a competitive cost.

No major scheme designed solely for the artificial recharge of ground water has been undertaken in the United Kingdom, although small-scale installations are being operated. One statutory water undertaking has confirmed the feasibility of recharging locally the chalk in the London area. Work on the hydro-geological aspects of possible recharge of the chalk of the London Basin has been initiated by the Water Resources Board and model studies are intended to investigate the possibilities of recharge in this area. Proposals have also been made by certain river authorities for recharge in limited areas.

Attention is also being directed at the possibilities of constructing barrages across a number of the larger tidal inlets around the coastline. Unlike the works carried out over the centuries by the Dutch these proposals are directed primarily at the provision of fresh water storage behind the embankment, as distinct from the reclamation of land (although this, and the provision of transport links would arise as by-products of the main proposals). Preliminary studies have been made of suggested estuarial barrage schemes for Morecambe Bay and Solway Firth (which forms part of the border between England and Scotland). Large freshwater yields appear to be possible from the larger barrages, and the Water Resources Board have recently been asked by the Government to proceed with a full feasibility study of one of these (the Morecambe Bay Barrage). A feasibility study is also being undertaken in relation to the Dee estuary, but here the water conservation interest is subordinate to regional development prospects. The practicability of actually constructing an embankment is dependent, essentially, on engineering considerations. However, before the overall feasibility of a barrage scheme can be determined full consideration must be given to such factors as siltation on the seaward and landward sides of the embankment, and the effects on navigation and fisheries; the presence of polluting matter in the fresh water impoundment; and affects on land drainage and the ecology of the surrounding areas.

Water supplies in the United Kingdom are generally adequate and, although future resource developments will be more extensive and costly than those carried out in the past, there are developable resources available to meet all foreseen demands. Some 99 percent of the population of England, Wales and Scotland has a piped water supply (although this need not, necessarily, be from the public mains) into their homes. In England and Wales some 40 percent of the total supply is derived from groundwater, the remainder from surface sources. In Scotland and Northern Ireland surface water supplies represent more than 90 percent of the total volume taken for public supply. As a result of the overdevelopment of groundwater resources in certain coastal areas saline infiltration has occurred locally. Mineralized groundwaters are also known to be present in other areas, particularly in certain triassic and coal measures strata. In 1750 the population of the United Kingdom was estimated to be some 6·5 million, by 1821 this figure had risen to 15·5 million, by 1901 to 38·3 million and by 1965 to an estimated 54·4 million. Economic growth after World War II, despite the coupling of legislation directed at the cleaning up of polluted rivers with expenditure on modern effluent disposal works, led to water demands on some areas approaching the limit of locally available supplies.

The pattern of water resources development envisaged in Britain has involved the storage of water to regulate the flow of rivers which would then function as conduits in carrying raw water in bulk to points close to the areas of demand. Such surface storage is likely, wherever practicable, to be supplimented by the use of groundwater storage, possibly replenished by systems of induced recharge. The surface storage could, within the limits imposed by physical, hydrological and economic factors, provide a measure of flood alleviation by retaining a portion of major flood flows until river levels have fallen sufficiently to permit the water to run away without inundating land and property. Provision for the alleviation of flooding in Britain has, in the past, largely consisted of works for containing flood flows within embankments but, in the past decade attention has increasingly been directed at the use of some of the storage of new water supply reservoirs for flood alleviation during part of the winter. The effects of flooding in Britain are minimized by warning systems operated by the river authorities, and the existence of embankment schemes in locations prone to inundation renders flooding, in all but exceptional circumstances, more or less a temporary disruption of normal life and communications than a serious hazard to life and property.

There are two main categories of body operating in the water resources field at the local level in England and Wales, the water undertakings with the responsibility of actually supplying water to the consumer, and the river authorities who are concerned with the wider problems of water conservation and management within river basins.

At the central government level, the Minister of Housing

and Local Government and, in relation to Wales, the Secretary of State for Wales are the Ministers primarily concerned with water conservation and supply. They have a substantial measure of oversight and control over the activities of water undertakings and river authorities, and are assisted in this by the Water Resources Board, which is a Government-appointed body with advisory and research function. In addition, there is a central advisory water committee, whose function is to advise them on central issues concerning the use and conservation of water. Roughly 80 percent of water supplied by undertakings in England and Wales is supplied by local authorities operating either singly or in joint boards or committees. These authorities are elected county borough, borough, urban district, and rural district councils, which have a wide range of other local administrative functions. The remainder of the water supplied is the responsibility of private companies. At the end of 1966 there were some 286 water undertakings in England and Wales compared with over 1,100 in 1945. This reduction has come about through a continuing policy of regrouping undertakings with a view to forming administrative units large and efficient enough to deal with growing and increasingly more complex problems of water supply. There has in particular been a sharp reduction in the number of private companies and smaller local authorities (mainly urban and rural district councils) operating as water undertakings. This process of regrouping takes the form either of amalgamation or the creation of joint boards of local authorities for the areas supplied.

Certain broad powers and duties of water undertakers in England and Wales are laid down in general statutes, the chief ones being the Water Acts 1945 and 1948. In addition, a number of local authorities (mainly urban and rural district councils) operate undertakings under a specific code of powers laid down in the Public Heath Act 1936. The remaining undertakers—including nearly all water companies—operate under local enactments, i.e. under individual Acts of Parliament or individual orders made in pursuance of general statutory powers by the responsible Minister (subject to the scrutiny of Parliament in certain cases where there have been objections raised by individuals or bodies affected). There are no private water companies in Scotland, all water undertakings being run either by local authorities operating individually or in joint boards subject to much the same sort of statutory requirements as those prevailing in England and Wales.

It is the duty of all county borough and county district councils, irrespective of whether they are themselves water undertakers, to ensure that all parts of their areas, where there are dwellings and schools, have a sufficient and wholesome supply of water. Where local authorities are not also the water undertakers for their area, they can fulfill their obligations by entering into an agreement with existing undertakers. In addition, water undertakers are themselves normally under an obligation within certain specified limits of operation to provide a sufficient wholesome supply of water to households for domestic purposes, and if there are no existing mains in the neighborhood, they may be required by owners and occupiers of premises to lay mains to those premises, and to provide any necessary service reservoirs, if the water rates (taxes) payable annually in respect of the premises will not be less than a certain fraction of the cost of the works. If the local authority are not the water undertakers for their area and a requisition fulfilling these conditions cannot be made the authority may undertake to make good the deficiency between the fraction of the cost and the revenue from water rates. Water undertakers are bound to accept such guarantees. Where new dwellings have been built, the landowner can require the water undertakers to provide a supply of water, but he must pay for the works necessary. Subject to their prior obligations to domestic consumers, undertakers are normally obliged on request to supply water to industrial and other non-domestic consumers on reasonable terms; disputes are subject to Ministerial arbitration. Water undertakers normally charge for water supplied as follows: in the case of domestic supplies, by levying a sum equivalent to a specified fraction of the rateable value of the premises in question (the rateable value is roughly equivalent to the annual rental and is the basis used by local authorities for levying the 'general rate,' this form of property tax being their main source of local revenue); for certain domestic purposes, e.g. car washing by hose, there is a surcharge; in the case of non-domestic supplies, by levying charges on terms agreed for metered supplies. Local authority undertakers can, in addition, raise capital by means of loans at fixed rates of interest which are secured on their revenue; they may raise the money by mortgage or the issue of stock, or may borrow from the Public Works Loans Board, a Government-financed agency for lending money to public authorities. All borrowings not specifically authorized by statute are subject to Ministerial consent. Statutory water companies are not subject to this form of Ministerial control, but they are subject to special restrictions designed to safeguard the interests of the consumer. The amount of their capital is prescribed by local enactment and normally consists of share capital, which may include 'preference' as well as ordinary shares or stock, and loan capital, such as debenture stock, mortgage loans etc. The dividends and reserve funds of companies are subject to stringent limitations. As already noted, there is Ministerial control over borrowing by local authority undertakings. In addition, Ministers have wide powers of control over the levels of rates and charges. More importantly, all major works and in particular new reservoirs are subject to Ministerial control, usually by means of an order and in certain special types of case, to scrutiny by Parliament. Control over actual abstractions of water by undertakers is exercised by river authorities subject to Ministerial right of intervention under the licensing system mentioned below.

Tennessee Valley Authority

The Tennessee Valley Authority (TVA) in the United States is a Federal public corporation device for coordination of water resources development and management activities on an interstate stream. Interest in improving the Tennessee river for navigation goes back to 1824, but it was not until World War I that the United States government became directly concerned with the river's development. In the Spring of 1933 Congress passed and on May 18 President Roosevelt signed into law the Tennessee Valley Authority Act.

The agency created by the Act has a number of features which are worthy of note. The TVA is a Federal organ; it is not connected in any way with any other Federal department or agency, but enjoys substantial administrative independence subject to control by the President and Congress. It is governed by a Board of Directors of three members, appointed by the

Water Resources Planning, Development, and Management

President with senatorial confirmation for overlapping terms of nine years. The Board in turn appoints a General Manager who, serving without term, operates as administrative head of the agency under general policy direction by the appointing body (Martin, 1960).

The position of substantial independence occupied by the TVA is abetted by the fact that it is a government corporation; it may sue and be sued and may acquire and dispose of property with substantial freedom. The TVA also enjoys more independence of action than most Federal agencies with respect to such matters as personnel, policy decisions regarding expenditures, and disposition of revenues.

While the TVA is a federal organ, it is also a regional agency. Concentration on the region has enabled TVA personnel to develop a technical competence with respect to regional problems not found in other river basins. TVA maintains its headquarters in the Tennessee Valley; it emphasizes its regional rather than its Washington orientation. The agency maintains a small Washington office, and its top executives journey to that city when the occasion requires. It is significant that the people of the valley regard the TVA as a local agency.

The Act of 1933 identified the new agency's central mission as that of bringing about the integrated development of the natural resources of the Tennessee Valley. The agency has brought a multiple-purpose, fully integrated approach to the river and its problems. TVA was charged with three principal responsibilities with regard to the river. These were the control of floods, the improvement of navigation, and the utilization of surplus power. The TVA undertook to employ the technique of multiple-purpose treatment not on one project alone but throughout the valley.

TVA fostered a sytem of cooperative administration and has entered into manifold negotiations with State and local governments active in the region looking toward the effectuation of cooperative arrangements for administration. Agreements cover all programmatic areas, and they involve such agencies as state departments of health, agriculture, commerce, forestry, and natural resources; state water resources boards, planning boards, and geological surveys; cities and counties (health departments, planning boards, public works departments, park departments, library departments); and local electric cooperatives (Martin, 1960).

A basic responsibility placed on the agency is control of the river to the end that danger from floods may be minimized. The TVA has built or acquired control over 31 dams, of which 9 are on the main stem and 22 are on tributary streams. Of these, the agency acquired one from the Federal government and 10 (either outright or for purposes of management) from private industry; the remaining 20 it constructed itself. For flood control purposes, all dams are integrated into a single unit under the management of the River Control Branch of the Division of Water Control Planning, Office of Engineering. So effectively has the system operated that there has not been a major flood on the river since it went into effect. Even 31 dams, synchronized into one system, cannot eliminate all floods; for on the one hand some minor watersheds are beyond the limits of the big dams' control areas, while on the other hand the continued practice of building on flood plains makes more and more property subject to damage by floods. With regard to the first problem, TVA from its beginning has recognized the significance for flood control of land and forest treatment in the upper watersheds, and has collaborated in demonstration small-watershed projects. With respect to the second, it has encouraged and has entered into agreements with a number of local governments looking to flood-plain zoning. In these ways the agency seeks to broaden its already successful river control program into a comprehensive program for flood damage reduction throughout the Tennessee Valley.

The Act of 1933 directed the TVA to dredge and equip with appropriate facilities a nine-foot navigation channel from the mouth of the Tennessee at Paducah, Kentucky to Knoxville, Tennessee, 650 miles away by river. This objective has been achieved, with TVA's nine mainstem high dams providing a series of lakes between the two cities. River traffic has responded to these navigation improvements in a manner exceeding all expectations. Repeatedly traffic engineers have seen their estimates far outstripped, with raw materials inbound and finished products outbound taking the place of the short-haul, low-value cargoes of earlier days.

The Act contained a directive to the TVA to produce and

market power, recognizing always the primary claim to water use of the river control and navigation. Only with the onset of the war, with its large new demands for electricity for defense plants located in the region, including notably the Oak Ridge and Paducah plants of the Atomic Energy Commission, did the TVA go intensively into the construction of stream-electric plants. The generating system now includes the 31 hydroelectric plants on the Tennessee and its tributaries, 5 hydroelectric plants on the Cumberland River, 8 steam-electric plants built by the TVA, including the largest known steam-electric plant in the world, and 7 small acquired steam-electric plants.

TVA operates a fertilizer-munition plant at Muscle Shoals and has an active research and experimentation program for testing and developing new fertilizer materials. In forestry as in agriculture, the TVA has limited its activities largely to demonstration, service, and assistance. Foresters have operated nurseries from which hundreds of millions of seedlings have been supplied for the reforestation of thousands of acres, and inaugurated and pursued a forest inventory which has already proved its utility and cooperated actively with state and private foresters both in research projects and in such practical areas as the prevention and control of forest fires and the extension of sound forest management practices (Martin, 1960).

TVA operates no recreational enterprises, though it lends continuing aid and encouragement to both public and private recreational bodies. As a result, there has been a spectacular increase, largely in water-based recreational activities, particularly in the last fifteen years.

The state and local governments of the Tennessee Valley as a general rule were not notably vigorous or effective when the Act was passed. Programs in important areas were ill-supported or even, in some instances, non-existent, while the basic tools of administration frequently were rudimentary and the practice sometimes primitive. Yet, it was to these governments that the TVA by deliberate choice entrusted fundamental responsibilities in some of its important program fields. It is wholly unlikely that, in the early years at least, the results which followed were as good as the TVA could have obtained through use of its own personnel. Further, it has been argued that the TVA sacrificed something of precision in program definition and something of vigor in execution through its reliance on existing governments and agencies with long-standing, traditional program commitments. The method of operation chosen by the TVA has strengthened and lent added validity to the Federal system. This result has followed first from the growth of a vigorous regional awareness on the part of both citizens and public officials of the Valley, and second from the improvement of state and local government in the region.

Genossenschaften *in the Ruhr industrial area*

There are several German water resources associations operating in the Ruhr industrial area. These are cooperative associations generally referred to as Genossenschaften. The small streams of the Ruhr not only support a tremendous industrial development and a massive population, but they do so while providing a generally high level of amenities and recreational opportunity. The Genossenschaften of the Ruhr area are the only organizations in the world that have designed, built, and operated regional systems for waste disposal and water supply. Of equal interest, they have developed comparatively sophisicated methods of distributing the costs of their operations by levying charges on the effluents discharged in their regions (Kneese, 1964).

There are eight large water resources Genossenschaften in the highly industrialized and heavily populated area generally known as the Ruhr: the Ruhrverband, the Emschergenossenschaft, the Ruhrtalsperreverein, the Lippeverband, the Wupperverband, the Niersverband, the Linksniederrheinische-Enterwaesserungs-gennossenschaft (lieng), and the Erftverband. These organizations were created by special legislation in the period from 1904 to 1958. There are thousands of water Genossenschaften in Germany, most of them created for special purposes such as the drainage or flood protection of specific and limited plots of land. The large Genossenschaften in the Ruhr, however, were given almost complete multipurpose authority over water quantity and quality in entire watersheds by their special laws. These organizations are henceforth referred to simply as the Genossenschaften. For almost 60 years they have made and executed comprehensive plans for waste disposal, water supply, and flood control, as well as for land drainage, which is a problem of great significance in the coal mining areas. This has involved the design and construction of a large array of quality management facilities, including large-scale measures of various types and most of the conventional waste-water treatment plants in the region.

The Genossenschaften are comparable to co-operatives in the Anglo-American sense, but voting power is distributed in accordance with the size of the contribution to an association's expenses, and membership is compulsory. Members of the associations are principally the municipal and rural administrative districts, coal mines, and industrial enterprises. General public supervision is in the hands of the Ministry of Food, Agriculture, and Forestry of the State of North-Rhine Westphalia in which the Genossenschaften are located. The Ministry's supervision is, however, almost completely limited to seeing that the associations comply with the provisions of their constitutions. The Genossenschaften have the authority to plan and construct facilities for water resources management and to assess their members for the cost of constructing and operating such facilities. A process of internal appeal to special boards and of final appeal to the federal administrative courts is available to the individual members (Kneese, 1964).

The statutes creating the Genossenschaften set forth the goals and responsibilities of those organizations in highly general terms. One general provision of the statutes has played a large role in successful and efficient operation. This provision specifies that the costs of constructing and operating the system are to be paid by those members who are responsible for them and by those who benefit. Over the years comparatively elaborate procedures have been developed for assessing the cost of land drainage and waste disposal.

The Ruhr area is one of the most concentrated industrial areas in the entire world. It contains some 40 percent of total West German industrial capacity and between 75 and 90 percent of West German production of coal, coke, iron, and steel. There are some eight million people in the Ruhr's 4,300 square miles. Water resources are extremely limited if the Rhine River is excluded into which the streams of the Ruhr area flow. Not only is the Rhine itself of very poor quality at the point where the Ruhr enters it, but the water from the Rhine must be lifted into the industrial area. The Ruhr area is much more dependent upon the Rhine for its waste carriage capacity. A large proportion of the wastes discharged from the industrial region into the Rhine now receive comparatively little treatment. However, after construction of a large new biological treatment plant on the Emscher, virtually all effluents reaching the Rhine will have been given far-reaching treatment, and the contribution of this area to the pollution of the Rhine will be comparatively small.

Five small rivers constitute the water supply and the waterborne waste carriage and assimilative capacity of the industrial area proper. In descending order of size, these are the Ruhr, Lippe, Wupper, Emscher, and the Niers. The amazing waste load which these rivers carry is indicated by the fact that the annual average natural low flow in the Ruhr which is heavily used for household and industrial water supply and recreation, is less than the volume of effluent discharged into the river (Kneese, 1964).

The Genossenschaften have made this small supply of water serve the needs of the mines, factories, and households of the great industrial complex, while permitting the use of streams for recreation and waste disposal. They have achieved this at relatively modest cost. Despite rather impressive attention to amenities and recreation, the combined expenditure of the Genossenschaften on building and operating all waste water treatment plants, dams, pump stations, etc., amounts to about 60 million a year, somewhat over half of which is for land drainage. The largest waterworks in the area is a profit-making enterprise delivering water for household use at 30 cents (2s. 6d.) per thousand gallons and for industrial use at 20 cents (1s. 8d.) per thousand. These are among the lowest water prices in any of the German metropolitan areas, despite the fact that the waterworks pays a share of regional water supply and quality improvement costs. The success of the Genossenschaften stems from the design and operation of an efficient system. Because of the regional purview of the associations and the dense development of the area, far-reaching use is made of collective abatement measures and stream specialization.

In the Ruhr River Basin itself, the general objective of the system is to maintain water quality suitable for water supply and recreation. In the Lippe, the objective is much the same;

the Lippe, however, is made largely unsuitable for drinking purposes by salinity arising both from natural sources and from the saline water pumped from coal mines. Some of the tributaries of the Lippe, notably the Stever and the Muehlenbach, are used for potably supply. The Emscher, by far the smallest of the three major streams, is used exclusively for waste dilution, degradation, and carriage. The Emscher, which has been fully lined with concrete and converted into a single-purpose stream, is sometimes referred to as the cloaca maxima of the Ruhr area. The only quality objective is the avoidance of aesthetic nuisance, and this is achieved by mechanical (primary) treatment of effluents entering the stream and by the rather slow rate of biological degradation in the stream itself. Also, by the use of plantings, gentle curves of the canalized stream, attractive design of bridges, etc., care is taken to give the Emscher as pleasing an appearance as circumstances permit. Since the Emscher can be used only for effluent discharge, the area is dependent upon adjoining watersheds for water supply and water-based recreation opportunities. This presents little hardship since the distances are small, and the streams are parallel. Near its mouth the entire flow of the Emscher up to about 1,000 cfs is treated mechanically to remove most of the suspended matter, thus making possible the realization of scale economies in treatment to a far-reaching extent. The heavy burden put on the Rhine both from upstream sources and from the Ruhr industrial area (largely via the Emscher) has caused great downstream costs. This is especially true in Holland where even recently introduced large-scale groundwater recharge projects are failing to supply water of a suitable quality. Consequently, the Emschergenossenschaft is now laying detailed plans for biological treatment of the Emscher, which experiments indicate will be highly successful (Kneese, 1964).

While formal optimization procedures were not utilized by the Genossenschaften, they have probably realized their major gains from viewing the problem of waste disposal and water supply as one of the integrated system design. They have made extensive use of scale economics in treatment by linking several towns and cities to a single plant in cases where the cost of transporting effluents to the plants was less than the additional scale economies that could be realized. In the case of the Emscher

The World of Water

they have linked an entire watershed to a single treatment plant.

Outdoor recreation is quite impressively catered for in the Ruhr area, partly because of the considerable power which the communities and counties exercise in both the water Genossenschaften and the Siedlungsverband (the agency responsible for land use planning in the Ruhr area). Coordination between the work of the Siedlungsverband and the Genossenschaften has contributed to the explicit weighing of recreational and aesthetic values against others in the development and use of water resources, and to the explicit consideration of industrial location as variable in water use and waste disposal planning.

References

'A Place to Live.' *The Yearbook of Agriculture* 1963. United States Department of Agriculture, Washington, D.C.

ARX, SC. D., W. S. VON. *An Introduction to Physical Oceanography*. Assison-Wesley Publishing Company, Inc., Wesleyan College Press, Buckahannon, West Virginia., 1962.

BENNISON, E. W. *Ground Water: Its Development, Use and Conservation*. Edward E. Johnson, Inc., St. Paul, Minnesota, 1947.

CARSON, R. *The Sea around Us*. The New American Library, New York, 1961.

CHOW, V. T. *Handbook of Applied Hydrology*. McGraw-Hill Book Co., Inc., New York, 1964.

CLAWSON, MARION. *Land and Water for Recreation*. Rand McNally and Company, Chicago, 1963.

DAVIS, K. S. and DAY, J. A. *Water: The Mirror of Science*. Anchor Books, Doubleday and Co., Inc., Garden City, New York, 1961.

DAVIS, S. N. and DE WIEST, R. J. M. *Hydrogeology*. John Wiley and Sons, Inc., New York, 1966.

DIETRICH, G. *General Oceanography: An Introduction*. John Wiley and Sons, Inc., New York, 1963.

ERIKSSON, E., GUSTALSSON, Y., and NILSSON, K. *Ground Water Problems*. Pergamon Press, London, 1968.

FAIRBRIDGE, R. W. *The Encyclopaedia of Oceanography*. Reinhold Publishing Corporation, New York, 1966.

FLAIR, T. A., and FITE, R. C. *Weather Elements*. Prentice-Hall, Inc., Englewood Cliffs, New Jersey, 1965.

GOODE, W. 'River Management in England and Wales.' Planning and Developing Water Programs, *Water for Peace*, Vol. 6, U.S. Department of State, 1968.

GUY H., S., ed. *Conservation of Natural Resources*. John Wiley and Sons, Inc., New York, 1965.

HATHERTON, T., ed. *Antarctica.* Frederick A. Praeger, Inc., New York, 1965.

HUTCHINSON, G. E. *A Treatise on Limnology.* John Wiley and Sons, Inc., New York, 1957.

HYLANDER, C. J. *Fishes and Their Ways.* The Macmillan Company, New York, 1964.

ISAAC, P. C. G., ed. *River Management.* Maclaren & Sons, Ltd., London, 1967.

KNEESE, A. V. *The Economics of Regional Water Quality Management.* The Johns Hopkins Press, Baltimore, Maryland, 1964.

LEET, L. D. and SHELDON, J. *Physical Geology.* Prentice-Hall, Inc., Englewood Cliffs, New Jersey, 1954, 1965.

LEOPOLD, L. B. and DAVIS, K. S. *Water.* Life Science Library, Time Inc., New York, 1966.

LINDUSKA, J. P., ed. *Waterfowl Tomorrow.* United States Department of the Interior, Washington, D. C., 1964.

LINSLEY, R. K. and FRANZINI, J. B. *Water Resources Engineering.* McGraw-Hill Book Co., Inc., New York, 1964.

LONG, Capt. E. J., ed. *Ocean Sciences.* United States Naval Institute, Annapolis, Maryland, 1964.

MARSHALL, N. B. *The Life of Fishes.* World Publishing Co., Cleveland, Ohio, 1966.

MARTIN, R. C., BIRKHEAD, G. S., BURKHEAD, J., and MUNGER, F. J. *River Basin Administration and the Delaware.* Syracuse University Press, Syracuse, New York, 1960.

MEINZER, O. E. *The Occurrence of Ground Water in the United States.* United States Geological Survey, Water-Supply Paper 889, 1923.

MEINZER, O. E. *Physics of the Earth — IX Hydrology.* McGraw-Hill Book Co., Inc., New York, 1942.

NAMOWITZ, S. N. and STONE, D. B. *Earth Science: The World We Live In.* D. Van Nostrand Company, Inc., Princeton, New Jersey, 1965.

Outdoor Recreation for America. A Report to the President and to the Congress by the Outdoor Recreation Resources Review Commission. Washington, D. C., 1962.

ORDWAY, R. J. *Earth Science.* D. Van Nostrand Company, Inc., Princeton, New Jersey, 1966.

RAIKES, R. *Water, Weather and Prehistory.* John Baker, London, 1967.

References

REID, G. K. *Ecology of Inland Waters and Estuaries.* Reinhold Publishing Corporation, New York, 1961.

Restoring the Quality of Our Environment. Report of the Environmental Pollution Panel, President's Science Advisory Committee, Washington, D. C., 1965.

RUTTNER, FRANZ. *Fundamentals of Limnology.* University of Toronto, 1963.

THOMAS, H. E. *The Conservation of Ground Water.* McGraw-Hill Book Co., Inc., New York, 1951.

TODD, D. K. *Ground Water Hydrology.* John Wiley and Sons, Inc., New York, 1959.

TOLMAN, C. F. *Ground Water.* McGraw-Hill Book Co., Inc., New York, 1937.

TREWARTHA, G. T. *An Introduction to Climate.* McGraw-Hill Book Co., Inc., New York, 1954.

Water. *The Yearbook of Agriculture* 1955. United States Department of Agriculture, Washington, D.C.

Water for Peace. *United States Geological Survey,* Washington, D. C., 1967.

ZUBOV, N. N. *Arctic Ice.* United States Navy Electronic Laboratory, Moscow, 1943.

Index

Acclimatization, 47
Air currents, 65
Air mass, 47
   Continental, 48
   Maritime, 48
Algae, 101
Alluvium, 138
Analog
   Computer, 161
   Hydraulic, 161
   Mechanical, 161
Angling, 238
Animals, sessile, 102
Antarctica, 122
Anticyclones, 56
Atmosphere, 45
Aquiclude, 134
Aquifer, 134
Aquitard, 134
Aufwuchs, 197

Barometer, 59
Basalt, 165
Basins
   Glacial lake, 179
   Stream discharge, 211
   Tectonic lake, 177
   Volcanic activity lake, 178
   Wind action lake, 181
Beach deposits, 75
Belts
   High-pressure, 49
   Low-pressure, 49
Bennison, E. W., 157
Benthic organisms, 100
Biochemical oxygen demand, 227
Blooms, algal, 272

Boating, 239
Bog, 199
Borehole diameter, 143
Bores, 91
Botulism, 259
Budget, glacier's mass, 121
Buoys, 109

Cable tool drilling, 157
Carson, R., 101–5
Cell, 69
Chow, V. T., 113, 115, 116, 120, 121, 176, 189
Chronometer, 109
Circulation, general, 56
Clawson, M., 240–2
Cliffs, wave-cut, 75
Climate, 53
Clouds, 60
   Altocumulus, 61
   Altostratus, 61
   Cirrocumulus, 61
   Cirrostratus, 61
   Cirrus, 61
   Cumulonimbus, 61
   Cumulus, 61
   Stratus, 61
Coefficient of storage, 147
Commisions, river basin, 287
Computer, digital, 210
Condensation, 67
Conservation, 261
Constituents, dissolved, 152
Currents
   Equatorial counter, 85
   Monsoon, 85
   Ocean, 83

313

Index

Slope, 187
Surface, 188
Trade wind, 84
Cycle, hydrologic, 13
Cyclone, 56

Dams, 203
Davis, K. S., 30, 32
Davis, S. N., 140–3
Decomposition
  Aerobic, 226
  Anaerobic, 226
Deposits
  Eolian, 164
  Unconsolidated, 138
Depressions, submarine, 79
Desert, 65
Development
  Groundwater, 167
  Basinwide, 285
Dew point, 64
Diatoms, 100
Dietrich, G., 72, 74, 78, 79, 80, 81, 82, 83, 84, 86, 87, 89, 90, 92
Discharge, stream, 209
Disease, 17
Doldrums, 50
Dolomites, 164
Drainage, 281
Drains, storm, 226
Drilling cuttings, 140
Drumlins, 118

Economic development and water use, 32
Economic, feasibility of river basin plans, 284
Environment, 262
Epifauna, 100
Epilimnion, 185
Erickson, E., 172
Erosion, 215
  Channel, 216
  Sheet, 216
Eskers, 119
Estuary, 77
Eutrophication, 272
Eutrophy, 195

Evaporation, 67
  Potential, 70

Fairbridge, R. W., 100
Faults, 139
Fauna, abyssal, 102
Fetch, 92
Fish
  Bony, 242
  Cartilaginous, 242
  Ears, 248
  Eggs, 249
  Eyes, 248
  Fins, 247
  Flying, 247
  Freshwater, 253
  Gills, 245
  Jawless, 242
  Locomotion, 246
  Marine, 244
  Population, 253
  Scales, 248
  Teeth, 246
  Teleost, 253
Fishing
  Areas, 105
  Methods, 106
Flair, T. A., 48, 49, 52, 57, 61, 62, 63, 65, 68
Folds, 138
Food chain, 101
Floods, 19
  Damage, 20
  Plain zone, 20
  Peaks, 220
  Recurrence of, 220
  Routing, 221
Floor, deep sea, 78
Fluctuations, water level, 145, 170
Flyways, 257
Fog, 67
Forests, 68
Forces affecting currents
  Coriolis, 83
  Tidal, 83
Formations, rock, 137–40
Fowl cholera, 260
Fractures, 139

Index

Fringe, capillary, 172
Front, 61
Frost, 116

Gages
   Coastal, 111
   Staff, 208
Geologic correlation, 140
Glaciations, 112
Glaciers, 113
   Cirque, 112
   Ice, 112
   Icecap, 112
   Transection, 120
   Valley, 112
Goode, W., 291
Gradient, thermal, 141
Graphs, streamflow, 209
Grasslands, 68
Groundwater, 133, 160
   Users of, 170
Gulf stream, 88
Guy, H. S., 275–8
Guyotts, 82
Gypsum, 164

Habitat, waterfowl, 282
Halibut, conservation of, 276
Hatherton, T., 122–8
Hutchinson, G. E., 177, 178, 180, 181, 182, 185, 186, 190, 191, 192, 199, 200
Human body, water in, 24
Hurricane, 62
Hydraulic-rotary drilling, 157
Hydroelectric power, 21
Hydrogen bond, 30
Hydrographs, 145, 182
Hygrometer, 59
Hylander, C. J., 232, 244, 245, 246, 248, 249, 251, 252, 253, 254

Ice
   Age, 116
   Arctic sea, 130
   Continental, 113
   Drift, 97
   Formation, 185

Frazil, 116
   Little Age, 122
   Mush, 97
   Pack, 97
   Regions, 132
   River, 116
   Shelves, 123
   Surface, 125
Icebergs, 97
Icecap, 131
   Islands, 131
Icemelt, 115
Infauna, 100
Infiltration, induced, 148
Insects, 235
Interflow, 205
Interstices, 133
   Original, 135
   Secondary, 135
Institutions affecting water utilization
   Cultural, 34
   Legal, 34
Instruments, oceanographic, 107
Intergovernmental groups on water problems, 43
Islands, 184
Isotherms, 48
Isotopes, 31
Issac, P.C., 208

Jet stream, 52

Kames, 119
Kneese, A. V., 304–7

Lagoons, 76
Lakes, 175
   Ice, 185
   Inland, 175
   Shoreline, 182
   Solution, 180
Lakeshores, 262
Leet, L. D., 113, 117, 118, 119, 211, 213, 217
Leisure, water and use of, 231
Leopold, L. B., 24–7
Limestones, 164

315

Index

Linduska, J. P., 234, 254, 255, 256, 257, 258, 259
Linsley, R. K., 207, 211
Log
    Electric, 141
    Flow-meter, 142
Long, E. J., 106–10

Management of water resources, regional, 285
Maps, geologic, 139
Martin, R. C., 301–3
Marshall, N. B., 233, 242, 244, 245, 246, 248, 249, 252, 253, 254
Meanders, 213
Meinzer, O. E., 134, 136, 137, 138, 139, 152, 165, 172
Metalimnion, 185
Meter, current, 208
Migration of birds, 233
Models, mathematical, 161
Moraine
    Ground, 118
    Terminal, 118

Namowitz, S. N., 112
Nektonic, 100
Nuclei, condensation, 45
Nutrients, 101

Ocean, 72
    Atlantic branch, 73
    Density distribution, 96
    Density stratification, 94
    Indian branch, 74
    Pacific branch, 73
Oceanography, 74
Oligotrophy, 195
Ordway, R. J., 112
Organisms existing in water, 100
    Faunal, 101
    Floral, 101
Orographic uplift, 61
Oscillation, tidal, 90

Paleolimnology, 199
Pathogens, 225
Pelagial, 192

Penguins, 129
Peninsula, 77
Permeability, 147
Phosphorus removal, 273
Photosynthesis, 151
Phytoplankton, 193
Plains, 162
    Outwash, 119
Plankton, 193
Planning for water resources, 283, 293
Plants, 68
    Aquatic, 272
    Sewage-treatment, 226
    Tissues, 68
Polar easterlies, 51
Policies, water, 34
Ponds, 175
Pollution, 267
    Groundwater, 271
Porosity, 136
Population, 14
Potamo-plankton, 214
Precipitation, 63
Permafrost, 116
Pressure
    Air, 47
    Artesian, reduction in, 171
Prevailing westerlies, 51
Priorities, 289
Processes, treatment, 271
Production, fish, 107
Project, multi-purpose storage, 285
Pulp wastes, 270

Radar, 60
Radionuclides, 269
Radio sonde, 60
Raikes, R., 56
Rainfall, annual, 65
Rain gage, 59
Ratio, benefit-cost, 284
Recharge, 148
Record
    Gage-height, 208
    Water-stage, 208
    Well, 140
Recreation, outdoor, 231

Index

Reef
  Coral, 76
  Oyster, 104
Refuges, waterfowl, 260
Reid, G., 235
Relative humidity, 63
Reptiles, 235
Reservoirs, 175
  Groundwater, 150
Resorts, 239
Resourse-based area, 241
Reverse-rotary drilling, 157
Ridge, oceanic, 80
River
  Authority, 291
  Banks, 262
  Basin requirements, 283
  Forecaster, 223
  International, 36
Rocks
  Crystalline, 165
  Layers of, 137
  Metamorphic, 165
  Specific yield of, 137
Rollers, 93
Root systems, 173
Routes, migration, 257
Runoff
  Groundwater, 149
  Surface, 205
Ruttner, F., 193, 194, 195, 196, 197, 215

Salinity, 98
Samplers, water, 111
Sandstone, 164
Scavengers, 245
Sea, 92
  Birds, 128
  Density, 93
  Invading, 77
  Marginal, 74
  Mediterranean, 74
Seashore, 262
Seals, 128
Season, growing, 69
Sediment,
  Load, 218

Samplers, 218
  Yield, 216
Seiche, 187
Seismic method, 143
Seston, 193
Sewage, 226
  Treatment of, 229
Sewer, sanitary, 226
Sextant, 109
Shale, 165
Shelves
  Continental, 78
  Underwater, 183
Shoal, 183
Shoreline, 183
Slopes, continental, 78
Snow, 114
  Boards, 115
  Line, 114
  Stakes, 115
  Surveys, 115
Soil
  Moisture, 173
  Water, 133
Solar radiation, 48
Soundings, echo, 79
Sphere, coldwater, 96
Stage-discharging, 208
Stations, gaging, 207
Streams, 203
  Systems of, 212
Streamflow, 205
Submarine, 108
Subsidence, 171
Surface, piezometric, 144
Surface tension, 30
Swamps, 200
Swell, 92
Swim-bladder, 246
Swimming, 231

Television, 60
Temperature, 47
Tests, aquifer, 147
Test hole, 156
Thermometers, 59
Thermocline, 185
Thomas, H. E., 162, 167, 170, 172

Index

Thunderstorms, 62
Tides, 89
  Lakes, 189
Till, glacial, 138
Todd, D. K., 142, 149
Tolman, C. F., 146
Tombolo, 76
Tornadoes, 63
Tracers, 143
Transpiration, 69
Trenches, deep-sea, 79
Trewartha, G. T., 48, 49, 53
Tripton, 193
Tritium, 144
Tropics, 66
Trophosphere, 48
Tychoplankton, 193

Vacations, 236
Valleys
  Abandoned, 162
  Buried, 162
  Intermontane, 162
Velocity, stream, 209
Vessel, research, 108
Von Arx, Sc. D., 72, 74, 78, 79, 80, 81, 82, 84, 86, 87, 89, 90, 92, 93, 94, 95, 98, 99

Wastes
  Agricultural, 270
  Industrial, 230
Water
  Bog, 198
  Budget, 67
  Chemical analysis of, 155
  Courses, 162
  Equivalent, 115
  Fresh, 22
  Gaseous, 28
  Latent heat, 29
  Liquid, 28
  Molecule, 31
  Rights, 34
  Saline, 22
  Sea, 98
  Skiing, 239
  Solid, 28
  Surface, 204
  Table, 144
  Undertakers, 299
  Vapor, 45
  Waves, 91
  Wells, 137
Waterfowl, 254
Waterways, 21
Waterworks systems, 225
Waves
  Surf, 93
  Surface, 186
  Tidal, 92
Weather, 56
  Charts, 57
  Cycles, 57
  Maps, 57
  Prediction, 57
  Station, 60
Well
  Drilling, 156
  Logging, 141
Wetlands, 258
Whale
  Blue, 128
  Hunting, 277–8
Wilderness, 238
Wildlife, 235
Winds, 47
  Antitrade, 52
  Direction, 58
  Northeast trade, 52
  Southeast trade, 52
  Trade, 50
  Velocity, 58

Yield, specific, 137

Zones
  Intermediate, 53
  Polar 53
  Subtropical, 53
  Transitional, 54
  Tropical, 53
Zooplankton, 193
Zubov, N. N., 130–1

DATE DUE

MAR 19 '75			
MAY 1 '75			
AP 26 '78			
GAYLORD			PRINTED IN U.S.A.